BOND OF PERFECTION

BOND OF PERFECTION

Jeanne de Chantal & François de Sales

Wendy M. Wright

PAULIST PRESS
New York/Mahwah

Library of Congress
Catalog Card Number: 85-61743

ISBN: 0-8091-2727-X

Published by Paulist Press
997 Macarthur Boulevard
Mahwah, New Jersey 07430

Printed and bound in the
United States of America

CONTENTS

DEDICATION

To my parents,
Walter and Elizabeth Wright,
with gratitude for their
unflagging encouragement
and love

PREFACE

This study, in a somewhat more unwieldy version, was originally a dissertation done in an Independent Interdisciplinary Doctoral program at the University of California at Santa Barbara. A desire to understand more about women in the Christian contemplative tradition led me to uncover and become enamored of Jeanne de Chantal. Through the encounter with her I formed a new desire to enter into her long friendship with François de Sales and to explore the phenomenon of heterosexual friendships, those intriguing relationships, all too-little examined, that frequent the pages of Christian history.

I was aided by several sources in the original work done on the dissertation. A Women's Studies Research Grant awarded by the Woodrow Wilson National Fellowship Foundation and a Graduate Humanities Research Grant bestowed by the University of California enabled me to travel to the sites of the friendship in the summer of 1981. A Charlotte W. Newcombe Doctoral Dissertation Fellowship provided support and encouragement for the writing done in 1981 and 1982.

Help of many kinds came from the faculty of U.C. Santa Barbara. I am especially indebted to Walter H. Capps (Chairman of my doctoral committee), Jeffrey Russell, Raimundo Panikkar, Ronald Tobin and Abraham Freisen, all of whom participated in one or more of the various phases of research, writing and editing. Special thanks also go to Sr. Patricia Burns of the Monastery of the Visitation in Annecy, France, for many hours of conversation about St. Jeanne and for careful reading of the manuscript in its dissertation stage.

The staff of the Interlibrary Loan Office at UCSB, Paul Lachance O.F.M., Robert Petty, and the Community of the Visitation

1

in the State of Washington are likewise due a debt of gratitude for their efforts in procuring materials for research, as is Cheryl Youmans for the laborious work of typing and retyping the manuscript in its numerous forms. Love and gratitude also go to my husband, Roger Bergman, for his unqualified support of this and my many other projects and for his long hours of careful editing, and to my eldest daughter, Emily Frances, who shared her nursery school years with her mother's passion for a saint.

INTRODUCTION

The following in its broadest conception is a study of the spiritual friendships between men and women that are found with surprising frequency in the history of the Christian contemplative tradition.[1] My method of approaching this neglected subject will be to focus upon one particular friendship—that of Jeanne de Chantal and François de Sales—in the belief that the detailed analysis and depiction of one relationship, though not exhaustive of this genre of friendships, can nonetheless be representative of those found in the tradition. This friendship is certainly unique in a number of ways yet it can illuminate the wider genre because it is primarily the Christian contemplative tradition, not the different cultures, eras or personalities of the friends, that defines this type of relationship. That tradition, although it has changed in response to differing historical climates, nonetheless retains in most periods and places a set of basic assumptions which seem to make the emergence of this type of friendship not only possible but probable.

Besides focusing upon the lives and letters of the early seventeenth-century couple, I have also chosen to direct my attention especially toward the woman of the pair. This is in part because the very essence of these male/female spiritual friendships is the transformation of the individual that they can facilitate. This personal transformation is of utmost importance for this study not simply because it is at the heart of spiritual friendship but because it is at the heart of the Christian contemplative tradition as well. And because of the nature of this couple's writings—his are generally intended for a wide public while hers are often composed for private reading—it is easier to see the radical personal transformation of Jeanne de Chantal's life than it is that of her friend.[2]

The fact that I have chosen to focus upon a woman, as well as the relationship which she enjoyed with a man, has consequences

for the direction of the study. In the contemplative tradition of the
Christian Church the general tendency in spirituality has been to
interpret and assimilate the symbols and language of the tradition in
a neuter fashion, as pertaining to either men or women. This is the
case despite the fact that there has existed a great deal of discrimi-
nation toward women as a class and toward women as equal participants in the life and administration of the church. Yet research
shows that in the past on the whole, men and women who were part
of this tradition did not necessarily differentiate themselves by gender in relationship to the central symbols and language of the faith.[3]
This could safely be said of the subjects of this study.[4] Yet because
it is the study of personal transformation within the context of a
mixed relationship, the dynamics of male/female interaction necessarily merit some sort of consideration here. Furthermore, it cannot
simply be assumed that, because both sexes tended to use the same
imagery to describe their contemplative experience, they necessarily
experienced these images in the same way.

A secondary focus of this study will therefore be the spiritual
development of a *woman* within the context of both a man/woman
friendship and the ideological enclosure of the Christian contemplative perspective. Jeanne de Chantal is an excellent subject for such
an effort as she was not merely a woman on account of her biological
endowments but because for the first thirty-eight years of her life
she defined herself by a wide range of the social roles traditionally
assigned to women. Even after entering the convent, traditionally
the one place in the church where the quest for holiness admitted
no distinction between genders, Jeanne de Chantal did not give up
her female roles. She continued to perceive herself always as a
woman undergoing the human transformation that the contemplative
life promised.

In approaching her personal development I will try to a certain
extent to look with fresh eyes upon a figure who, because she has
been deemed a saint, has often had her life reread through the lenses
of the church's canons of sanctity. It is not possible to divest her
entirely of these canons, nor do I want to do so simply because she
understood herself in great part within these same canons. Therefore I will try to discern what her own perception of herself was in
contrast to the pious interpretations of her given to us by her admirers. The names she gave her own motives and the judgments she

made about herself will be deemed normative in my interpretation.[5] While I will sometimes have recourse to more contemporary language used to interpret the workings of the human being, I will try not to superimpose the assumptions of any particular school of psychology upon my subject.[6] I will, however, assume a certain fluid distinction between what might be called psychology and spirituality, the former referring more to the workings of the human psyche, the latter to the movement within that psyche that reveals a transcendent and transpersonal element.

This is, then, a study of a woman experiencing a personal transformation within the embrace of a particular type of friendship found in the Christian contemplative tradition. It also probes the phenomenon of spiritual friendships between Christian men and women. Since the particular as well as the general nature of the study is of such importance I have tried to set the story accurately in its historical context. The study will therefore begin with a general consideration of women and of male and female relationships in the Christian past, attempting to outline what attitudes and assumptions inherited from religious tradition and the socio-cultural setting of the seventeenth century Jeanne de Chantal and François de Sales would bring to their relationship. In the course of the study itself I have included information about the political, social and religious contexts of the time as well as the history and development of the idea of friendship in the Christian church. I hope that an awareness of the context that emerges from this effort will aid in understanding the rich and many-faceted nature of the friendship that this early seventeenth century man and woman shared.

The Contemplative Vision

Most of the religious traditions of humankind have contained a disciplined approach to the cultivation of life. Sometimes this has involved the articulation and formation of what could be called a contemplative life, which in its broadest sense can be described as an orientation: a centering and centered perception of the person in his or her relatedness to all things. Through the contemplative eye, humankind is known in its true relation to itself and to what is other than itself. In this relational seeing a knowledge is discovered which profoundly informs the ways in which the individual lives his or her life.[7] This may take many forms depending upon the culture and period. The contemplative life often necessitates a highly structured discipline of life and a sensitivity to a rhythm that is perceived as flowing from a deep and primal rhythm. It may also involve an inward journey which begins with a profound self-knowledge and discovers through it a different level of reality (or non-reality) which, when grasped, becomes the perspective from which the contemplative experiences all life.

Thus the contemplative life can be seen as disciplined life directed toward the total transformation of the individual. This life may have many dimensions but, fundamentally, it is constructed to aid the person to perceive the various levels of existence and to change him or her into the ideal model of the human person proposed by the particular religious tradition. This individual would, in living out the structured life proposed by the ideal model, achieve truth or liberation or enlightenment or salvific insight that would so inform him or her that he or she would be utterly responsive and conformed to the contemplative insight and would live continually out of that perception.

In the west today when we speak of the "individual" we generally mean not only what constitutes a person, but also a particular self, unique and unlike other selves. So when we speak of the development of the individual we often mean something open-ended.[8] This is not the case with the Christian contemplative tradition, within which the goal of self-development is not the cultivation of a unique and even idiosyncratic individuality but its transcendence and the discovery of a more primal self common to all humans. Moreover, there is a tendency today to presume that people, and especially religious "mystics," develop most authentically without the structure of a particular set of assumptions and a language that articulates these.[9] Not only does this fly in the face of historical data, it does not take into consideration the integrated relationship between "raw experience" and language, neither of which can be considered as primary in the activities of human beings, for each shapes the other in the process of living.

When considering the transformation of the individual in an historical context, one must accept, with the individual herself, that the ideas of religious tradition may be encountered as correspondents to an interior reality (which itself has been given form by the assumptions of the prevailing world view) that can lead to human fulfillment. The contemplative life is not then solely speculative, but first of all experiential, so that the authentic discovery of self occurs simultaneously with the discovery of the living truth of the assumptions of tradition.

A model has traditionally been a way of gaining access to the true contemplative level of perception of the true human self, which is discoverable in models precisely because it is not something idiosyncratic but something profoundly and commonly human.[10] Thus, in most historical religious traditions, the model in relation to which the contemplative experienced his or her transformation was understood to reveal and liberate the "real" personality and embody the "real" human meaning and intent of the individual's life. This point of departure for human development also assumes that the individual was part of a larger collective which did not exist in opposition to the separate person but which existed for the true realization of all its members.

Each religious tradition has its own set of assumptions which determine the shape, the goal, and the process of the contemplative life as well as the physiognomy of the ideal model of human development.[11] Similarly each religion has a plethora of images and symbols and a language that articulates its assumptions and gives the individual access to the centered seeing that is the contemplative life. The Catholic Christian tradition provides the backdrop against which the scenario of Jeanne de Chantal's and François de Sales' story plays itself out. The early seventeenth century French variant of Counter-Reformation Christianity can be rendered as follows.

The two central figures of this Christian drama are the deity and the human soul. Deity or God in Catholic theology of the period was a triune reality consisting of a unity of Father, Son and Holy Spirit. It was thought that God was unknowable in His essence but that His existence and something of His nature could be deduced by human reason from the nature of the created world. God revealed Himself most fully in the person of Jesus Christ who is fully God and fully man, and in the inspired books of the Scriptures. The human person was believed to have been created by God in His own image and likeness to share in and enjoy divine life. However, with the fall of the first man, who opposed himself in pride against God, the very nature of the human person was altered. This nature was "wounded" to the extent that, although it still retained its divine likeness, the image was so tarnished as to be virtually unrecognizable. It was through the revelation of Jesus Christ that the way to the restoration of this broken image was shown. Fully God and fully man, Christ was believed to have entered history and through His death and resurrection to have redeemed fallen humankind. He established a church which was conceived to be His own mystical body through which His salvific grace flowed in the seven sacraments.

The early seventeenth century Catholic saw the drama of the redemption of the human soul by God primarily from the human point of view. Human beings were called upon to respond to the love shown by God by cooperating with the plan of salvation that He held out to all. God offered His grace to assist human beings to reconstruct their original divine likeness, but while He desired human love, He did not coerce anyone, for the human person had been created with free will and was given leave to use it. Thus the relationship between humankind and God was essentially a love relationship, a marriage, and the person was called to be the most fervent lover possible.[12]

The love relationship between God and the human soul involved the whole personality but the relationship had its genesis and progress in the inner person. While inner and outer were never conceived of as divorced from one another, the distinction was made and the inner was given priority as the location where humankind encountered God. Prayer was the activity proper to the interior life, and since the heart of the divine/human love relation was carried out interiorly, prayer was of utmost importance. Indeed, the varieties of prayer described during the period and the subtlety of interpretation given to them is remarkable. In its broadest sense, however, prayer was simply the way in which the soul achieved closer and closer intimacy with its divine spouse. Because the growing intimacy was conceived as a movement of the *whole* person beginning with the inner core, prayer could, in a fervent lover, become an entire way of life. In a Catholic context this often meant the embrace of the monastic life. Although, in the period with which we are concerned, the active dimension of Christian vocation, which was associated with the outer man, was coming to be seen as equally as important as its contemplative counterpart, still the contemplative life of prayer that the monk or nun undertook was generally seen as the crown of religious achievement. The contemplative formed himself or herself upon the model of human actualization that was found in the person of Jesus Christ. The modeling that went on was not only a formal imitation but also a subtle restructuring of both the inner and outer person through the images presented by the life of Christ. These images found their outline in Scripture but were fleshed out and given color and texture by the accumulated doctrinal and devotional life of the church. Central to these images was the death and resurrection of Jesus Christ, which the contemplative experienced not simply as a metaphysical event changing the course of human history but as a primal rhythm in response to which his or her own life would be patterned. This modeling of the self on the pattern of Jesus Christ, the primary task of the contemplative, was not to be done in an idiosyncratic way, although every person brought a unique personality and life-situation to the task.

For the Catholic Christian at the beginning of the seventeenth century, the soul of a man or woman was indivisible from its body and with it created a composite which was one single being. The human soul was intermediate between inanimate or animal being and divine being and was thus capable of moving both "above" itself to God and "below itself" to the lower forms of the created world. Indeed, it was in constant tension, for it found itself deeply attracted by both. In its "lower" or "inferior" part it was drawn by the senses, emotions and purely human considerations; in its "superior" part it was pulled by the intellect informed by spiritual considerations and God.[13] Both intellect and will, its two major faculties, participated in this double tension.

There were, of course, depending on the particular orientation of the interpreter, a number of ways to envision the activity of this soul and its relationship to the divine. For François de Sales the superior part of the soul was the location of human/divine interaction.[14] According to him, the soul had a tripartite division of inferior soul, superior soul, which was illuminated by natural light, and superior soul illuminated by supernatural light. At the summit of this last was a spiritual faculty known as the "supreme point" or "fine point"[15] of the spirit which did not operate by the light of discourse or reason but only by a simple apprehension of the understanding and a simple orientation of the will by which one acquiesced to faith, hope and divine love. It was at this "fine point" that the divine entered the human soul. This summit or supreme eminence of the human soul, since it involved both reason and will, was, in François de Sales' eyes, both intellectual and volitional and its proper activity a simple encounter and acquiescence to the transcendent presence it experienced.

Thus the full development of the human person, which began with an interior impulse and involved the reconstruction of a wounded soul that in its disfigurement had lost its perfect likeness to its Creator, was the task of a loving individual who, with grace aiding, would bring himself or herself closer and closer to a divine intimacy through a cultivation of a simple apprehension of the understanding and a simple orientation of the will. The interior task was one of learning to distinguish the movements of God and the divinely illuminated superior part of the soul from the movements of the inferior part and to conform reason and will to the superior's wisdom.

This was the technical theory of the journey of humankind as understood by François de Sales and Jeanne de Chantal. In practice, the imagery and language of the Christian contemplative tradition, rooted in the Scriptures and developed and nuanced through the centuries, provided the means of the journey and the guidance by which it could be successfully completed. Potentially, a radical transformation of the person could take place; the man or woman, while still retaining his or her distinctive personal individuality, could become one who mirrored the Christ that he or she so ardently loved.

Women and Men in the Christian Contemplative Tradition

With this background in mind, a brief and general survey of the relationship between the sexes in the Christian past will complete this preliminary stage-dressing that must precede the opening of the curtain on the drama of the friendship between Jeanne de Chantal and François de Sales.

Christianity in its infancy was a radically counter-cultural movement which posited a view of humankind and of social relationships that was in opposition to the prevailing views of the Judeo-Hellenistic cultural matrix out of which it sprang.[16] Although the earliest Christian ethos in many ways reflected the society which gave it birth, it was an ethos more of contrast than of similarity. Membership in this new movement was not limited by a person's race, class or gender. Both men and women were attracted by the call of Christ and seem to have found in this new visionary group a place where gender did not impose all the limitations on individual participation that it usually did in the larger society. The Pauline formula found in Galatians 3:27ff—"For as many of you as were baptized into Christ, have put on Christ. There is neither Jew nor Greek, there is neither slave nor free, there is neither male nor female, for you are all one in Christ Jesus"—is one crucial passage that supports this understanding of early Christianity. It is not generally agreed by scholars that this seemingly egalitarian message was meant to have any social implication for women.[17] But some scholars have asserted that the purely spiritual interpretation of the Galatians text was not the only interpretation given by the community itself; for the early Christians tended to live out their faith in very concrete ways.[18]

Indeed, what evidence there is does suggest that within the early Christian fold women as well as men assumed positions of leadership and shared responsibility for the functioning of the church. Women were referred to by titles that suggest leadership positions; during the first two centuries they acted as missionaries and as prophets and their duties seem not to have been significantly curtailed by their sex; after the second century they assumed positions as widows, deaconesses, prophets and teachers and seem to have had a central role in the establishment and maintenance of "house churches."

There was in the earliest Christian ethos some profound understanding of the nature of the Christ event that utterly overturned the world as it was known. Under the new covenant, people were to be born again through Christ and were, as a community and as individuals, to throw off their old ways of being and emerge into a new reality. Everything was overturned, including the distinctions by which society evaluated and treated people. One of these distinctions was the distinction of gender. In many cases the attempt to minimize the differences between the sexes became an attempt at the celibate life. The new covenant was felt to restore humankind to a paradisiacal state in which women would no longer be subject to the curse which branded Eve and so would escape the subordinate marriage relationship and the pain and danger of childbearing.[19] Thus the way was opened for the establishment of relationships between men and women which were not defined by sex roles or patterns of relationships current in society but which were defined by the couples' shared vision of religious commitment. A second century document, the *Acts of Paul and Thecla* (which in many regions was considered canonical during the first three centuries), shows Thecla, a female missionary and companion of the apostle, engaged in the propagation of the faith with a commission from her friend to teach the word of God.[20] Supported by the assumption that in the new dispensation men and women were partners in bringing that dispensation to its fullest expression, women like Thecla in the early church not only could act as responsible and authoritative individuals within their communities, but the possibility was open for the formation of lasting friendships with the men who shared their hopes.

As time passed, the hopes nurtured by the advent of the new kingdom came to be redefined in the Christian community. More and more, the views of women and relationships between the sexes came to be reshaped by the prevailing cultural standards.[21] In Jewish terms this meant that while marriage and family were upheld, woman was nonetheless seen as definitely and rightly subordinate to man. The Jewish woman's legal and religious rights were traditionally less than a man's. In the Hellenistic world, women may have had more social freedom than their Jewish sisters, but the legal system did not allow for equality. Moreover, the philosophical tradition which was so important to the formative church had little esteem for marriage and sexuality (which in itself may have affected the status of women as a class) and also a negative evaluation of womanhood in general. The most prominent example of this is Aristotle's view that women were intellectually and morally as well as biologically inferior to men and that, because of this, male domination was the will of nature.[22]

At the same time that culturally-defined theories about the nature of women were profoundly modifying the radical vision put forth in the earliest church, women were also less and less accepted

as co-workers in the church's practical life.[23] Suffice it to say that by
the fourth century the tradition not only of female leadership but of
the eschatological hope for a shared life beyond the distinction of
gender had faded from the mainstream of the Christian church.

Despite this, the hope remained alive in some quarters. In the
patristic era there were chagrined rumblings about attempts on the
part of men and women to live out their paradisiacal relationship
outside of the traditional confines of marriage.[24] We know of these
"agapatae" or female Christian ascetics who attempted to live a con-
tinent life with similarly committed male companions chiefly from
the attacks of church councils and individuals writing during the
period when the practice had fallen into disfavor. Apparently, the
custom was of earlier origin and presumably received its impulse in
a prolonged millenarian quest for a new reality. These female ascetics, who were also known by the terms *virgines subintroductae* and
Syneisaktoi (which have derogatory overtones), found male companions in a number of different settings in Christian antiquity. Early
Syriac-speaking Christian communities in northern Mesopotamia
anticipated the future kingdom of the resurrection by taking upon
themselves vows of celibacy. The couples either started as virgins
or modified the actual married state by renouncing sexual relations.[25]
Among ascetics in the Egyptian desert the practice was likewise not
uncommon, the women often living with or near male solitaries who
acted as their spiritual directors. In urban as well as rural settings,
the impulse to spiritual friendship took concrete form as priests in
the early centuries accepted virgins as spiritual companions and
housekeepers. Sometimes wealthy widows or unmarried women
took in monks or clerics to share their homes. Often two lay ascetics
might live together as brother and sister for mutual support and edification. It is possible that the custom of men and women sharing
the religious life also existed in the ancient Celtic church, though
this is debated.[26]

The custom did have its pitfalls and cases were reported which
caused scandal. As the practice became widespread and potentially
embarrassing for as well as a threat to the spiritual overlordship of
the ecclesiastical hierarchy, which was not clearly established as the
heir to the Christian legacy, pronouncements began to be made
against the *virgines subintroductae*.[27] From the beginning of the
fourth century, councils laid down decrees against the practice,

bishops inveighed against it, and finally, with the aid of the civil power in 420, a law was enacted which once and for all prohibited the practice of sisterly cohabitation. It is of great interest that Jerome and Chrysostom, two of the most prominent of the church fathers and men who themselves enjoyed close friendships with women (that did not involve cohabitation), were two of the most articulate critics of the *subintroductae*.[28]

If the patristic era witnessed the demise of this one form of relationship, it also witnessed the rise of another lifestyle that, in a somewhat different way, rose to the challenge of the Christian life as one in which women as well as men were to have a place. The flight to the solitude and simplicity of the desert which had occurred with the legalization of Christianity in the fourth century gradually took an institutional form. The communal celibate experience—monasticism—was not new to Christianity but it had never been so widespread.[29] Christian monasticism in many ways seems to have retained much of the early church's liminal view of itself and of the nature of human society. The monk was, to quote a modern monastic, the "marginal man" who rejected the assumptions of "the world," put on the new man and attempted in a radical way to live out a new life in Christ.[30] Monasticism was in many ways a movement which envisioned the coming kingdom in a new way. Once anticipated as an imminent historical event, the kingdom was now anticipated in a present but more individualized and spiritualized fashion. The monastery was par excellence the place where the cultivation of these hopes continued, where a person's entire life might be given over to the schooling that the transformation in and into Christ required and where some foretaste of the community of God's kingdom might be found.

In the nascent monastic world women played a large part. The call to become neither male nor female was heeded and members of both sexes were drawn to the schools of the Lord. It should not, however, be inferred that in this early period women *as females* were given freedom of expression and an equal place in the kingdom. There was no such thing as a simple mutual embrace of the celibate life which would elevate both men and women above their biological differences. Women had to, as it were, "become male," the inherently more spiritual gender, by denying the bodily functions unique to women and the natural affections proper to motherhood and marriage in order to be invited into the new community.[31] The period thus provides many examples both of imagery in which women see themselves as men in their religious quest and of inverted language which makes of this transsexual process a reality in the minds of those undergoing it.[32]

This attempt on the part of women monastics to resex themselves has its basis in the Hellenistic philosophical tradition that so informed the patristic church. It also corresponds to the whole notion of Christian perfection assumed during the period. The perfect follower of Christ was at that time embodied in the figure of St. Antony, the warrior-ascetic doing battle with demonic forces[33] who represents a preeminently "masculine" model of spiritual growth. Any person aspiring to Antony's heroism would necessarily take up a life of ascetic rigor and spiritual warfare.

But this becoming male for women did not necessarily mean simply self-denial, for in most cases the change was a profoundly liberating one, giving the woman new access to a realm of personal development and life-mission unavailable to her before her change.[34] In this new world men and women shared the task of bringing the Christian monastic vision into its fullness. That great champion of the monastery, Jerome, was followed from Rome to the Holy Land by a band of female ascetics intent upon living out the life he wrote of so enthusiastically.[35] Chief among these was Paula, a noble widow who with her daughter Eustochium joined Jerome's female supporters. With her mentor, Paula labored to found monastic communities for men and women in Bethlehem. The friendship that these two shared was central to the great churchman's entire life's vision. He nonetheless suffered the disapproval of some of his contemporaries for his relationships with the opposite sex.

Contemporary with Paula, another Roman widow, Melania the Elder, established a double monastery with facilities for both men and women with her spiritual associate Rufinus. Melania's granddaughter, Melania the Younger, likewise aspired to the anticipated life of the kingdom and with her husband Pinian took a vow of chastity, founded two monasteries at Tagaste, and later joined Jerome's communities in Bethlehem.[36] These male and female ascetic couples were in the forefront of monastic development in the west, yet, as in Jerome's case, their relationships were often suspect. Such was also the case of the friendship between John Chrysostom and Olympias.[37] The golden-mouthed bishop enjoyed a relationship of mutual respect and moral support with this woman. She received from him spiritual instruction and edification; he received emotional and spiritual support from her when he was in exile as a result of his disagreements with the Byzantine primate and empress. She also provided financial support and supervision for a convent in Constantinople which he had established. Yet Chrysostom was publicly censored for his practice of meeting with her (and other women) alone.

Within the contemplative tradition a woman could be esteemed for her own merits. She could be a sister or a companion to men who might look upon other women who were not transformed by the vision of the kingdom as inferiors. This negative evaluation of womankind running through the patristic world did not remain simply an unexamined assumption but received theological justification in the writings of Augustine of Hippo.[38] The African doctor set the tone for much of later theology's understanding of the nature of woman when he claimed that in the spiritual sense women were, like men, created in the image of God, but in body were unequal. The woman together with her husband was seen to be in the image of God, but when she was separate from him she was not, while the single man was the image as fully and completely as when a woman was joined with him. Further, women as a class received a blow from Augustine when he identified the primary sin of humankind against God as concupiscence. This hardened disposition of the human being found its most obvious expression in lust. Wrestling with his own relationship to what he considered a prime obstacle to the true life in God, the bishop of Hippo cast a skeptical eye upon human sexuality. While he could not deny the ultimate goodness of the created world, which included sexuality, he could see that humankind's agency could come between the true source of humankind's life and love, God. This was sin, and the close connection between sin and sexual intercourse in Augustine's thought added the great bishop's authority to the already strong antipathy toward sexuality found in many of the patristic writers.[39] This had its effect upon the general Christian view of women as a class and upon marriage.

Yet despite a tenacious misogynist tendency within Christian tradition, the monastic world continued to produce evidence that a more balanced view of womankind (and of humankind) was still very much alive and well. Monasticism provided an alternative lifestyle in which many women achieved a full development of their personal potential. History provides evidence of these women cultivating lifelong friendships with their male counterparts. One example is the eighth century Anglo-Saxon nun St. Lioba who with her fellow missionary St. Boniface traveled to Germany to establish the Christian religion in that as yet pagan land.[40] Lioba was not only a soul mate for her friend, but was also his intellectual equal, being a classical scholar of some repute. She was entrusted with the governance of a woman's community founded by the bishop on German soil, and so close was their friendship that Boniface granted her permission to pray at his monastery of Fulda, a favor never granted to any other woman before or since that time. Apparently the two of them experienced their relationship as one that was of an abiding quality, for Boniface made a formal request that when Lioba died she be buried beside him "so that they who had served God during this lifetime with equal sincerity and zeal should await together the day of resurrection."[41] Suffice it to say that the monks of Fulda did not carry out the request after Boniface's death.[42]

It is indisputable that in the medieval world women often found a sphere of creativity and personal expression in the monastery that was unavailable to them elsewhere.[43] But it is not her achievements in the realms of literature, philosophy or the arts that gave the medieval nun her true influence and stature in the eyes of society. Nor was it her social status, for many of these women were drawn from the ranks of the nobility and exercised authority over large communities of women and vast material holdings. It was rather the values she embodied in her contemplative life. It was holiness that gave the medieval contemplative woman's life meaning, power and authority.[44] Certainly not all medieval female monasteries endeavored to inculcate the values requisite for holiness: any cursory study of the practices of recruitment and administration or of the political and economic basis of monasticism during this period should make that clear. Nevertheless, it was the veneration that the medieval world in general gave to the canons of sanctity and to holy persons that established the basis of religious and moral authority that authenticated those contemplative women who did embody this ideal. That the criteria for holiness did not include any notion of gender is evidenced in the influence of the life of Catherine of Siena, who was low born and possessed no other claim to the notable political and religious power she wielded than the evident sanctity of her life.

The late medieval world also witnessed a new more "feminized" devotional atmosphere that spread through Christian culture. In its most obvious manifestation, this interest in "feminine" imagery is seen in the flowering of the cult of the Virgin and the popularity of growing numbers of female saints.[45] Perhaps less well known is the rapid rise of devotional language utilizing images derived from woman's experience: maternity, birth, lactation and nurture.[46] This feminized devotional language, which was evident both in conceptions about the nature of God and humankind's relationship with God, must be seen against a wider picture of a generally humanized piety which began in about the eleventh century and which focused upon the humanity of Christ, utilized analogies from human relationships and developed a sense of God as loving and accessible. This piety did not necessarily originate with women, and in fact seems to have had greatest popularity among male contemplatives, especially the Cistercians.[47] Whatever its origins, the new interest in female imagery gave to the Christian contemplative repertoire a new androgynous flexibility which symbolically made possible a new self-image for both contemplative men and women and gave them a new sense of the nature of the quest for God.[48] Becoming neither male nor female still generally presupposed the adoption of a celibate life, but now this did not imply "becoming male" to the extent that it had in an earlier Christian world. Both men and women identified with a wider range of human capacities in their devotion to a God who was Mother as well as Father.

It is not possible to claim that the feminization of Christian devotion in the late medieval era coincided with any improvement in theological attitudes toward women. The great schoolman of the thirteenth century, Thomas Aquinas, essentially reiterated the sentiments about womanhood expressed by Augustine. His Aristotelian insistence that the end of man is fully achieved by the operation of the rational soul, when joined with an Augustinian notion of the nature of the soul in the sexes, did not do much to improve theological thought on womankind. For, although he claimed spiritual equality for the sexes, Thomas also claimed that a man was in possession of the *imago dei* in a different and superior manner from a woman.[49] He also, through his adoption of Aristotelian biology which viewed woman as a defective male, strengthened the andro-centric anthropology that already dominated medieval thought.[50] Thomas' theological formulations did not dominate the century in which he lived. Nonetheless, his views on women are evocative of views held during the period and his systematization of the faith did become the dominant Catholic theology after the sixteenth century.

Despite the subordinationism found in the theological tradi-tion, women in the medieval contemplative world continued to flourish. The late Middle Ages saw the emergence of a number of new vocational alternatives alongside the monastic alternative. In northern Europe, informal communities of women—Beguines—dedicated to lives of prayer and charitable activity sprang up. In Italy, both the Dominican and Franciscan families provided a third religious option—the tertiary life—for those men or women not able or willing to embrace the lives that the first and second orders of the mendicants offered. A century later, in the Lowlands, the pop-ular piety of the *Devotio Moderna* was given an outlet in the quasi-monastic association of the Sisters of the Common Life. There are also examples during the Middle Ages of what is known as a double monastery: a monastic community which housed both men and women. Chief among these were the Order of Fontevrault in France and the Gilbertine Order established on English soil. The impulse behind these double foundations may have had less to do with any kind of equalitarian vision than with the practical necessity of pro-viding male spiritual direction and manual labor for groups of high-born nuns, and does not suggest anything but a strict separation of sexes.[51] In fact, one order presumably attempting some sort of dou-ble community, the Premonstratensions, within a decade expelled all females from the premises, and accompanied their departure with a downpour of verbal abuse.[52]

Still, the medieval era witnessed to a good number of male and female spiritual friendships whether women as individuals or as a group did or did not escape the denunciations often flung at them. In the contemplative world friendship between the sexes was pos-sible. The first names that naturally come to mind in this regard are Francis and Clare of Assisi.[53] Their story is well known: lovely Clare of the noble Favarone family fled from her father's home and her privileged life one night in the year 1212 to live in prayer and poverty near the wealthy merchant's son turned beggar. Adopting a strict regime of penance, Clare was established by Francis as the foundress of the second order of the Franciscan family. Clare seems to have shared Francis' most intimate vision in a way no one else did. Although she and her nuns remained cloistered in their convent of San Damiano while Francis and his brothers adopted the mendicant life, Clare was in constant contact with her friend and they considered their work as one. In conformity with the customs of the period, the physical contact between Clare's cloister and the outside world was restricted, yet in the legends about the Franciscan founder, Clare figures as a main persona in the drama and it is clear that she, as well as he, was instrumental in nurturing and furthering the Franciscan charism. After Francis' death it was Clare who quite alone and valiantly fought for the continuation of the privilege of absolute poverty in her community, about which her friend had felt so deeply.

The mendicant orders also produced another spiritual friendship to rival the beauty and intensity of the one between Francis and Clare. Jordan of Saxony, the successor to the generalship of the Dominican Order after the death of Dominic, came to know of Diana of Andalo from his predecessor.[54] It seems that Diana, a young Lombard woman of notable lineage with a passion for the contemplative life, had for several years attempted to enter religious life much to the dismay of her family. Under Dominic's guidance she had led a mortified life in her home and had gathered about her a group of women followers. Refused admission to a nearby convent, she planned a country outing with friends in the course of which she sought refuge with a community of Augustinian canonesses. Enraged, her brothers dragged her physically from the property and confined her to her room for one year. But Diana's determination was undaunted. At this time Jordan entered the scene. Through his efforts she became a member of the Dominican family and succeeded in establishing herself and a small band of friends in the convent of St. Agnes, thereby founding the Second Order of St. Dominic. Jordan and Diana exchanged a series of letters throughout the years 1222–1237 which attest to the depth of their relationship. One quotation from Jordan must suffice to give some flavor of this friendship:

You are so deeply engraven on my heart that the more I realize how truly you love me from the depths of your soul, the more incapable I am of forgetting you and the more constantly you are in my thoughts, for your love of me moves me profoundly and makes my love for you burn more strongly. . . .[55]

The friendships between Clare and Francis and Diana and Jordan existed not simply as relationships between individuals but were supported by the current understanding of the nature of Christian vocation. For both Franciscans and Dominicans the aim of the mendicant existence was to pass on the fruits of contemplation to Christendom at large. Or to put it another way, its aim was to fully live out the charism of both the active and the contemplative vocations. It was felt that the church, which was conceived to be the mystical body of Christ, was one unity with many members of which Christ was the head. Within the organism all parts sustained and participated in the whole. With this in mind it is possible to perceive how both Dominic and Francis understood the establishment of a second order of cloistered women. These women were to be the contemplative fire, drawn from the deepest source of all life, that would animate the active lives of the brothers.

It would be a mistake while surveying the period to avoid another famous and slightly earlier medieval friendship, that shared by Abelard and Héloïse.[56] More complex in its genesis and conforming less to the typical pattern of spiritual friendships, this clandestine affair-turned marriage-turned celibate relationship has gripped the imagination of centuries of admirers. Well known is the story of how Abelard, the brilliant scholastic and tutor of the young Héloïse, fell in love with his pupil, how they married secretly when she became pregnant (despite the stain this would place upon his clerical status), how they were discovered together by her uncle and protector, how Abelard was castrated for his offense, how they entered separate religious communities, and how, years later, Abelard became the provider for the community of nuns of which Héloïse was abbess. It is the later phase of this relationship that is of particular interest here, for it is from that period that any extant correspondence dates. The letters we have, if indeed they are authentic, are revealing of this man and woman's attempt to come to terms with the many facets of the love they had shared and to balance the tension (which in their case was heightened in a particular fashion) between love of God and love of one another.

One more friendship from the twelfth century is revelatory of a different type of tension potentially inherent in male and female spiritual relationships. The story of Christina of Markyate and two men with whom she was closely aligned, the hermit Roger and the Abbot Geoffrey, shows the sometimes terrible obstacles such relationships had to surmount in order to exist.[57] The young Anglo-Saxon noblewoman from an early age had desired monastic life but was forced into marriage by her family. Refusing to consummate the union (for it violated private vows of chastity she had taken), she fled to a community of hermits and came under the direction of the venerable Roger. For two years they had contact only through third parties but, following a prophetic dream of Roger's, the two of them came into contact. The mutual recognition of their shared aspirations was immediate and lasting. According to Christina's biographer:

> The fire which had been kindled by the Spirit of God and burned each one of them cast its sparks into their hearts by the grace of that mutual glance and so made one in heart and soul in chastity and charity in Christ they were not afraid to dwell together under the same roof.[58]

Christina and Roger might not have been afraid for themselves but so antithetical was prevailing monastic opinion about contact between the sexes that Christina was forced for four years to live secretly in a tiny closet attached to Roger's cell where there was neither heat nor water nor any way to care for bodily functions. They met only during the cover of night. After Roger's death, Christina finally made her way to the vicinity of the monastery of St. Albans and became a professed religious. There she met and formed an equally impassioned friendship with one Abbot Geoffrey. Due to her influence this worldly administrator experienced a conversion which led him to prayer and solitude. Through the years he became dependent upon her for advice and direction, and she in turn cherished him as a companion on the spiritual journey. But this friendship too was not free from the suspicious meddlings of others, and Christina and Geoffrey were openly accused of all sorts of impropriety.

Such was the fate of some of these friendships. Others enjoyed a much freer existence. Because of the tremendous veneration afforded to holiness during the medieval era, it was possible for women of reputed sanctity to come to public attention and attract to themselves followers or disciples who sought spiritual aid. Catherine of Siena and Catherine of Genoa are two women from the Italian peninsula who come to mind in this regard. The first of these Catherines is well known to history, for she not only enjoyed the reputation of sanctity during her life but received the acclaim of succeeding centuries, becoming one of only two women in the Catholic tradition to be officially decorated by the title "Doctor of the Church." This daughter of a Siennese dyer and Dominican tertiary is remembered for her diplomatic missions as well as for her extraordinary insight into the ascetic and mystical life. Catherine attracted around herself a number of followers, many of whom were men. Of these individuals, one, the Dominican Raymond of Capua, may be seen to be a friend of unusual closeness and importance. He was her spiritual director for six years as well as her treasured friend. It was Raymond she referred to as "the father and son given to me by that gentle Mother Mary," and her designation of him in this dual relational role is evocative of the specific nature of their friendship. For Catherine was perhaps, of the two of them, the dominant spirit at least in the contemplative realm. After her death, Raymond devoted eleven years of his life to recording her memory for posterity, and his *Legenda Major* remains as one of the chief and most reliable sources for her life.[59]

The other Catherine, who lived a century later in Genoa, also enjoyed the friendship of a man who first came to her as disciple. Ettore Vernazzo was twenty-three years younger than his friend. When they met she was already matron of a hospital in the city and had experienced, a number of years earlier, a profound conversion to a life dedicated to love of God. She belonged to no religious community or organization but was self-authenticating, attracting followers by visionary and penitential gifts with which she was abundantly endowed. The two friends met during an outbreak of the plague, and he, a young lawyer with a desire to lead a holy life, offered himself as an aide at her hospital. Their friendship was close for many years and extended itself to Ettore's wife and daughters. His more active orientation complemented her contemplative gifts. Ettore served as Catherine's amanuensis and historian during her lifetime and was instrumental in compiling the "Life and Doctrine" which forms the backbone of the source material that exists on this Genoese holy woman.[60]

This account brings us to the beginning of the sixteenth century and thus to a new era in Christianity: the Renaissance and Reformation. It is a period of great importance for the history of women generally, for it witnesses, at least in some circles and locations, an increased appreciation of the female sex as seen in growing educational opportunities afforded women as well as an enlarged sphere of legitimate female influence beyond the home or the cloister. It consequently also signaled changing opportunities for women drawn to the contemplative life and new opportunities for the development of friendships between women and men.

That the Renaissance was a period of some major shifts in viewpoints about women is evidenced by the three-century-long literary debate known as "La Querelle des Femmes."[61] The very insistent mysogynist tradition which painted women as cursed by Eve's sin, as concupiscent, crafty and essentially depraved, was countered by lively efforts to establish the nature of female capabilities. Authors such as Christine of Pisa and Erasmus lent authority to a more dignified image of womankind, argued for the full equality of their souls, insisted that they were not only educable but deserved education, and gave women an explicit role outside of the family household or the cloister.

The Protestant Reformation likewise had an impact upon the lives of women, although its importance was more long-range than immediate. The Protestant world was for the most part opposed to the monastic and ascetic ideal of medieval Christianity.[62] In place of celibacy, marriage became dignified as the proper life for a Christian. While this did much to raise the status of many women who were wives and mothers or destined to become such, it also reduced the options a woman might have open to her for some role other than a domestic one. To counter this however, educational opportunities came to be extended more liberally to women because of the Reformers' insistence upon the importance of the scriptural word and individual access to it. There were numerous examples of women in the Protestant world who wielded considerable influence and who shared the religious aspirations and work of their male counterparts.[63]

The changing views of women during the period in question could not fail to have their effect upon the contemplative world. In the Catholic arena, women who might otherwise have sought monastic enclosure for the satisfaction of their religious impulses turned now to a new alternative, the congregation, which gave expression to the still celibate but now more active and militant spirituality of the Counter-Reformation Church.[64] Angela Merici in Italy founded the Ursuline community, Louise de Marillac was foundress of the Daughters of Charity in France, and the English woman Mary Ward instituted a congregation in honor of the Blessed Virgin Mary in her country. All these groups, while not new in conception (witness the Beguines and the tertiaries), did offer women an important celibate option.

In terms of the relationships between the sexes, the entrenched anti-feminism of centuries, while somewhat mitigated by the intellectual world of the Renaissance and Reformation, still continued. The year 1600 in France marked the publication of *La Sagesse* which disseminated the view that women were biologically and morally inferior to men. These opinions were given something of a boost by the moral rectitude of Counter-Reformation Catholicism. The church at the time was leery of any infringement of the rule of clerical and monastic celibacy and thus tended to view any attempt at less than strictly regulated contact with suspicion.

Still, at least in some parts of Europe and in some segments of society, women came to be more socially visible, more influential, and more accepted as equal partners in many matters. This was especially true of France at the turn of the seventeenth century.[65] Although their juridical status (both civil and canonical) was nonexistent outside the protection of a father, husband or convent and much poular sentiment denounced them as inferior, women in French society were extremely influential in shaping the mores and culture of the period. Moreover, they were given a relatively wide berth in their spheres of operation, afforded educational opportunities, and allowed a fair amount of personal mobility, especially if they happened to belong to the upper classes. This social acceptability of French women could not help but have an effect upon the relationships between men and women in the contemplative life. Despite the Counter-Reformation impulse to reform which strengthened the tradition of claustration for contemplative nuns and the reaffirmation of the chief features of medieval doctrine concerning women,[66] friendships between the sexes in the religious life seem to have been reasonably frequent, although there was not infrequently public concern about them and although there was inevitably a caution expressed about them both in theory and between the individuals.

The French examples of these friendships appear to be most numerous.[67] There is the friendship between Vincent de Paul and Louise de Marillac which, while colored by a certain austere reserve reflective of his personality, was long and faithful. Together this peasant-turned-priest and illegitimate daughter of the French aristocracy founded the congregation of the Daughters of Charity, which gave expression to their mutual passion for charity and ministry to the sick and dying. Although Vincent was originally Louise's director, he soon recognized her maturing spiritual gifts and gave her a wide sphere of freedom in the direction of their congregation. She was even given his blessing to conduct retreats for her spiritual charges, a practice reserved at the time almost exclusively for men.[68]

Other French couples of the period likewise joined together to found religious communities. Joseph du Tremblay and Antoinette d'Orléans, the marquise of Bellisle, founded a contemplative order for women, the Daughters of Calvary, remarkable for its austerity.[69] Similarly Madame Acarie, in whose salon could be found the most luminous stars of France's spiritual renewal, and Pierre de Bérulle established a long-term relationship which resulted in the importation of the Spanish contemplative order, the Discalced Carmelites, into France.[70]

Other friendships bore fruits different from new religious communities. The illiterate but mystically-graced Marie de Valence enjoyed a close relationship with one of the luminaries of the contemporary religious renaissance, Pierre Coton.[71] She was an obscure young widow, a convert from Calvinism, whose tender, almost idyllic mysticism had gained her a modest local reputation. When she happened into the confessional of Coton, a bond was formed which lasted for the rest of her life. Impressed and moved by her rustic wisdom, the priest never missed a chance to stop at Valence, wrote to her regularly, and requested that all her private papers be sent to him. Marie had another lifelong friend in the person of her biographer, Louis de la Rivière. For her he was local confessor and spiritual child. By her side she kept another companion, her secretary Marguerite Chambaud who, in her turn, formed an abiding friendship with de la Rivière. For thirty-six years these two "loved each other like brother and sister, with a holy and constant affection. . . ."[72]

Equally notable was the relationship between Jean-Jacques Olier and the abbess of a Dominican community at Langeac, Mère Agnes. As a young abbe, this future founder of the Society of St. Sulpice led a dissolute life. Mère Agnes, learning of this young man's talents and lack of self-discipline, dedicated herself to a program of prayer directed toward his conversion. With her spiritual aid he eventually dedicated his life to parish ministry under the direction of Vincent de Paul.[73] There were also the two friendships of Jean Eudes: with Madame de Camilly and with Marie des Vallées. Eudes was a missioner and member of the Oratory, an organization dedicated to the spiritual nurturance of the priesthood instituted by Bérulle. With Madame de Camilly the austere Eudes shared not only a common zeal for his reforming work but a tender affection as well. In her judgment and religious integrity he had a boundless confidence, and this friend soon became virtually the manager of and his right hand in the Order of Our Lady of Charity, which he founded for the care of fallen women. Together they held a veneration for Marie des Vallées, a woman of flamboyant mystical gifts whose periods of "possession" by God (some critics thought by the devil) were much regarded in religious circles. Marie became Eudes' inspiration. He called her "the eagle," and under her influence his later life took a new direction.[74]

Not all friendships shared by men and women in the French contemplative world of this period fared as well as the above-mentioned. Two infamous stories tell of couples whose religious vision had joined them together but who found not only their relationships but their own personal lives severely tested in the political and theological controversies of the later seventeenth century. The couples in question are of course Madame Guyon and Fénelon and Angélique Arnauld and St. Cyran.[75] Buffeted by the controversies ranging around the soon-to-be-heretical Quietist and Jansenist movements, the partners of these couples, each in quite distinct and personalized ways, established with each other a religious vision that ran counter to the prevailing orthodox doctrine. Doggedly and with loyalty they supported one another. Their lives were sometimes bitter, always difficult, but the friendships that these two couples displayed are among the most heroic in the literature.

Outside of France during the period of the Counter-Reformation other spiritual friendships flowered as well, despite the fact that women did not enjoy the same freedom of movement or social influence as they did within France. The most luminous of these relationships was undoubtedly that between Teresa of Avila and John of the Cross in Spain. Although there exists only limited data about the nature of their personal exchange, their common work and individual literary outpourings testify to the depth of their shared passion for things of the spirit and the heights to which they raised each other. For six years John of the Cross was Teresa's confessor while he was in residence at her convent in Avila. She was the elder of the two, a prioress who had initiated him into the disciplines of the spiritual life and who was aflame with a passion to restore the primitive austerity of the Carmelite life. He was to be her counterpart in the men's branch of the order. It was during their shared years together that Teresa wrote what is perhaps the most beautiful of all her works, *The Interior Castle,* and John began writing his astounding poetic celebration of the love of God, the *Spiritual Canticle.* Teresa also shared a special and intimate friendship with another Carmelite actively involved in the work of their order's reform. Father John Gratian was for a number of years the nun's director and they experienced together the pain and frustration produced by the vigorous opposition mounted against their efforts on behalf of monastic renewal.[76] Equally notable if less luminous examples of male and female friendships are found in sixteenth century Spain among the "beatas," charismatic women who developed spiritual friendships with Franciscan priests.[77]

As the modern era dawned, the contemplative tradition continued to spawn spiritual relationships between men and women. Certainly, as the western world in general relaxed its more severe attitudes toward any type of sustained contact and women came more frequently to occupy positions of authority outside the home and had equal access to education, the ground was prepared to allow for the growth of these friendships. Yet despite this secular readiness to till the soil for their flowering, men's and women's friendships did not receive the same encouragement from within the Catholic Church. The tenacious anti-feminine tendency discernible throughout Christian history seems to have lived on into the modern period.

Nevertheless, the contemplative world continued to produce examples of these friendships. The theory of the organic unity of the Church found undergirding the relationships of Dominican and Franciscan friends in the Middle Ages was renewed in the relationships established between the cloistered Carmelite nuns and the missionary community of Maryknoll. In this relationship the concept of radical self-gift embodied in the image of martyrdom, which was a cornerstone of modern Carmelite spirituality, found a resonant response in the missioners.[78] Well-known is the turn-of-the-century life of the young Carmelite, Thérèse of Lisieux, who was deeply bonded in her extraordinary prayer life to the overseas missionaries whom she considered her spiritual brothers and with whom she founded a relationship based on their common zeal for souls.[79]

In the English-speaking world, the relationship fostered between Herbert Vaughn, founder of the Mill Hill Fathers and later cardinal of Westminster, and Lady Herbert of Lea bears noting. A deeply felt and long-term bond united these two individuals and gave to the Victorian world a remarkably frank and affecting correspondence from which the cardinal's letters have survived. Like the much earlier missionary Boniface and his friend Lioba, they desired to be buried next to each other. Their wish was granted and their bodies rest together at Mill Hill.[80]

Several other contemporary examples of remarkable friendships bear mentioning. Teilhard de Chardin, the visionary anthropologist-philosopher exchanged a memorable correspondence and maintained a fruitful relationship with Léontine Zanta, the French Catholic intellectual.[81] Less explicitly philosophical but no less visionary were the friendships of Dorothy Day and Peter Maurin and Catherine de Hueck Doherty and Eddie Doherty. Both of these couples' histories are rich mines for any understanding of the nature of spiritual relationships and of the type of ventures to which they may give rise. Dorothy Day, political activist and convert to Catholicism, found a friend for her radical social and religious dreams in the unkempt hobo-philosopher Peter Maurin. Under his prodding she set her principles into action and founded the Catholic Worker

Movement to which they were both devoted until their deaths.[82] Catherine de Hueck Doherty and her second husband Eddie Doherty likewise gave their lives to the establishment of a Christian alternative lifestyle. Influenced by the contemplative wisdom in her native Russia, Catherine late in life founded a Friendship House whose aim was to provide a living example of Christ's message to feed the poor. Her life was active but rooted in the wisdom of solitude and prayer. To this venture her husband, with whom she took a vow of chastity, gave himself wholeheartedly.[83]

This survey has not exhausted the examples of spiritual friendships between the sexes found in the history of the Christian contemplative tradition. The purpose of this overview was rather to suggest the wide range of historical circumstances and personalities that have produced these friendships and to suggest something of their variety. What they all have in common is their genesis in the Christian contemplative life, sometimes monastic in form and sometimes not, and in the unwavering commitment of both the woman and man of the pair to the vision that that life revealed. The contemplative world was in many essential ways counter-cultural. Like the millennial community gathered around Paul and his companions, the contemplative tradition lived with the urgent expectation that the kingdom of God was at hand. This expectation, for most of the period we have been discussing, was understood in an interior and spiritual fashion. The coming of the kingdom was less a future event of history (although it was also this) than a vibrant awareness of its constant and ever-awaited coming in the human soul.[84] The kingdom came to sweep away much of what the ordinary world held dear, and, in the words of St. Paul, it would result in a reality in which there was neither Gentile nor Jew, neither servant nor freeman, neither woman nor man.

That the contemplative tradition should have preserved the impulse that sustained the counter-cultural vision of the early church, which included (at least as a possibility) the overturning of established relationships between the sexes, is not surprising. Like the early Christian community, it was created to be an alternative society of believers in contradistinction to the rest of society. Perhaps even more importantly, it was the one place within the entire Christian world in which prayer, especially in its contemplative form, was preserved and cultivated. At least in its periods of vitality and renewal it was in this tradition that men and women sought through prayer to become transformed by the new life proclaimed in the gospels and who surrendered themselves with abandon to the life of Christ and the reality of the kingdom. The tradition taught that deep within the individual one finds an image of God. When the many levels of self-absorption were peeled away this magnificent and simple core was revealed. Rather than distinguishing people from one another this revelation united them, for the realization was that the *imago dei* is not unique to the individual but is shared by all, most fully by those who have searched for it. The contemplative vision brought a deep and gripping realization of the Galatians formula which swept away human distinctions derived from race, class or gender.

The contemplative vision was not simply an ideological stance but a wholistic vision that demanded expression in a way of life. It would appear that, despite the strong mysogynist tendency of much of Christian thought and the cultural practices that supported this tendency, the transformed perception of many of those deeply immersed in contemplation led to a profound minimization of the prevailing views of womankind. This made it possible for genuine friendships between the sexes to emerge. The Christian contemplative world produced a good number of these surprising relationships and gave to women, because of its vision of the human person, a place of freedom to develop themselves in many personal ways as well as to become the transfigured human beings they sought to be. These friendships proclaimed the advent of a new world in which barriers drawn between the sexes could no longer impede the intense and deeply Christian impulse to love one another and to become as one person in the profoundly human task of recreating life in the image of God. These friendships were given shape by shared assumptions about the value and proper orientation of human life and brought many couples to the mature fulfillment of the potential with which they were singularly and mutually endowed.

1.

The Beginning[1]
(1604–1605)

I

The devout of Dijon in the somber March weather and penitential mood of Lent were greatly anticipating the series of sermons of that year, 1604. The notables of the ancient city of the dukes of Burgundy had invited the bishop of Geneva to preach. Monseigneur François de Sales, a Savoyard, was rapidly gaining a reputation in France both for the reforming zeal of his episcopacy and for his charismatic preaching. It was said that when he spoke, he spoke directly from his heart to the hearts of his listeners and that the power of his presence was greatly affecting. That Friday, March 5, Jeanne-Françoise Frémyot Baronne de Chantal was among the crowd surging into that monument to ducal splendor, the Sainte-Chapelle, to hear the words of the good bishop. She was thirty-two, a widow of three years with four small children. Her father, Bénigne Frémyot, president of the Dijon parliament, had urged her to leave the country residence of Monthelon where she was staying with her father-in-law and join him in the city of her birth for the duration of the Lenten sermons.

She, perhaps more than anyone that day, came with eagerness and an attitude of receptivity for what she was to hear. Since the shattering death of her much-loved husband in a hunting accident she had been in inner turmoil. It would have been logical and, in the eyes of society, desirable to be considering remarriage. But Jeanne had discovered within herself a restlessness as a result of the tragedy. What was formerly a sincere but predictable religiosity that she had inherited from her family had become a painful yearning, an urgent necessity of her most private self. She did not understand the depth or shape of her desire for God or know the form that her longing was to take. But she had vowed to herself that she would never marry again and had ardently prayed for a director of some sort to help her make sense of the chaotic impulses that raged within.

Her anticipation for finding such a spiritual counselor had been heightened several years before while riding in the meadow near the mill on the estate of Bourbilly where she had lived with her husband. The figure of a man appeared at the foot of a small hill. He was wearing a black cassock, surplice and headcovering that a priest would don before stepping into the pulpit to preach. As she beheld him a certainty overcame her in the form of the knowledge that "this is the man, beloved of God and men, into whose hands you must entrust your conscience."[2] The experience had held her elated for some time but the weight of her grief and her uncertainty about the nature of her vision caused it to fade. At the urging of some pious Dijonnaise acquaintances she revealed her pressing interior concerns to a priest at the nearby shrine of the Black Virgin at Notre-Dame-d'Etang. He undertook her direction by burdening her with a great many formal exercises of devotion: long vocal prayers, elaborate meditations and mental considerations sealed with the stipulation that she speak to no one else but him of her spiritual life. The rigidity and exteriority of this director's scheme served only to increase her anxiety and alienate her from the drama going on within.

So when she made her way from her family home opposite the imposing facade of the Palais de Justice through the narrow streets of the mercantile city to the Sainte-Chapelle that March 5, Jeanne de Chantal was unknowingly prepared for what was soon to take place. She arranged her seat directly beneath the pulpit that rose into its prominent position in the church. When the visiting ecclesiastic mounted the steps to begin his address, she recognized him as the figure she had seen in the meadow at Bourbilly.

His preaching was indeed riveting and novel for its time. His aim was to stir his audience to action, to inform the will, to inflame the heart. As a preacher he spoke plainly and directly; his teaching was simply the gospel-inspired precepts of love of God and neighbor expressed in a manner that would have consequence for his hearers beyond intellectual assent. In this design he was a trend-setter, for the popular and accepted form of preaching at the time was a sermon constructed on the model of closely reasoned scholastic argument. Its aim was to convince the listener as well as to impress with erudition.[3] François de Sales broke with this tradition and became part of a trend that was to have its adherents throughout the century.[4] The assurance with which he spoke and the authenticity of person that communicated itself to his audience were overwhelming.

Jeanne's close attention to all he said was obvious enough to cause the bishop himself to remark upon the continued presence of "that young widow with light brown hair who seats herself across from me during the sermon and who listens so attentively to the words of truth."[5] He questioned his host, André Frémyot, the archbishop of Bourges and Jeanne's brother, about this woman. The ecclesiastic was proud to introduce her as his sister.

Jeanne recognized the wisdom of François de Sales' preaching and longed to speak to him privately about the confusion of spiritual impulses to which she had been subject. But she was constrained by her vow to her first director that she not reveal herself to anyone but him. Throughout Lent she was torn by this conflict. She had many opportunities to see the bishop socially, for he was often a guest in the homes of the first families of Dijon to whose society she belonged. On the Wednesday of Holy Week, she managed to free herself from the companion provided for her by her first director and, with her brother's help, gain a brief interview with François de Sales. The next day the bishop, who had been moved by the intense if fleeting encounter with the young widow, overheard her remark that she was planning a pilgrimage to the shrine of St. Claude in the Jura Mountains. As he and his mother, he said, had been considering a similar excursion, perhaps they might arrange a meeting there later in the year.

Encouraged by this, Jeanne sought the Savoyard out for a full confession the week after Easter. She sought not only to unburden herself of the grief that she felt at her husband's death, not only to lay bare the painful and as yet unclear emotions and thoughts that she felt were leading her to some new depth of encounter with God. She sought, although she only dimly perceived this, another person whose vision of the spiritual life was as radical and committed as hers was to become. She sought a friend, a companion for the life journey she was beginning. François hesitated but a lengthy interview did take place and Jeanne bit by bit unfolded the drama of her interior life. Her confessor was struck by the sincerity and vitality of this woman's quest for God. He, cautious by nature, must have spent a good many reflective moments considering his moving encounter with the widow, for when he left Dijon the Sunday after Easter he took a moment just outside the city gates to write her a brief note, "It seems to me that God has given me to you; I am assured of this more keenly as each hour passes. This is all that I can say; commend me to your good angel."[6]

This was the beginning of the friendship that was over the years to transform the lives of both. It belongs to the larger genre of spiritual friendships between men and women that have appeared with surprising frequency in the Christian contemplative tradition. But the friendship between Jeanne de Chantal and François de Sales was also a particular friendship that took shape at a unique moment in the history of western culture and of the Christian Church. Without an understanding of this historical matrix we will not be able to envision the architecture of their relationship.

The place was southeastern France and Savoy at the dawn of the seventeenth century. The overriding historical realities of the period were the aftermath of the grim civil wars in France and the renewed vitality of religious life that occurred in the wake of the reform efforts of the Catholic Church. Since the mid-sixteenth century, French society had found itself divided into two intractable camps: the adherents to the Church of Rome and the followers of the Reform. While the religious loyalties of other European nations and principalities were determined primarily by the persuasion of their rulers, France was racked by seemingly insoluble conflicts between the varieties of Christian practice. The struggles were armed as well as ideological and few communities or families were left undivided and unscathed. Losses in life and property were immense. The issue was given political prominence by the fact that the French monarch, Henri III, was childless and his direct heir, Henri of Navarre, was of the Reform faith. Much popular sympathy was rallied around the Holy League, a political association headed by leading French families and backed by many local parliaments whose goal was to ensure a Catholic succession to the throne of

France. The maneuvers of the League were complex. All the complexity came to a head when the new monarch succeeded to the throne in 1593 as Henri IV, abjured the faith of his upbringing and proclaimed himself the Catholic ruler of the realm. While this was a victory for the Catholic cause, the Huguenot element of society was too strong and entrenched to be easily overwhelmed. In 1598 the Edict of Nantes decreed the legal co-existence of both the Catholic and Reform faiths. But this truce was not an easy one and feelings ran high on both sides. The bitterness of the wars was still freshly implanted upon the hearts of the French in 1604 when Jeanne de Chantal and François de Sales met. It imparted to the Catholic mood of the age an intense loyalty to the Roman cause conceived in both personal and political terms and a deep devotion to the traditions and teachings of the church.

Devotion to the church was not forged only out of this negative material. It was born as much if not more out of the renewal of religious vitality sweeping Catholic Europe. Since the fourteenth century the reform impulse in Christendom had been felt in the sporadic renewal of religious orders and the emergence of new spiritual movements. Voices had been raised in protest against the corruption of the Christian vision: Savonarola called for Christian repentance, John Colet cried out for a reform of the clergy, Egidio da Viterbo demanded a church council to restore the moral fibre of the church, Erasmus challenged the ecclesiastical hierarchy to resemble their mentor, Christ, and Lefèvre d'Etaples sought a return to the pure gospel faith through the translation and critical analysis of the texts of the early church. Other voices and presences set the stage for new life, but the government of the old church was unable to respond to the renewed spirit, and the force of Lutheran, Calvinist and other reform efforts split Christendom in two.[7]

When finally the Council of Trent was convened in 1545 by the papacy to resolve the conflicts, the lines of division were too deep to be healed and Trent became not a truly representative Christian council but the instrument of reform for the Catholic cause.[8] The shadow that Trent cast upon the following century was long and wide. The aims of the council were multiple and reform efforts were expended in many directions. A number of doctrinal issues came to debate and official positions were propounded: original sin, justification and the sacraments were the focus of the council's attention. In the area of ecclesiastical reform, Tridentine directives were many and sweeping. The papacy was to reform itself in both morals and organization. The Vicar of Christ was enjoined to be a worthy representative of his Master, and indeed this period saw the ascension of men of earnest intention and exemplary life to the chair of Peter. Rome was to become a fitting pilgrimage center, building projects were begun, and the city was renewed. The entire curial government underwent a radical reorganization. Centralization and uniformity of belief and practice were the underlying aims of much of this reform work.

The state of the episcopacy likewise came under fire. The Counter-Reformation bishop was to be the delegate of the Pope in his diocese. His life was to be a model of Christian devotion and reforming zeal, that is, he was to stay in his diocese and truly take upon himself the role of shepherd to his flock; he was to preach—often and well; he was to supervise the reformation of the religious orders and clergy under his jurisdiction; moreover he was to see to it that the laity were well schooled in their faith and given places of worship and leaders worthy to guide them in undertaking the devout Christian life.

As for the lower clergy, they too were the concern of the Council of Trent. Priests were to be instructed in their faith and were to live within the structures of celibacy. They were to be worthy and knowledgeable dispensers of the sacraments. To this end the construction of seminaries began, and what had been the haphazard making of priests became a serious business. Religious orders too, many fully decadent in their practices by the sixteenth century, were to experience renewal through a strict observance of the order's original rule. The prohibition against owning property was to be enforced. Nuns were to be reestablished in their cloisters while abbots and abbesses were to be worthy individuals of sufficient age and experience to undertake the spiritual direction of their communities. Profession into religious vows was not to be forced by relatives or others, nor could an individual be professed at too early an age.

These were then some of the directives of the council. A long and hardly representative gathering of the Catholic world, the Council of Trent nonetheless was illustrative of the vigorous renewal going on within European religious life at the time. It should be noted, however, that the wholesale reception of the council's decrees throughout Europe did not take place. In France, the heads of state were unwilling to integrate Tridentine decisions into the constitutional laws of the kingdom. Centuries of privilege and prerogative of the monarchy in regards to the appointment of high ecclesiastical position as well as a Gallican sense of independence from the authority of Rome made this impossible. Nevertheless the French clergy went on record (1615) as accepting the council's decrees that dealt with faith and pastoral activites. And Tridentine observance did become a reality for most of the populace in France.[9]

Beyond the centralized directives of Trent and perhaps even independent of them was the more general upsurge of interest in Christian values and spirituality among the laity. The late sixteenth and early seventeenth centuries in France stand out as a period in which the call to a radically-lived Christian commitment was strongly felt. Certainly, the church had a long history of this periodic calling to renewal. This time, the call to renewal was distinguished by the scholarly legacy that the preceding century had bequeathed. There had been for some time a growing consciousness among Europeans of the historical progression of religious tradition and an increasing appreciation of the evolution of ideas and language when perceived in historical perspective. The Renaissance individual was concerned to return to the roots of western culture by exploring the texts of antiquity. This meant, for those who found their work defined by specifically Christian issues, a return to the wisdom of the Bible and the early church fathers. Critical editions and new translations were fashioned.

The Catholic Church was deeply touched by the Renaissance impulse to seek renewal from the past. This was particularly true because of the imprint of the humanist culture of the period. It has been called an era of "devout humanism."[10] This trend of Christian thought, perhaps best represented in the writings of Capuchin author Yves de Paris, was based upon several tenets. It believed that humankind possessed "relative sufficiency" to act in behalf of its own salvation. Human nature for the Christian humanists was not utterly corrupted by the fall, but merely wounded. There remained to it a natural orientation to God as its supernatural end. Further, in the view of this type of humanism, God "predestined" individuals by taking into consideration their efforts and merits. God did not predestine arbitrarily. Moreover, humans could and must cooperate with divine grace in the accomplishment of saving works, which makes the efforts of creatures something extremely important in the Creator's scheme. A final tendency of Christian humanism was the appreciation of the wisdom and works of the classical world.[11]

In this broad form Christian humanism became the common property of the entire period not only through the influence of specific authors but through the educational efforts of the Society of Jesus. This formidable society of priests became the backbone of the educational system of the Counter-Reformation. Its founder, Ignatius Loyola, had drawn deeply from the springs of humanist learning in his native Spain where such currents were strong in the sixteenth century. The society became an important instrument of the new reforming spirit issuing from Rome. In their curriculum at the numerous teaching facilities that they directed all over Europe, the Jesuit fathers taught their variety of Christian humanism.[12] The legacy of antiquity as well as the truths of Christian revelation formed the basis of the curriculum. Moreover, the ancient languages of Greek and Hebrew were taught alongside Latin. With these language skills students read not only portions of the biblical text and the church fathers but the literature of Greece and Rome.[13]

The imprint of the Renaissance can also be seen in Catholic theology. There was a tendency to view all theology, including metaphysics, from the point of view of man. Of the two terms central to Christianity—God and the soul—the soul received the larger share of theological attention. At the same time, a move away from the principles of scholastic argumentation was accompanied by an enthusiasm for rhetorical modes of writing and reasoning.[14]

The Renaissance spirit also made its presence felt in the debate over grace and predestination. There emerged a new position on these issues that bears the name of Molinism.[15] Molinism, briefly, is the teaching that the freedom of the human will is an essential factor in the divine plan of salvation. God does not predestine individuals to either heaven or hell. Molinism posits a special type of knowledge attributable to God by means of which He infallibly knows those possible events whose future occurrence is conditioned by the self-determination of man's free-will. Thus, whatever occurs in the future is determined by human free choice. God is not the cause of choice nor does God predetermine any particular choices made.

Nonetheless, He does see the future as it will occur. While Molinism certainly does not represent a humanist position in the modern sense of the word, it did contribute to some philosophies and spiritualities of the period an ideological optimism that stands in contrast to much of the church's earlier ambivalence on the topics of predestination and grace.

All of this provided a background for the popular religious movement of which we have spoken. It was a movement with personal origins and practical application. It was a thirst for devotion and a hunger for surrender to the spiritual values of the Christian faith. In France it had full flowering between the years 1550 and 1650—the years that span the lifetimes of François de Sales and Jeanne de Chantal.[16] There, it was Lefèvre d'Etaples and his followers who had led the way in the literary rejuvenation of Christianity.[17] Attracted to the simple piety of the fathers and convinced that the discursive, rhetorical method of the ancient authors was preferable to the formal, logical modes of scholasticism as a means for conveying wisdom, they undertook to translate many works from their original languages. The Lefèvre d'Etaples group was an important sign of the times, for it was not part of any order, congregation or institution. It reflects the fact that the interest in the restoration of Christian life was becoming the concern of all Christians, whether in vows or lay.

The language of the devout life catalyzed many in France into action.[18] There were improved hospitals and congregations formed to staff them; there were schools and teaching orders established to teach in them; there were foundations for abandoned girls, for the victims of war and for rural evangelization. Representative of the new social concern of the Christian community was the community of the Sisters of Charity, co-founded by Louise de Marillac and Vincent de Paul. A simple congregation rather than a full-fledged order, the Sisters of Charity banded together to give themselves to the service of the sick and poor. They did not observe the traditional enclosure of women's orders but moved about in society dispensing their charity to those in need. In the area of education, the Ursulines, founded by Angela Merici, were active. This order had as the justification for its existence the establishment of schools for the education of young women. Furthermore, with the exploration of the non-European world that was being pursued with gusto in the sixteenth century, a new field for active endeavor opened up—foreign missions. The Society of Jesus especially found fertile ground for the expansion of their energies in missionary work.

The zeal that thrust Catholics into social action was nourished by the deep currents of contemplative life that undergirded French society in this period.[19] There was a widespread interest in the vast devotional literature that was in circulation. Many of the works were newly translated into either Latin or, for lay consumption, into French. They represented an eclectic gathering together of the church's centuries of interior experience. Many of the works were Spanish; the Rhineland and Italian mystics also made a representative showing.[20]

The marked interiority of this type of religious literature captured the imagination of the age. There was a vogue for mysticism and a taste for the visionary, the supernatural, and the miraculous. There was also an upsurge of interest in the monastic life. The nobility and well-to-do families of the realm became the patrons of many reformed or new monastic foundations. The early part of the century saw the implantation onto French soil of the austere order of the Discalced Carmelites that was renowned for the purity and ascetic rigor of its life of interior prayer. The new era also witnessed the reformation of many traditional contemplative houses, notably the Benedictines, through the efforts of their inspired abbesses or abbots.[21]

The Counter-Reformation had as a primary aim the infusion of Catholic spirituality into all levels of society. That it was highly successful in this regard is seen by the extent to which lay persons took the injunctions of contemplative literature seriously. Perhaps the best example of this popular embrace of a highly exacting spiritual vision is the salon of Madame Acarie in Paris. This extraordinary woman attracted attention because of the profound holiness of her life and because of the ecstatic quality of her experience of God. The leading lights of France's religious renewal gathered in her home to imbide her presence, to explore with her the subtleties of the interior pilgrimage and to design the architecture of the church's new life. François de Sales came there, as did Pierre de Bérulle, Dom Beaucousin, Benoît de Canfield and other seminal figures of the era.

The Acarie salon was the hub of a wheel whose spokes radiated out to penetrate the life of the period. From this center what is known as the Abstract School of mysticism emerged. Profoundly influenced by the spirituality of the Rheno-Flemish writers, this highly refined school of interior experience was best represented by Madame Acarie and Benoît de Canfield.[22] Similarly, the very Christocentric spirituality of Bérulle also emerged from within the circumference of Madame Acarie's circle.[23] His spiritual teachings radiated out through France by means of the Oratory, a community of secular priests dedicated to the rehabilitation of the priestly office among the laity.

The end product of all this ferment was a society within the Christian fold charged with spiritual vitality, hungry to explore all dimensions of the Christian life, full of optimism and earnestness and girded for the real sacrifice it knew that life entailed.

II

When Jeanne de Chantal left Dijon for her country residence in Monthelon in the spring of 1604, she felt that her life had taken a new and dramatic turn. But the certainty about a new life which François de Sales in some unclear way seemed to represent had not come easily. Her first response after making contact with the bishop was to suffer much anxiety about her disloyalty to her first director. Jeanne was, and would always be, a woman of great fidelity. The fact that she had promised not to reveal her conscience to anyone but her too-strict mentor, and then had sought and obtained an audience with another for expressly that purpose, haunted her. Unable to resolve in her own mind whether or not her actions had been appropriate, she sought the advice of a respected Jesuit priest. He listened carefully to her story and offered his opinion: her relationship with the bishop was the will of God. What she had intuitively felt received confirmation. She was able to return to Monthelon full of anticipation and a renewed hope.

Hope was needed in her case, for life had not dealt her the easiest of hands.[24] She had been born in Dijon in 1572, the second child of Bénigne Frémyot, councillor and afterward president of the local parliament, and Marguerite de Berbisey. Her family was of the "noblesse de robe," the emerging class in French society that owed its position to the talents and industry of its members rather than to the inherited properties and titles that ensured the social status of the ancient "noblesse d'épée." She had lost her mother at the age of eighteen months, and she, her elder sister, and her infant brother André, who survived the birth his mother did not, were brought up in part by their paternal aunt, in part by their father. The elder Frémyot greatly loved his children and included them in the political and religious discussions that often went on in the house.

The Frémyot household was devoutly Catholic and had inherited from the civil wars a fierce loyalty to the orthodox cause won at the expense of suffering and risk. Her father for some time had been forced to flee Dijon and live in exile, and her brother André had been held captive by League opponents and his life threatened. Jeanne herself inherited from this time of strife an intense loyalty to the Catholic cause conceived in both personal and political terms. Her early memories of the wars were emotionally charged. Riding through the countryside she would often come upon the remains of some church or monastery violently razed by the Huguenot forces. She would weep uncontrollably, gathering into herself the clear religious identity that a sense of persecution seems to bestow.

If the civil wars had divided France, they had also forged networks of allies whose futures seemed linked by a common cause. Bénigne Frémyot had joined energies with Baron Guy de Chantal, an irascible nobleman whose wealth, like that of many French aristocrats, had been greatly reduced by the years of armed conflict. For these two men to consider the union of their respective children was natural. So a marriage was arranged between Jeanne-Françoise Frémyot and the young baron, Christophe de Rabutin-Chantal. It was a good match and much to the liking of twenty year old Jeanne. Christophe was a handsome man of twenty-eight, lively of temperament, affectionate, mixing a flair for the soldier's vocation and the gallant life in society with a certain reflectiveness which gave weight to his character. He liked to read and was sensitive to the arts and literature. He was a loyal if not overly observant Catholic.

They married just after Christmas in 1592. The religious ceremony took place in the baron's fortified castle of Bourbilly in the country west of Dijon. It was mid-winter and the countryside was not yet entirely free from strife, but much of the danger had receded from the area, and the mood that accompanied the sacramental joining of these two was optimistic and gay. Jeanne began the life to which she had always assumed she was destined. Bourbilly was to be her home, the place where she would raise children and fulfill the duties of the wife of a provincial aristocrat of the time. The castle was far out in the country, isolated a good distance even from the nearest town. It was a great contrast to the bustling life of Dijon. There her own home had been situated squarely in the middle of the district dominated by the Palais de Justice and the activities of the local parliament.

Jeanne, as was her fashion, applied herself with energy to the duties set before her, and it did not take long for her to discern their scope. The baron's affairs were in terrible disarray, since the devastating wars had reduced the family inheritance and had necessitated prolonged absences by the heads of the household. The former baroness had applied herself to the righting of this situation, but since her death ten years before the situation had become critical. Christophe took his new bride on a tour of the properties and carefully laid out in detail the indebtedness and grim toll that lack of management had taken on the family holdings. Would she undertake the restitution of their fortunes? He would be unable to do so because he was required to spend much time away on campaign in the service of the king. She balked. The project seemed overwhelming. But gradually he convinced her that her managerial talents were desperately needed. She began the difficult task.

Despite the fact that all her life Jeanne expressed a distaste for administrative business, she did have a talent for it. Moreover, she was devoted to her husband and serious about her responsibilities as the Baronne de Chantal. Among those responsibilities was the management of the baronial property. Her handling of this task gives some insight into her character. She began by establishing a routine to the day. The practice of daily morning Mass, long lapsed at Bourbilly, was reinstated. She then had all servants, laborers and stewards come to her for instructions of what tasks were to be accomplished during the day. She personally oversaw work going on both within and outside the house. And she supervised the accounts, perfecting the tedious skills of bookkeeping to the end that she could set aside money for the payment of the many debts the family had incurred. Moreover, she cut back considerably on household expenditures by simplifying her own style of life: linen and wool clothing instead of a noblewoman's silk and velvet sufficed.

Orderly she was, and a capable manager. But while she took her duties seriously, she carried them out in a spirit of fairness. She had a remarkable talent for identifying with people, taking upon herself, in ways that were appropriate, their care and governance. It is reported that she used to take her own spinning into the maids' room and talk or read to them from edifying literature. She was also deeply moved by the plight of the sick and poor. Much of her spare time she spent visiting them. This was not mere piety on her part nor is it the wishful hindsight of hagiography. Jeanne appears to have been drawn to those less fortunate than she in a genuine way. She saw the suffering of others and felt it as her own. Then she acted to the extent that it was within her power to alleviate it. A continual bread-line formed behind the kitchen door at Bourbilly to receive the food the baroness offered. The sick of the region as well as the hungry had reason to rejoice that Jeanne Frémyot was the Baronne de Chantal, for she was a skilled nurse with a wide knowledge of medicines and treatments and the compassionate nature of a true healer. She did not find even the most loathsome diseases repellent but visited their sufferers and anointed their victims.

Through all this she remained a companionable wife. Christophe was away a good deal of the time, and her charitable activities occupied her in his absence. But upon his return she became a lively hostess and eager friend. It is worth noting that her interior religious life seemed most active when he was away. She spent time then reciting prayers, mostly for him. But his presence once more assured, she was swept up in the round of social life that presented itself. Women of the time were expected to revere and devote themselves completely to their spouses, and Jeanne certainly did this, but there was nothing forced about her acquiescence.[25] Duty for her emerged naturally alongside great affection and appreciation. Christophe on his side returned her feelings, and the two enjoyed a fine friendship and mutually satisfying life.[26]

This life together was fruitful. During their wedded years Jeanne was pregnant six times. The first two infants died at birth, a fact which could only have been very disheartening to the young baroness. The next four babies, one boy and three girls, survived. Celse-Bénigne arrived in the world in 1596, Marie-Aymée followed two years later, Françoise one year after that and Charlotte in 1601.

It was less than two weeks after the birth of their last child that this domestic world to which she was so totally committed came crumbling apart. The baron had been home for some time, an unusual state of affairs that greatly pleased his wife. He had retired from life at the court following his refusal to obey an order he considered unjust. He was also suffering from a case of dysentery he had contracted while on campaign, and Jeanne had been nursing him back to health. His mood was reflective, if not somber, for the illness and the deflection of his career gave him much opportunity to evaluate his life. For a while he was dangerously ill and his thoughts turned to death and its preparations. Jeanne was alarmed by his gloom and refused to let him dwell upon these topics.

Soon his health improved and the thirty-five year old baron began to tire of his sickbed. He planned a deer-stalking expedition with a close friend, a pleasant recreation that suited his returning high spirits. The baroness was still convalescing after a successful childbirth, content with her life and full of her domestic joys. It was an autumn morning when the hunters set out toward the forest, dogs and servants in tow. The two were a little distance from one another when the companion's gunstrap caught on a protruding branch. His weapon went off, scattering shot, some of which pierced Christophe's thigh and buried itself deep in his abdominal cavity. The baron knew the wound was mortal, forgave his distraught companion, sent for a priest and gave instructions for a message to be taken back to Jeanne at Bourbilly. But she was not to be alarmed: the messenger must say that the accident was not serious. With a cry of foreboding the young wife leapt out of bed, dressed and hurried to the little cottage at the edge of the forest where her wounded husband had been brought on a stretcher.

The next nine days were an agony for her. The baron understood the true nature of his injury. Bravely and with a calm deliberation he readied himself for death. She must accept this as a reality, he insisted; she must make her peace with it and make the necessary preparations. She must never speak a word against the unhappy friend whose accident had been the cause of his injury and she must resign herself to her new life. Jeanne resisted him. She refused to believe he was not going to recover. She sent for every doctor available and told them bluntly that the baron *absolutely must* be healed. But try as they might the men of medicine could do little for the dying man. The wound was too deep for them even to attempt to remove the shot.

Until the very last the young baroness refused to submit to the fact of her husband's death. At first she tried direct denial. When he spoke of his approaching end she spoke only of his continued life. While he was turning his thoughts away from earthly concerns she was fiercely trying to will him into engaging with them. At last desperation seized her. She fled from the castle to the solitude of a nearby wood. There she cried aloud to God,

> Lord, take everything I have in this world, my relatives, my goods, my children, but leave me this precious husband you have given me.[27]

When Christophe de Ratutin-Chantal died, his widow was unconsolable. She wept until her friends feared for her health. They came to visit her to distract her from her grief. But this was not what Jeanne needed, and for once her perceptive intuition, which she seemed at other times never entirely to trust, held in her stead. She knew she needed to be alone, and so when friends kept her from the full expression of her grief during the day, she stayed awake all night in mourning. When she could during daylight hours, she rode on horseback into the solitary splendor of the Burgundian woods to be alone with herself.

It is said of her that during this period of mourning, God took command of her life and oriented it in a new direction. This is the way that she came to understand what happened to her, although at the time she was uncertain about the particulars of the reorientation. Jeanne had loved her husband unreservedly. The fact of his death plunged her down an inward spiral from which she was to emerge a different person, a person who now understood and perceived things differently than she had before. All the neatly arranged jigsaw pieces of her world were thrown into disorder, and as she attempted to reconstruct the picture she found that the pieces did not fit as they once had.

What emerged from her solitude was, first, a certainty that she could never marry again. She took a private vow of chastity and, as we have seen, she did not lightly underestimate the importance of vows. We can only surmise that in part this vow was motivated by loyalty to her first spouse. Perhaps too she unconsciously shrank from any new commitment which could expose her to the pain of separation and death that she now felt. But her embrace of the chaste life had other motives, too. She reported in later years that, in the midst of her grief, she experienced a certain relief, a freedom that beckoned her to a new life. This could not have been a freedom from the burdens of the marital state, for she still had the responsibilities for her children and for the estates. A remarriage would in many ways make her situation easier. The new freedom that she sensed was of a different nature. It was less a freedom from burden than a freedom to expand the perimeters of her present person. The jigsaw puzzle had been overturned, and when she righted its scattered pieces, one by one, she began to discern not a familiar portrait but a new visage whose dimly perceived features, though recognizable, suggested a new richness and a new maturity of self.

She had always been a person for whom relationships were profoundly important. In her letters one can clearly discern a wealth of warmth and attachment for those closest to her.[28] Her vivid personality and talent for leadership in no way kept her from expressing herself as a woman who entered deeply into the bonds of intimacy with others and who allowed those relationships to affect and change her profoundly.[29] Sometimes the roles of mother and administrator that she played necessitated her taking a position in relation to another individual that precluded the intimacy that equals can enjoy. But in these cases she did not display her most essential self.

Christophe's sudden death unmoored her. With him she had shared companionship, love and mutual responsibility. There are no letters that survive this early period of Jeanne's life, but as the reports of her contemporary biographer testify, she was well aware of the meaningfulness of that intimacy for her own life. It would seem as though what she had built with Christophe had touched a deep spring in herself, for when he died she did not seek to replace him with a new partner who could fulfill the ordinary functions of a marriage; she sought instead an ultimate relationship. Inchoately, she felt that the new self she was becoming could no longer be satisfied or defined by any less an intimacy.

Her awareness at the time, of course, did not come in such a highly articulated manner. She found herself plunged into an abyss and in the terror of a darkness where she knew nothing but the yearning of her own heart. Her childhood piety, fashioned in adult years into a loyal observance, opened wide. She knew, somehow, although it made no sense, that she would not marry again. She would give herself to her God. Her religion was not primarily solace at this time; it was identified with the emergence of her new person.

> ... Our Lord increased in me my desire to serve Him; the attractions I received from God were so great that all I wanted was to leave everything and flee into a place of refuge so that I could do this totally and perfectly, without any external obstacles. I believe that if I had not been restrained by the consciousness of my responsibility toward my four small children, I would have secretly escaped to the Holy Land there to end my days. I felt such indescribable longings to know and follow the will of God, whatever might happen, and it seems to me that this desire was so great that it was consuming and devouring me from the inside.[30]

But she had very little encouragement for her emerging dreams. The religious atmosphere of the time was conducive to the call of the celibate life, as we have seen. But for a young widow with small children a supposed call to celibacy was not necessarily sufficient, in the eyes of society, to override the primary responsibilities that she faced. This she knew, and the conflicting knowledges that she lived with at this time were a source of great pain. She began to search for someone who could help her untangle the complex issues with which she struggled. She began to look for a spiritual director. But she was very isolated at Bourbilly, both physically and emotionally, and she did not know of any individual to whom she could turn.

Nonetheless, the desire was strong enough in her that she continued to nourish it. It was further strengthened by the startling vision that she had in the meadow beyond the mill at Bourbilly. But circumstances conspired to obscure her reveries. Just months after Christophe's death the elder Baron de Chantal summoned her to him. She was told that she must come with the children to live on his rustic estate at Monthelon. If she refused, he would disinherit his grandchildren. Monthelon was, in spirit as well as distance, far from either the verdant if lonely beauty of Bourbilly or the familiar warmth of busy Dijon. The old man presents himself unattractively to history. Retired from his years of soldier's service, he had sequestered himself in his rural properties. There he had fallen under the domination of a housekeeper by whom he had sired several children. He seems to have cared little for Jeanne's personal needs or concerns. Besides, legally (and the accepted custom of the time reinforced the legality), women in France were, like their children, the wards of their male relatives.[31] Jeanne dutifully fulfilled his command.

The situation at Monthelon exacerbated Jeanne's inner anxiety. Accustomed to the free exercise of her position as baroness in the management of her affairs at Bourbilly, she found herself reduced to the status of an unwelcome guest at her new home. The housekeeper seems to have resented the widow's presence and made things extremely unpleasant for her. The old man was quarrelsome. She was given no domain for her own personal expression save an upstairs attic which she converted into a sort of apothecary's storehouse. It served as her refuge from the unhappiness around her and as the center for her charitable activities into which she threw herself with renewed vigor. With great tenderness she sought out the victims of the most loathsome maladies, visited them and cared for them. She also attended to the upbringing of her children as well as the tutelage of the other children on the estate.[32]

We know that it was a painful time for her. Yet she set herself the task of carrying out her duty with grace and courage. She did not even tell her own father, whose solicitous response could only have been outrage, of her plight. Instead, she swallowed her pride and tried to respond as best she could to the call that she felt from God.

She was still searching for a director. As we have seen, at the advice of some pious acquaintances she attached herself to the entourage of the priest at Notre-Dame-d'Etang. She carried out his rigid spiritual disciplines in her typical spirit of careful observance. But she was not at peace, for there was a nagging certainty that a dramatic change of some kind was needed. When she saw François de Sales in the pulpit during the Lent of 1604, when she hung upon his words, when she listened to the restless yearning of her own heart, she sensed that through this man she would discover the secret of her emerging identity. After her Easter confession and his suggestion that they should meet again on pilgrimage in St. Claude, she was confirmed in her intuition. The Dijon Lent had become for her what a Christian Lent is intended to be: a period of preparation for new birth. In rhythm with the liturgical year, she had emerged from the husk of her old self into the Easter light of life begun anew.

Four months were to pass before François and Jeanne were to meet again. During that time they began the correspondence that was to unite them, at times despite geographical separation, over the course of the next eighteen years. He had encouraged her to write to him as often as she was able if her first director felt this was advisable. He was much moved by the spiritual potential that he sensed in his correspondent.

> ... having seen in you the tree of desire for holiness that Our Lord has planted in your soul, I cherish it tenderly ...[33]

he wrote to her in May. He wished to be of service to her in any way he could.

She responded by taking up her pen and somewhat hesitantly revealing more and more of herself to him. Many of the letters that she wrote during the years of their friendship, much to the historian's dismay, are lost to posterity. After François de Sales' death all the numerous papers that had been in his possession were sent to Jeanne for sorting and editing. Included were packets of the letters she had penned to him annotated in the margins in his own hand, for he had planned at some point to write an account of her soul-story for the edification of others (a fact of which she was presumably unaware). She separated out and then burned much of her own part of their correspondence.[34] We have, therefore, little written by her before 1611. Fortunately, from his letters to her one can clearly deduce the content of her portion of the correspondence.

Her scruples about a possible violation of her vow of confidence returned when her first director learned of her encounter with the illustrious prelate. This jealous priest tried to pressure her into renewing her promise. Another round of worried consultations with respected advisors followed. Now she wrote frankly to her new correspondent about the situation. He responded that he greatly admired her candor and praised her for the horror of duplicity she displayed. But he was becoming more uncertain about the methods her guide seemed to be employing. Moreover, the prelate saw no reason why an individual could not consult more than one advisor on spiritual matters while still maintaining a primary allegiance to one's selected director. He saw the bond that united director and directed not in terms of dependence but in terms of a mutual and ultimately free relationship in which the director aided his charge to discover within himself or herself the will of God. There could be no oppression in such a relationship, only the loyalty and obedience that mutual trust involve.

These first letters to Jeanne are filled with the solicitous advice of a man practiced in spiritual consultation. François was above all gifted in the art of directing souls.[35] His calm and insightful guidance of his new friend is admirable. She was overly scrupulous about her first vow, too easily distracted from the real inner movement within her, her increasing desire for God, and by her fretful impatience to know how her future was to be arranged. She was also very unsure of her own intuitions. With a sure hand the bishop began to teach his friend a confidence in her own inner resources. He began to turn her attention from the externals of the life of piety to the less tangible movements of God's Spirit within.

He also drew up the blueprints for what was to be the architecture of her lifelong spirituality.[36] Her devout life was to be supported by what he referred to as two columns: her desire for Christian perfection and her love of her widowhood. With one deft stroke François de Sales created the rendering. The life that she was to live for God was to be an affair of her whole person. The love of God which she felt from within must be allowed to emerge and inform the direction of her outer world. Likewise, the immediate situation in which she found herself—for the present, her widowhood—was to be embraced as a revelation of the will of God. She was, simply, to nurture her sensitivity to the *presence of God* in its infinite modalities. The practice of this presence was to be the one constant theme of her spirituality from this time on.

They agreed to meet again in late summer at the Shrine of St. Claude high in the Jura Mountains. It was an ancient pilgrimage center of a late seventh century abbot whose relics were legendary for their miraculous curative powers.[37] Although it was a center of popular devotion, Jeanne had had little or no knowledge of the cult of St. Claude until, in the early years of her widowhood, she had become interested in it as a result of a dream that she had. She had seen herself in a carriage full of travelers who passed by the open door of a church where worshipers were praising God with great joy. Wishing to join the throng, she pushed forward but was stopped as a voice announced to her:

> You must pass by and go farther; you will never enter into the sacred repose of the children of God except through the gate of St. Claude.[38]

She began to research the cult and had been planning a visit to the shrine itself when she met François, whose mother, Madame de Boisy, had requested of him that he accompany her on pilgrimage to the site.

They met on August 24. The widow de Chantal had made the arduous journey of three days on horseback accompanied by two of her childhood friends, the sisters Marguerite and Rose Bourgeois de Crépy who had been part of the admiring audience at the Lenten sermons in Dijon. She was keenly anticipating this Alpine encounter with her new mentor. He seems likewise to have been engrossed in the thought of her during her absence. They met soon after their arrivals. He wasted no time. She was to report to him all that was going on within her. This she did, it is reported, with candor, clarity and simplicity. The prelate did not respond with even a single word but gravely left the room and his confidante till their meeting of the next morning. When she saw him the following day, her director had obviously had little sleep during the night. He had pondered her case, he said, for he wanted to be sure that what he was undertaking was indeed the will of God. That is why he had waited so long and delayed his decision. It was truly the will of God that he become her spiritual director. He considered her previous vows null and void. From now on she should rely upon his advice. Later in the morning she made a general confession in his presence and he wrote up a formal statement of his acceptance of this responsibility.[39]

The commitment for both of them was a serious one. While he regularly undertook the direction of souls, François always did so with the sense that he was to play the part of facilitator. God, acting in the person, must be allowed ample room for activity. The director, informed by the principles of asceticism and prayer taught by the church, aided the individual to discern in himself or herself the authentic will of God. This was no light task, and the prelate knew it. He was aware of the sacred trust that he held. He was not to act in his own self-interests or even in the self-interests of his charge. His responsibility was to something greater than either of them.

It is probably safe to say that in this early stage of their friendship, François was more emotionally distanced from the relationship than was Jeanne. To be sure, this ardent woman's vehement impulse toward sanctity drew him irrepressibly. He must have sensed in her a rare potential for spiritual authenticity similar to his own. In Dijon he had reported to her that while celebrating Mass he had felt the presence of her spirit not as a distraction but as an aid in attaching him further to God. But at first he saw her as primarily his charge. "God has given me to you," he had written. This was not always to remain the case.

She embraced the bond between them with equal seriousness. Whatever her personal feelings about their coming together might have been—there was after all a mysteriously fated quality to it all—her primary motive in becoming his protégée was her overwhelming love of God. Jeanne was deeply concerned about her state in life. God was calling her to a deeper intimacy, a more mature love. How could she best give concrete expression to this call? In her mind this call was linked to the person of François de Sales, but she did know that this holy individual was not the source of the call but the conduit through which she was better to listen. She returned to Dijon full of joy.

At the Shrine of the Black Virgin at Notre-Dame-d'Etang she wrote out her own version of their agreement:

> All powerful and eternal God, I, Jeanne-Françoise Frémyot unworthy of your divine presence, yet confident in your infinite goodness and mercy, in the presence of the glorious Virgin Mary and all your triumphant celestial choirs, make a vow to your divine Majesty of obedience to Monseigneur, the bishop of Geneva, subject to the authority of all his legitimate superiors. Humbly entreating your immense goodness and clemency, by the precious blood of Jesus Christ, may it please you to receive this sacrifice of sweet fragrance and as it has pleased you to give me the grace to desire and offer it, may it also please you to give abundantly to me in order that I may accomplish it.

Amen. Written at Notre-Dame-d'Etang the second of September, 1604.[40]

III

When Jeanne passed through the gate at St. Claude she journeyed west to the Burgundian valleys. Her newly-commited director made his way south and east to the mountainous lake country of Savoy. It was here that he had been born and raised, here that he exercised his episcopal duties. François de Sales, named for the great saint from Assisi, was born in 1567 at the Château de Sales, the first child of François de Boisy and Françoise de Sionnaz. His family line was old and distinguished. Much was to be expected from the talented and ingratiating boy. He was, at his father's insistence, sent to the Jesuit college at Clérmont in Paris to study philosophy and the humanities and then to the University of Padua to apply himself to the study of law. He returned to his native Savoy at the age of twenty-four with a degree in civil and canon law. At his own instigation he had also extensively studied theology, for he was determined to become a priest. With his mother's assistance he convinced his father that his future lay in ecclesiastical life. In 1593 he was appointed provost of the cathedral chapter of Geneva. He was to serve the bishop of that diocese, de Granier, in his exile in the little hill town of Annecy. For many years now the bishop of that once thriving Catholic diocese had been forced into exile beyond the Swiss border, for Geneva had no use for the representatives of Rome. François was familiar with Annecy, for his family home was in the area and as a boy he had been schooled there. François took holy orders later in the same year as his appointment as provost.

Not soon after this, Bishop de Granier called upon his young provost to undertake a missionary campaign in the neighboring Chablais region where Catholic observance had become virtually non-existent. His assistant was remarkably successful in this sometimes harrowing mission of reconverting the area to the orthodox faith.[41] It was during this time that François began his career as a writer, penning polemical tracts for the instruction of possible converts in the Chablais. By 1599 he had been named coadjutor of the episcopal see. His duties (a diplomatic mission) took him to Paris and the French court in 1602. There he met and made a positive impression upon that enigmatic monarch Henri IV. He also came to be included in the devout circle gathered at the house of Madame Acarie. There the young provincial mingled with the guiding lights of the French religious renewal. His gifts were so recognized that Madame Acarie herself chose him for her confessor. The talk at the Acarie household was of the writings of Teresa of Avila. It was in this circle that the Savoyard became acquainted with Carmelite spirituality and, through Teresa and other representatives of the mystical tradition, with the rich possibilities of contemplative prayer. At the same time he was composing material for the book he was soon to begin writing, and which was to gain wide recognition, *The Introduction to the Devout Life*. François held that the devout life should not be the prerogative of a select few cloistered persons or the business only of priests. So he began to compile a book of meditations and instructions for people in other walks of life.

Upon his return to Annecy and the death of the presiding bishop, François was consecrated to the episcopal post. The ceremony took place on the feast of the Immaculate Conception, December 8, 1602. He vigorously undertook the work of reforming his diocese. Monasteries were visited and enjoined to return to an exact observance of their original rules. Places of devotion were reestablished and the work of religious instruction began for clergy as well as lay parishioners of all ages, and he began to preach all over his diocese. Clearly, directly from his heart to the hearts of his listeners he spoke of the word and work of God, moving his auditors to emulate the holiness he radiated.

It was to his busy life as bishop that François de Sales returned from St. Claude. But he did not forget Madame de Chantal. On the contrary. Their correspondence grew in importance. The rendering of the devotional architecture that he had begun in the summer months he now continued. In October 1604 he wrote her a long letter of advice. Remarkably precise, it shows her by concrete example how to order her day to facilitate the life of devotion. At the same time it clearly delineates the broader principles of spiritual growth by which the bishop operated. He communicates to her both the concepts into which he hopes she would be initiated and the methods she should adopt to facilitate this initiation. The tone with

which he writes is enthusiastic. The profound attraction that he felt
toward Jeanne is evident as well as his sense that this was a woman
capable of receiving the full force of his radical vision.

The October letter begins by assuring her, once again, that her
choice of him as director is legitimate and beyond question the correct choice for her. In part he is assured of this by the fact that he
himself experiences such certainty and such feeling for her. A new
quality of affection emerges which he finds difficult to name but
whose effect is:

> . . . a great interior warmth that I have to wish for you a perfect
> love of God and other spiritual blessings. . . . This feeling is dif-
> ferent from others; the feeling I have for you has a certain par-
> ticularity that consoles me no end, and to tell the truth, it is
> extremely profitable to me.[42]

Clearly, the director was beginning to perceive that this relationship
was going to be different from others he had known. He says that
he finds himself, while celebrating Mass, envisioning her as he prays
with the congregation, "give us," "grant us." The "us" before had
been, he claims, a general pronoun. Now it was taking on a personal
connotation.

The letter proceeds, after this arresting beginning, to be less
reflective and more directive. She had been suffering what she called
"doubts against the faith." No light matter this, in an age when the
Catholic Church was defining itself in terms of particular articles of
faith. François de Sales does not dwell upon the exact content of
these doubts, but we can be fairly certain that they centered upon
the mystery of the Eucharist.[43] Her director was less concerned that
she have doubts than that she learn to keep them from impeding her
spiritual development. He counseled her instead not to engage in
inner argument with her doubts.

> Temptations against the faith go directly to the mind in order to
> lure it into argument, reflection or daydreaming on the subject.
> Do you know what you should do while the enemy is occupied
> trying to scale the wall of the intellect? Go out through the door
> of the will and fool him by so doing.[44]

She should simply accept the fact of these troubling doubts but not give them undue attention. Instead she should humble herself before God, asking His help and leaving it up to Him to do something about it.

It was profound advice, advice that he would continue to offer Jeanne for many years in response to diverse spiritual crises.[45] François had the perceptiveness to know that one cannot, without violence to self, ignore the crises that occur in the inner life. "Temptations" of all types occur. But he concluded that to do battle with these temptations was to invest too much energy in them, to turn one's focus from where focus should be directed—to the love of God. Instead, one chose to live with the painful reality of such intrusions, letting them exist but, through acts of the will, permitting them neither free expression nor undue prominence. One did not ignore them but made a rational decision, based on criteria that the church had long taught, as to what were to be the priorities of the interior life.

The bishop himself had undergone an agonizing spiritual crisis as a young man and had, after painful months of struggle, discovered that a total acceptance of the situation in which he found himself was the path to spiritual healing. While a student at Paris he had been terror-struck at the doctrine of predestination that the theological masters Augustine of Hippo and Thomas Aquinas had formulated in early centuries. According to the revered doctors, God had predestined certain individuals to be the elect and one had actually no sort of assurance beyond faith that one might be one of the chosen number. It seems to have been the spectre of eternal separation from the God he loved above all else that caused the youthful student to quake. For several months he was obsessed with his fear; then a resolution to his tension was offered to him. Interestingly enough, the resolution was not in the direction of certainty. If he was predestined to enjoy the presence of God forever, so be it. If he was to be denied that unexpressible joy, so be it. At least, in this lifetime, he had the opportunity to love God with the full force of his capacities. He was free, not in knowing, but free to love. All the rest was unimportant, for what was most essential for him was the *pure love* of God. Pure love or love oblivious of any motives of reward or pleasure for the self was a doctrine that Christian mystics had long taught. At this important life crisis, the young François seems to have been totally converted to this attitude. It was to extend to all aspects of his life. He refused to engage with his terror of separation or his desire for eternal proximity. He surrendered to the ambiguity, the uncertainty of his doubt, and accepted it as a tension with which he was willing to live. But that was not to be the focus of his life. God was. For it was in a human being's power to love, and love he would, to the full extent of his capacity.

This brings us then to an awareness of the Salesian theology that undergirded this heroic detachment and embrace of pure love. Despite his genuine indifference even to the issue of his own salvation, François de Sales was profoundly optimistic about the forces that motivated the universe. He shared with other Christian humanists a firm faith in the capacity of humankind to influence its own destiny and the assurance that God wished the ultimate salvation of all His creatures.[46] When he wrote "I am a man, nothing more" he artfully implied that to be fully human is to be capable of loving God.

The love of God, he believed, is the purpose and fulfillment to which mankind was created. To incline to this love is not something foreign to human nature but intrinsic to it: it flows naturally from the human heart. This inclination is met on the other side by the graciously inclining love of God Himself, who desires humankind to rise to the fruition of their mutual love. The lover and the beloved are alike in that the one is created in the image and likeness of the other and in that they receive from each other their mutual perfection: the one a perfection necessitated by lack, the other a perfection fulfilled in bestowing abundance. But although the inclination to love simmers just below the surface of all human experience, humankind does not have the power to catalyze that inclination into activity. Original sin has so wounded nature that both the understanding and the will—the two essential elements of the soul—are paralyzed. The understanding must be educated as to humankind's essential nature and destination and the will reformed to respond to divine promptings rather than to its own misdirected urgings.

The reconstruction of the soul into its intended integrity is the task of the spiritual life. Like his predecessors in the contemplative tradition, François de Sales taught that the Christian life was a gradual but radical process of personal transformation through and into the image of God known in Christ. He advised as the means to that end the essential principle of Christian spirituality that is encoded in the life and death of Jesus of Nazareth—death to self and resurrection to a life in God. He framed the entire picture in the language of love. The Genevan prelate saw the spiritual life as a continuum of love. One moves "up" or "down" the continuum either nearer to or farther away from the loving perfection that is God to the extent that one loves God above all other loves and thus perceives other loves in and through God. An ascent is what is required. But as far as the person is concerned this upward movement is paradoxically also a downward movement: resurrection and crucifixion are inseparable. One dies to self-love as one surrenders to the love of God. Just as one is resurrected into God through the exercise of love, so one dies to self through the same medium. God wishes this for each individual and has endowed him or her with the capacity to cooperate with Him in the work of salvation.

It was this expansive trust in the ultimate beneficence of God and the innate capability of humankind, coupled with a radical surrender to whatever events or states one might experience during a lifetime, that François de Sales set out to teach his new friend. She had doubts, profound doubts, and was troubled and distracted by them. But her task was to love God in and through the circumstances in which she found herself. Hers was to be a naked love, a love not necessarily clothed with the consolation of certainty.

His October letter moves on from this reflection on how she should meet her doubts to an outline of the devotional activities with which she should occupy herself, which are to include daily prayers and attendance at Mass. The director further suggests a devotion to the suffering Christ. Jeanne is on five consecutive days imaginatively to enter into each of the five wounds inflicted upon the Savior at the time of the crucifixion. On the sixth day she is to retreat to the thorns of His crown, on the seventh to the wound in His side. In this way she will bring herself into an empathy with the crucified God she worships. Each day is to end with an examination of conscience and the recitation of various litanies.

Her director reveals his predilection when, after outlining this program, he underscores for her the spirit in which these exercises are to be carried out.

Everything must be done with love, nothing with force; it is more important to love obedience than to fear disobedience.[47]

It was not to be the specific externals of devotion that she was to strive for so much as the interior attitude with which they were to be carried out. That this emphasis on the interior meaning of acts of piety was transformative for her is seen by the testimony of her servants.

> Madame's first director only made her pray three times a day and we were all annoyed by it, but Monseigneur de Geneve makes her pray all the time and no one is inconvenienced in the least by that.[48]

Prayer was not to be an end in itself but the environment in which she allowed herself to touch and be touched by the God who is love. Through that love her very person and everyday routine was to be transformed.

Not that François de Sales had any disregard for the exercise of exterior acts of piety or asceticism. He simply did not want these externals to take the place of the authentic interior growth they were designed to facilitate. He does recommend a moderate use of the "discipline" and of fasting for Jeanne. In his moderate asceticism the bishop was something of an anachronism for his time. The new spiritual vitality of the Counter-Reformation had brought with it a zealot's taste for extreme bodily mortification both within and without monastery walls. The Savoyard, incomparably zealous when it came to interior discipline, was more generous when he preached exterior acts of penance.

Continuing with his practical advice, François encourages the widow to continue the visits to the poor and the sick that she had been accustomed to making. He further exhorts her to fulfill her responsibilities to her family. She is to pay particular attention to Celse-Bénigne, her eldest and only son, to see that he, little by little, acquires a taste for a life of devotion and a distaste of purely worldly ambition.

The long letter closes with a discussion of the spirit of liberty with which he wished her to embark upon her new life of devotion. This liberty he defines as "a detachment of the Christian heart from all things so that it might follow the will of God." It is the spirit that the good bishop himself exuded. A heart having such liberty will not be attached to spiritual consolations, he instructs her, but will receive even afflictions with gracefulness. Neither will it be attached to devotional practices. Rather it will be willing to leave these at any moment if duty or illness necessitates. Moreover, such a heart is never sad but continues its joyful celebration of the love of God in all circumstances.

A new vista was opening up for Jeanne de Chantal. For she was a woman of great potential but without the experience or confidence to allow her potential to bear fruit. Her friend could teach her to step boldly, to follow courageously the hidden life emerging from within her. The vision of the Christian life that Monseigneur de Sales was communicating to Madame de Chantal was distinctly his own. It was not a monastic spirituality. Neither did it resemble the superficial injunctions to pious observance that passed for lay religious instruction at the time. François de Sales drank deeply from the springs of the contemplative tradition and had extracted from that tradition the essence of the contemplative life which he managed to make applicable to persons in all walks of life.

The literary sources of his teaching are varied.[49] He lived, as we have seen, in a period of religious ecclecticism. Having read widely in the contemplative tradition, he had assimilated the teachings of a good number of authors. The Flemish mystical writers' influence can be seen in his thought, as can the imprint of Italian and, particularly, Spanish religiosity. François de Sales' spirituality evokes that of Teresa of Avila,[50] and he kept as his constant companion a little volume entitled *The Spiritual Combat*, a work of Italian and Spanish origins.[51] His sources were many, and his genius was to assimilate and integrate into one unified teaching the vast and varied heritage with which he was familiar. His teaching emerges as at one and the same time profoundly traditional, in that it embodies what is most distinctive and essential in the tradition, yet also highly unique.

The basic pattern he taught was traditional: death to self, rebirth in God through surrender in love. But his spirituality retains its own flavor and nuance. The bishop was raised in the mountainous regions of Savoy, and it has been said that the teaching he imparted bears a striking metaphorical resemblance to the geographical contours of his native land. This seems true enough. On first encounter, the countryside of Haute Savoie is ingratiating and hospitable. But the gentleness of what is at first presented to the eye belies the real nature of the landscape. Beneath bucolic meadows and streams are the powerful bodies of the Alps. The rock is ancient and immovable. In winter blinding snows can render the region perilous. It is a wilderness, after all.

Like his native land, François de Sales' spirituality conveys an impression that is deceptively understated. The gentlemanly liberality of his voice, his fabled "douceur," is not incompatible with the most austere and rugged of spiritual disciplines. His goal was utter denudation of self to the end that the presence of God be realized in the most perfect way possible. He was uncompromising in this quest. Jeanne in later years quotes him as exclaiming:

> We belong completely to God, without any other claim than to the honor of being His. If I had one slender thread of affection that was not for Him or from Him, I would tear it out at once. Yes, if I had one fiber of my heart that was not marked by His crucifix, I wouldn't want to preserve it for even the least moment.[52]

Moreover, as we have seen, the denudation he sought was first and foremost an interior matter. For this reason it is often overlooked in his spirituality. But it is the bedrock upon which his teaching is structured. Moreover, in the realm of the interior he preached the acquisition of what he calls the "little virtues" as opposed to their heroic counterparts. He wished the process of denudation to remain so hidden (in its operation, not its fruits) that the devotee could never fall into the subtle web of spiritual pride that can so easily entrap one if one seeks heroic denudation as an end in itself. Thus humility, meekness of heart, cheerful forbearance with neighbor, compliance with others, poverty of spirit, modesty and simplicity were the virtues he championed. Jeanne was to write, a number of years after his death:

> ... he preferred mortifications which presented themselves, little though they might be, to the great ones which one could choose saying "where there is less of our own choosing, there

is more room for God." In this way our Blessed One never went an hour without practicing interior mortification, using every opportunity that offered itself to him. . . .[53]

Total denudation he did advocate, but his style of advocacy at first encounter tends to belie the radical nature of his vision. François de Sales has been called the "gentleman saint," and indeed his style is gentlemanly if one understands that word in its full Renaissance implications. The society of his day had inherited the tradition of "l'honnête homme" from its cultured predecessors whose ideal was the man who fully realized his innate potential through the actions of daily life. The seventeenth century was preoccupied with the working out of this ideal of "l'honnête homme": "A wellborn man who knows how to live well"—Bussy-Rabutin was to neatly encapsulate the tradition. François was not outside of this concern. In his gracious manner with people, in his insistence on "douceur" as the appropriate attitude of the spiritual life, in his assertion that a Christianity overtly expressed is one mark of a fully realized man, in his reasoned good sense, one sees the melding of this tradition with the practical spirituality of the Counter-Reformation.

But his gracious manner was much more than a decorous posture toward the world. It was a total orientation of person. A marvelously balanced personality, François consciously strove all his life to achieve a proportioned exercise of all elements of his character. This balanced personality lent itself easily to the decorum for which he was noted:

The manner and the speech of the Blessed were majestic and serious yet at the same time completely humble, as calm and candid as one could imagine; he was completely unaffected. No one ever heard him say anything offensive to others nor anything unsuitable or flippant. He spoke quietly, thoughtfully, deliberately, gently and wisely always conveying his meaning but without recourse to fine phrases or any affectation; he loved directness and simplicity.[54]

There was a theoretical dimension to his orientation as well. It can best be perceived in his mode of communication. He speaks in all his works—letters, treatises, sermons—as a man intimately concerned with the direction of souls. Thus, he was primarily concerned to inform people of the truths of the Christian faith as taught by the church and to initate them into the life of the spirit as known through the contemplative tradition. Therefore, as with his preaching, he used methods of communication designed to inflame the heart, and thus the whole person, to stir his listeners to action.

His literary style is likewise informed by the same rhetorical emphasis. His prose is notable for its gracious use of metaphor, the unexpected turn of phrase and image. This aesthetic is not some mere ornament upon his thought but the vessel which gives form to content and upon which the particular nature of his thought depends for transmission. He cultivated this aesthetic at Paris and Padua where he was schooled. The perception of beauty is at its core. In France he learned that rhetoric and poetry are an integral part of logic, that argument is carried forward and made persuasive through images and metaphor. In Italy he imbibed the Renaissance atmosphere of Neo-Platonism which linked love with beauty and took as canons of truth the aesthetic categories of harmony and proportion. Furthermore, he came to see that beauty has a mission to mark out the way toward love, that creatures first ascend to God through aesthetic appreciation of the created world, although later this experience must surpass itself and yield to the experience of the source of beauty alone.[55]

Theory and character combined in a rare way in the bishop of Geneva. His person and his spiritual vision were like the Savoyard landscape: delicate and inviting to the eye, yet resting upon a rugged, sometimes treacherous foundation. And this he brought to his relationship with the widow de Chantal. In his unique personal style he stands out in contrast to her.[56] They were complementary. This perhaps was one of the great strengths of their long friendship. The steady and reasoned discipline in the life of the spirit that he taught her served as ballast for her impulsiveness and impatience. On the other hand, her extraordinary ardor and her capacity for radical intimacy was to leaven his already deep religious commitment, making him ready to experience the love of God in a newly heightened way. Moreover, they seemed to appreciate in each other these complementary qualities. These were just the beginnings, but they were soon to deepen into an intimacy that was to make of the director and his penitent spiritual friends.

2.

Hidden Growth
(1606–1610)

I

It had been decided, by confessor and penitent, that Jeanne should from now on more equally divide her time between Dijon and Monthelon. This meant that she must often be on the road, taking with her four young children and their attendants. Yet this new arrangement meant more contact with her father and her circle of devout friends in Dijon. In the eyes of the world there was nothing unusual in her situation. She was simply fulfilling the duties that her state in life required of her. For the spiritual life that she was nourishing in private was not to take her away from her family responsibilities. François de Sales impressed upon her the close connection between her public and private lives: the Christian vocation was for him both inner and outer, and love of God and of neighbor were the two inseparable elements of that vocation. Jeanne was to continue in her widowhood, looking to that state to provide for her the material out of which her growing desire to serve God unreservedly was to be fashioned.

This was because a fidelity to the situation in which one finds oneself was, in the bishop's eyes, the perfect opportunity for the self-denial that was necessary for growth. The prelate himself practiced this obvious yet unglamorous form of asceticism. In his opinion, it was a great aid not only to self-discipline but to humility as well, and for him an honest recognition of one's limitations and dependence was the basis of any authentic relationship with God. Salesian asceticism also assumed a strong faith in a loving, compassionate God who treasured each individual, so when one gave of self, the giving came not as duty but as a joyous and grateful response.

The subtle discriminations that the Genevan bishop was able to make in his direction of Madame de Chantal show how artful was his implementation of these principles. Alongside his attempt to instruct her in the principles of self-emptying, he continually buttressed her flagging self-confidence and encouraged her true sense of self-worth, transforming overly scrupulous fears about her "doubts" into a courageous liberty of spirit that allowed her the room for the development of which she was capable. It is interesting to note that François de Sales specialized in the direction of women.[1] His insightful handling of innumerable female penitents over the years is worth exploring. For he had a sensitivity to the particular difficulties that women are prone to encounter in the spiritual life. One of these is the issue of lack of self-worth which masqueraded as selflessness.[2] The bishop clearly knew the dangers of this personal orientation and sought to correct it in his penitents so that the genuine selflessness that arises out of love and gratitude, and not out of fear or servitude, could emerge.

True selflessness, he felt, could be achieved in any vocation. The life-situation in which one found oneself—and in Jeanne's case it was widowhood—was always the best. Jeanne's situation, in her friend's eyes was also appropriate to the pursuit of spiritual growth because the facts of her situation so closely resembled the very attitudes she was attempting to cultivate. Her director knew that Jeanne's spiritual state was deeply affected by her state in life, and from her lack and her perplexity he called upon the capacity for self-transformation that she held in reserve.

> It's not remarkable that a poor widow's spirit should be weak and miserable. What would you have it be? Far-sighted, strong, unshaken and self-sustaining? It is fitting that your mood match your condition: a widow's spirit, that is, lowly and totally abject except that it gives no offense to God. . . .[3]

The humbleness of her circumstances was perfect for the cultivation of the interior humility that is the foundation of Salesian spirituality. It was this humility that would open her to the free operation of God. Her continued realization of God's plan for her was to be a lowly occurrence, a matter of hidden growth.

Though this growth would be hidden from the eyes of her contemporaries, it would be far from hidden from her. She knew, if only intuitively, how profoundly she was being called to a new selfhood. The work would indeed take years. Now she knew only that she must live each day in the difficult reality of her widowhood: continue nursing the sick and feeding the poor, caring for her children and their grandfather, struggling with her own doubts. Her director asked all this of her and patience—a joyous, generous patience that desired nothing more. Jeanne found it difficult. For all her unquestioned dedication to her duties, she longed to be on with it, yearned with all her natural impetuousness to fling herself into the arms of her Lord.

In the years after their meeting at St. Claude, the letters between Jeanne de Chantal and François de Sales were long and frequent. Still, for her it was not enough. So it was agreed that she should come to the Sales family home in the mountains near Thorens in May 1605. She would be well cared for by the bishop's mother, Madame de Boisy, whom she had met on the pilgrimage the previous year. The visit lasted for ten days, during which time François and Jeanne walked the length and breadth of the family lands, deep in conversation. They often sat among the remains of a little pagan temple that stood on a hill not far from the main houses,[4] she pouring out her concerns to him, he listening and responding. As a result of these interviews with her mentor, Jeanne proceeded to write for herself a little booklet, the *Petit Livret:* bits of advice and imagery which emerged from the May trip to Savoy. She began to envision her interior landscape in monastic terms: Monica, the patron saint of widows, was to be her novice-mistress, the Virgin Mary herself her Abbess. Values generally reserved for monastics were to inform her life in the world. The contents of the *Petit Livret* are varied, but the one sentiment supporting it all is her desire to give herself completely to her God. The following spontaneous petition is revealing:

> Lord, consume me, ingest me, annihilate me in yourself. I want nothing but God; to rest in him, completely, being strengthened more and more to serve him by my total dependence on his

divine Providence, always more firmly anchored in the faith of
his true word, and completely abandoned to his mercy and care.
Oh eternal and fatherly goodness! My heart opens itself to you.[5]

The widow de Chantal left the springtime countryside of
Thorens to return to her duties at home. She took with her Jeanne
de Sales, François' young sister who was headed for convent school
in France. The older woman had been entrusted with the care of
this favorite child. Besides her youthful charge, Jeanne carried home
with her a new certainty that she was indeeed following the path
that God had marked out for her. This new certainty brought with
it the courage to cut through the remaining knots of emotional
entanglement that still held her to her role as wife or potential wife.
She had not made her final peace with her husband's death, particularly because she found herself still unable to reconcile herself to
the unfortunate friend whose weapon had discharged the fatal shots
that had killed Christophe. François de Sales knew of her unre-
solved anger toward this fellow and advised her about how she
might approach this issue.

> You needn't try to find a particular time or opportunity to seek
> him out; but if he should come to you himself, I would like you
> to greet him with a gentle, gracious and compassionate heart.
> Doubtless it will be uneasy and agitated and your blood will boil,
> but, what of it? . . .
>
> So it is, my daughter: through our emotions God makes us see
> that we are flesh, bone and spirit. . . . I repeat: my intention is
> not that you seek out an encounter with this poor man, but that
> you yield to those who might wish such a meeting to take place
> and that you show that you are capable of loving all things. Yes,
> even your husband's death or the deaths of your father and your
> children and those closest to you. Yes, even your own, through
> the death and love of our sweet Saviour.[6]

The advice was simple—she was to learn to love beyond her
present capacity. She was eventually to learn to love all that life presented to her. By doing this she would open herself radically to the
presence of God in all events. She, like the Savior she adored, would
stretch out her arms to embrace all her "crosses," knowing that in

the act of authentic loving, resignation in its most profound sense, she was being fashioned in the image she loved and bringing that image into the world. But now, in these years of hidden growth, she knew that primarily as a matter of principle, not of experience. By letting go of her pain and anger toward her husband's unwitting murderer, she began to let go of the emotional hold that her married life still had on her.

But moving out of the past was not all that was asked of her at this time. Her hand was asked for in marriage. The suitor was more than eligible and her family pressed her a bit to accede to this most attractive offer. She struggled with it. There were her young children to think about, and her own desire to remain unmarried she found hard to reconcile with her strong sense of obligation. The bishop knew what she herself knew but was afraid to articulate to her family—that she had gone too far in the process of self-definition to go back. The road on which she was headed was a road that required of her a vow of chastity and a total commitment to surrender herself to the unfolding will of God. Only she was not yet far enough along in that process to be able to easily withstand the pressures, especially since they were intended for her good. Her mentor's written words emboldened her in her refusal. Employing the metaphor of Solomon's temple to refer to the spiritual architecture they were fashioning, he wrote:

> Who are these reckless persons who want to strike at and destroy that white column of our sacred tabernacle? Well, it only amounted to a little vanity, a little flattery, a little something or other. Now, it is nothing. Courage. Our columns are well grounded, it seems to me, a little wind will not topple them. Really, my daughter, a person must be clear-cut and resolute on these occasions: you mustn't encourage solicitors at all, because you don't have to offer what they are asking for. You must tell them this in such a way that they will go look elsewhere. It is true, our way is not theirs, in the same way that the ivory in Soloman's throne no longer belonged to the elephants who carried it in their jaws.[7]

She felt that, quite literally, her heart was meant for God alone. This was not a protective withdrawal from reality. Rather, this was a genuine response to the call to a deeper engagement with reality for which she was being prepared. But the call, although it was strong and ardently felt, had almost to be burned into her consciousness before it could be heard amid the din of ordinary perception. She was being called, not merely to a new way of life, but to an utterly new modality of being in which the usual values and concerns she had known would be swept away by a new set of priorities and a new pattern of meaning. This she could feel. She could also feel the profound disparity between what she presently was and what it was she was challenged to be. François de Sales had written in his *Introduction to the Devout Life,*

> ... I have wished above everything else to engrave upon your heart this sacred motto "Live, Jesus!"[8] I am sure that after that your life, which proceeds from the heart as an almond tree from its kernel, will produce all of its actions, which are its fruits, inscribed and engraved with the same word of salvation, and just as this sweet Jesus will live within your heart so he will also live in all your conduct, he will appear in your eyes, on your lips, your hands and even the hair on your head. You will be able to say in imitation of St. Paul, "I live now, not I, but Christ lives in me."[9]

Soon after she returned from Thorens, Jeanne took a sharp metal object and knelt before the crucifix she kept among her private effects. She bared the flesh above her heart, heated the metal instrument in the fire and etched in letters about an inch high the name of Jesus.

This incident became infamous to later generations. It was cited to illustrate her extremes of temperament that she is thought to have had.[10] Certainly the event is arresting. She burned the letters deeply enough that they were permanently engraved. They were perfectly visible to the nuns who prepared her body for burial some thirty-six years later. But extremes were not her habitual mode, and the act of burning her own flesh was certainly not in the Salesian spirit. She had received permission to perform the act from a local confessor, but François de Sales' response to the event was cool. He chose to redirect her focus to the interior dimension of the act she had performed.

... who will give me the joy of one day seeing the name of Jesus engraved on the inmost depth of your heart as it is branded on your breast? Oh, how I have longed to have the iron of Our Lord's lance in one hand and your heart in the other! How I would have undertaken this task![11]

His response was predictable and his view of her action in keeping with his insistence on the paramount importance of the inner dimension of the Christian life. But one suspects that there is more to the event than the fact that an as yet untempered penitent acted impulsively and unwisely and her director sought to turn the event into a lesson on the true meaning of mortification. Jeanne, while vigorous of temperament, as a woman, had been trained from an early age to rely upon the direction of others where the major decisions of her life were concerned. The small insistent voice that told her she must go against the will of family and society in choosing a life of celibacy may have been what had brought her this far. But it needed great determination for her to follow that voice to the length it was calling her. She had the bishop for support, this was true. But he was far away and her family close around her. She, more than François, must have sensed how hard it was going to be for her to resist the pressures leveled at her. It was as though she needed in some way to convince not only her contemporaries but herself that she was in earnest in her total love of God. She needed to bear her beloved's imprint as concretely as a wife bears her husband's—in a new surname, a wedding ring, a belly swollen with child.

In the same letter François also made the following statement: "You must no longer be a woman, you must have a man's heart. . . . "[12] He meant this metaphorically in that he encouraged her to remain virilely courageous and firm in her desire to serve God. It was a meaningful statement for her. She would have to learn to do what she, as a woman, had seldom been encouraged to do:[13] to act in accordance with her own deepest truth whether or not this was what others found acceptable.

She would have to learn this lesson in another arena as well. Her tendency was to overlook her own innate capacities and to look to persons outside herself to supply her with direction and reinforcement. Because of this she tended, in the beginning especially, to be too attached to the advice of her director. Her mentor cautioned her against this:

> Certainly it is a great abuse to so bind oneself to a confessor that
> if he happens to be unaccommodating, one is troubled and upset.
> This is to attach oneself to the instrument of well-being and not
> the source, who is God and consequently to lose true liberty.[14]

Jeanne had vowed obedience to Monseigneur François de Sales and he did expect from her faithfulness and earnest cooperation. What he was in the process of aiding her to discern was the vital distinction between the letter and the spirit of observance. She did tend to want so scrupulously to fulfill all her duties that she could lose sight of the spirit they were designed to facilitate. He was helping her to separate her own interior movements from the advice of her director which she was internalizing and then to use the advice to facilitate the movements.

This was no easy task, and one that was made more difficult in her case because during the period following her return from Thorens she suffered acutely from spiritual "dryness." The interior certainty that had carried her thus far, difficult as it was to maintain her course amid the conflicting influences from outside, had previously had a comforting warmth and sweetness to accompany it. Now she didn't feel the way she had before. All that seemed to be left was a bold certainty with nothing pleasant to entice her to commit herself to it. Jeanne resisted the dryness. Longing to recover what she seemed to have lost, she became agitated and worried. She yearned ahead of herself, wishing to, as it were, leap over the distress to a comforting oasis of inner reassurance. But François de Sales was aware that the spiritual landscape through which he was guiding her had dark valleys as well as spacious plateaus. Her task was to be present to the situation as she found it. To ignore or be agitated by it would be to obstruct the process itself. Furthermore, the dryness she felt was far from meaningless, as it was very much a sign of growth. Self-love needed to die in order to make room for the expanding love that God was bringing to bear in her.

> Be attentive to the way in which you proceed in this situation.
> Perhaps you might see that you bind your spirit too much to

your desire for this most excellent taste which affords the soul the feeling of firmness, constancy and resolution. You have the firmness—what is it but firmness that would rather die than offend or abandon the faith? But you lack the feeling, because if you had it you would have a thousand joys. It is important that you are not over-eager; you will discover that you will be better off and that your wings will be more readily supported. This over-eagerness then is a fault in you, and it is this—I don't know why—that is never satisfied because you lack resignation. You resign yourself readily, only it is with a "but," because you want this thing and that thing and you argue in order to get it. A simple desire is not contrary to resignation, but a panting heart, fluttering wings, an agitated will, too much straining ahead, this is unmistakably a lack of resignation. Courage, my dear Sister, since our will belongs to God, no doubt we belong entirely to Him. You have all that is necessary, but you have no feeling that this is so there is no great loss in this.[15]

What was occurring was that Jeanne de Chantal was in the process of reenvisioning herself, articulating to herself in a new language, her own understanding of her experiences. On the one hand, this process took a certain toll. To surrender her own innate or learned cluster of responses and perceptions was at best disorienting. It meant the death of the self-identity that up until this time had formed the backdrop for all her actions. On the other hand, although death was the price of new identity it certainly was not the final goal she sought. The image of the dying and rising God through which Jeanne was beginning to articulate and interpret her own experience contained within itself an intimation of the radically transformative potential of those processes. An entirely new order of being was encoded there. The resurrection, as a symbol of the new identity that was emerging for this woman, was powerful and liberating.[16]

What made the whole issue more perplexing is that for the resurrection to find authentic expression in the individual, the death endured had to be a conscious and mature one. When Jeanne de Chantal surrendered her former identity, she was not letting some new role or set of ideas "carry" her psychic life for her. To counter this notion we have only to recall how arduously her director worked to put her back upon her own resources and to instill in her confidence in her own unique inner voices. He had firmly directed her away from her own tendency to overscrupulous observance and to superficial encounter with the truths he wished to impart.

To keep from stopping at the point of formal but unliberating realization, the process of death and resurrection—the incorporation in Christ—had to engage her on all levels. It was not a matter of intellectual assent or even of performing the right actions. The crucified Christ had to be experienced by her whole person. She was to be turned inside out, destroyed and remade. When the restructuring would be over she would find all her talents and resources brought to the full maturity of which they were capable.

It was a long process facilitated on the one hand by the self-emptying that was already taking place and on the other by the conscious attention to the images of Christ that she found in the Scripture, the liturgy, the devotional literature, and the iconography of the religious world in which she lived. This attention was like the slow spinning of a new garment. François, who knew the symbolic power of metaphor, seized the opportunity for instruction when Jeanne, who was accomplished in the sewing arts, wrote to him that she wanted to make for him a worsted vestment.

> It seems that the cross is the beautiful distaff of the holy bride of the Song of Songs—the devout Sulamite. The wool from the Innocent Lamb is carefully threaded there: that merit, example and mystery.

> Now, reverently place this distaff at your left hand and spin continually with your spiritual considerations, aspirations and exercises: in other words, by a holy imitation. Spin, I say, and draw all this white and delicate wool into your heart's spindle. The cloth that you make in this way will cover and save you from shame on the day of your death. It will keep you warm in winter and, as the wise man says, you will fear neither cold nor snow. This is perhaps what that same wise man was thinking, when, praising this saintly housewife, he said that she sets her hands to the distaff and her fingers grasp the spindle. Because, what is this audacious business which the spindle creates, if not the mystery of the Passion spun by our imitation?[17]

Through the use of other images François de Sales encouraged his protégée in her incorporation into the reality of the passion of

Christ. Devotion to the wounds of Christ was not uncommon at the time, and the bishop did not hesitate to initiate Jeanne into its deepest significance.

> ... go farther and farther, my dear daughter, in establishing your holy purposes and resolutions. Plunge your thinking deeper and deeper into the wound of Our Lord where you will find an abyss of reasons which will confirm you in your generous enterprise and will make you realize once again that the heart that dwells anywhere else, that builds its nest in any other tree than the cross, is empty and worthless. O God, how happy will we be if we live and die in this holy tabernacle![18]

When the bishop painted the metaphor of spinning, he used the term "imitation" to describe the relationship that Jeanne should have with the Christ image. But the term does not fully encompass what was occurring in her. When François used the devotional image of Christ's wounds, he was closer to expressing the actual process transpiring within Jeanne. She was entering into the deepest, most essential reality of the image and letting it surround her. She was becoming intimate with the very source of its life. The Christ image, especially as developed within the contemplative tradition, was multivocal. Jeanne was, with intellect, will, memory and emotion, allowing the many messages of the image to give meaning to what life presented her with and to form her sense of direction and perspective. She was being transformed by and into it.

Yet this, in the understanding of the Christian tradition, was not a one-way process. The image represented a living presence that could enter into the course of human history through the hearts of men and women. Christ not only was being born in Jeanne, but, through and in her, was being born into the world. In a letter of 1604, her director had enthusiastically proclaimed:

> Our souls must give birth, not outside themselves but inside themselves, to the sweetest, gentlest and most beautiful male child imaginable. It is Jesus whom we must bring to birth and produce in ourselves. You are pregnant with him, my dear Sister, and blessed be God who is His Father.[19]

Clearly, Salesian spirituality was marked by an emphasis on the humanity of Christ. "Vive, Jésus" was François de Sales' motto, and

the realization of this living presence depended, in his mind, on
familiarity with the human life, passion and death of Christ. In his
prayer, and the prayer that he recommended to Jeanne at this time,
there is an insistence that one must never abandon the "lowly valleys" of meditation,[20] that the spirituality of littleness so dear to his
heart implied a fidelity to the humble human Jesus. To prayerfully
consider the events in the life of Jesus, to make use of intellect and
imagination in prayer was the tried and true method of devotion.

Jeanne was steeped in this thinking, and we have seen how her
conscious attention to the imagery of tradition was radically transforming her person. But other spiritual influences were entering her
life at this time. The Carmel had come to France. In October 1604,
under the auspices of Madame Acarie and Pierre de Bérulle, a small
band of Spanish Carmelites observing the strict reformed practices
instigated by Teresa of Avila established themselves in Paris. French
thirst for the radical austerities of the life outweighed public opinion
hostile to all things Spanish. The Carmel grew rapidly. In 1605 a
foundation was made in Dijon. Jeanne, like many other women in
the town attracted to a life of devotion, was drawn to the convent
parlor.

Her restlessness and desire to leave the world was fanned by
her contact with the Carmelites. These fervent women were the talk
of the devout in society, and Jeanne could not miss the opportunity
to sit at their feet to learn of the life of contemplative prayer they
led. She spent a good deal of time in that Dijon parlor conversing
across the grilled aperture that separated the community of sisters
from those who remained outside. She seems to have questioned
them closely on their prayer and to have spoken quite openly of her
own interior life. She wrote of her new friends enthusiastically to
François. He, for his part, although he was always open to her con-
sulting others in spiritual matters and having a regular confessor
beside himself, was at first mildly reserved about Jeanne's contact
with the Carmel. First, he was concerned that she not lose the
patient acceptance of her widowed state. He had told her that he
was sure that sometime she would be called to change her situation.
But the time was not ripe. Her children were young. Besides, she
herself was not ready. And how could she use the present to grow
if she was always "somewhere else"?

... I am firm in my advice not to sow our neighbor's field, however beautiful it might be, while our own needs sowing. A distracted heart is always dangerous: having your heart in one place
and your work in another.[21]

Moreover, Jeanne had received advice on prayer about which
the Genevan bishop was reticent. We know that she spoke to Marie
de la Trinité, who in 1605 was a young French initiate to the Dijon
Carmel. Marie spoke to her of the methods of prayer practiced
within the cloister. It has been said that she judged Jeanne's dryness
in prayer, coupled with the obvious virtue of her widow's life, as a
sign that she was ready to move on to less discursive, more truly
"contemplative" prayer. She counseled her to avoid using the imagination or understanding while at prayer. When François was
informed of this he responded:

> So the good Mother says that there is no need to employ the
> imagination in order to envision the sacred humanity of the
> Saviour. Not, perhaps, for those who are already far advanced
> along the mountain of perfection. But for those of us who are
> still in the valleys, although desirous of mounting, I think it
> expedient to employ all our faculties, including the imagination.
> Nonetheless, I have already stressed in another letter that this
> imagining must be very simple and, like a humble seamstress,
> thread affections and resolutions onto our spirits.[22]

François de Sales' response to these suggestions has been much
discussed. Most frequently, he is seen as having as yet an incomplete
understanding of the nature of contemplation into which Jeanne
would initiate him in later years.[23] It has elsewhere been asserted
that the spiritual perspective from which Marie de la Trinité was
speaking when she conversed with Jeanne across the grille in Dijon
was not Teresian, as one would expect from a Carmelite, but deriv-
ative of the abstract school of French mysticism espoused by
Madame Acarie.[24] Teresian spirituality does not absolutely eschew
the use of human faculties. The abstract school does. In its focus on
Christ's divinity—his purely spiritual dimension—the French
school of spirituality places the locus of human-divine encounter
clearly outside the human faculties of the individual.

Marie de la Trinité was apparently counseling Jeanne consciously to avoid exercising her imagination in prayer. Certainly

Jeanne was, at this time, naturally drawn to a very simple non-dis-cursive prayer—what she called the "prayer of simple surrender." Her director had already heartily approved of her approach; in the *Petit Livret* there is a passage that indicates as much.[25] François de Sales in all probability did not redirect Jeanne's attention away from Marie de la Trinité's advice not because he did not understand its import but because he felt that, for Jeanne, the deliberate avoidance of the use of her faculties would serve to destroy the spirit of liberty that was desirable in prayer.

That she was drawn to a non-discursive prayer is clear. Even at this early stage the type of prayer that was all her life to charac-terize her inner attitude made itself manifest. She herself later summed it up in a single phrase: "a simple and single-focused atten-tiveness to God, through a complete surrender of the soul into His hands."[26] Hers was not a method of prayer so much as a posture in relationship to the divine. This posture was at one and the same time intellectual and volitional.[27] It was an orientation of her entire per-son, a conscious and continual gathering-together of the disparate elements in life and a giving over of them in love. It was, quite sim-ply, the practice of the presence of God in all things and at all moments. She was to write later in her life:

> The essence of prayer is not to be found in always being on our knees but in keeping our wills closely united to God's in all events. The soul which holds itself ready and open to yield itself obediently on any occasion, and which receives these occasions lovingly as sent from God, can do this even while sweeping the floor.[28]

But in 1605 and 1606 Jeanne de Chantal was not yet called upon to speak out about methods of prayer. She was very much a novice, eagerly seeking instruction from the cloistered Carmelites in Dijon, writing concerned queries to François in Annecy, carefully reading and rereading his replies, waiting in the perplexing but exhilarating state of not yet knowing how the new self emerging would be called upon to show itself. These were years of hidden growth. They were laying the foundations for what was to come next.

II

The bishop and the widow had hoped to see one another again in 1606, but circumstances did not conspire to make this possible. It was to be the summer of the following year before they would again have an opportunity to converse face to face. In the meantime, their correspondence continued their exchange of thoughts and deepened the relationship between them. He continued to advise her on the value of her widowed state. It was for her an opportunity to cultivate the virtues essential to an authentic life of prayer.[29] But this cultivation, though it was occurring on many personal levels, was to be undertaken simply, very simply. Virtues were not to be sought as an end in themselves but in order to reorient the individual to be more receptive and compliant to the divine will asserting itself in the events of everyday life.

> In order to practice the virtues it is not necessary to be attentive to all of them all of the time. In fact, this tends to turn one's thoughts and affections back on oneself so that they become entangled. Humility and charity are the dominant chords; all the other virtues are overtones of these. It's only necessary that these two be carefully observed: one very lowly, the other very lofty. The preservation of an entire structure depends upon the foundation and the roof. If you continue the exercise of these two with conviction, when you come up against the others, they won't give you any difficulty. These are the mothers of the virtues; the others follow them as little chicks follow mother hens.[30]

At the same time that François de Sales was instructing his protégée, he was also allowing the new life in her to take shape. The process he observed was as remarkable as the woman herself, and as variable. He wrote to her that all the seasons were seen in her soul: winter with its cold hands, its distractions and tedium, spring with its sweet flowerings of holiness, summer with the heat of her desires to please God. What remained to come was autumn, the time of harvest when all that she had planted would bear fruit.[31] What was the direction her life would take? Jeanne, as we have seen, was consistently moved toward a contemplative type of life. She kept pressing her mentor for his opinion on the subject. He had indicated his feeling that at some point she would indeed leave her present state for a new one, but that the time had not yet arrived. She gave herself up to the situation as it was.

> The hope that the Blessed One gave me [she confided to her biographer], that one day I would leave the world, consoled me no end. . . . I remained as my director had taught me, resting in God's hands, often offering Him the remainder of my days, asking that He employ them in the way of life that would be most pleasing to Him; refusing to be concerned with idle promises of the tranquility, attractiveness and obvious merit of the religious life. Instead, I tried to offer my heart empty of any other affection except that of pure, chaste love and of obedience.[32]

She was waiting, and her friend was waiting with her. He, with exquisite sensitivity was listening, sensing, making himself vulnerable to her as yet unspoken dreams. He believed that it was in that radical openness, that absolute suspension of self-will that one encountered the will of God. He too was preparing himself in the same way. Together they would discern the shape of her new life.

He wished to see her once again, so a visit to Savoy was planned for her in June 1607. It would be her first visit to Annecy, the theater of the bishop's episcopal activities. Annecy, "dear Nessy" as they would affectionately refer to the town in years to come, was nestled at the northwest end of Lake Annecy in the Alps about fifty miles south of Geneva. In the early seventeenth century it had a population of roughly four thousand five hundred. Compared to the metropolitan activity of Paris and Geneva or even the mercantile prosperity of Dijon, it was a modest, provincial hamlet. However, the little Savoyard town was the seat of the exiled bishop of Geneva, and so the pomp and ritual of the Counter-Reformation church played itself out along its narrow cobblestoned streets and along the banks of its quaint canals. At the time of the expulsion of the bishop from the magnificent Cathedral of St. Pierre in Geneva, the refugee hierarchy had sought shelter in a church belonging to a monastery of the Cordeliers in Annecy. Compared to the lofty structures that housed other bishops, this church wedged between canals and storefronts was hardly imposing. But it sufficed, and in

François de Sales' mind was ideal. All his life he loved Annecy. It was his homeland.

Jeanne arrived in town in early June. It was early summer and the Alpine countryside would have been verdant, the lake tranquil in its nest of towering mountain peaks. From the water one could see the towers of the ancient chateau that dominated the town. Beneath the chateau, Annecy was settled at the foot of the gentle slope of a hillside. Outside the town's stone walls the countryside was cultivated, fields and gardens bordering the shores of the lake. In Annecy Jeanne had the opportunity for the first time to view her friend in the full import of his official capacity. Here he was not a visiting, if esteemed, preacher, nor was he in the rural graciousness of his familial environment. Here he was surrounded by the elegance that an episcopal court required, by the splendor of a church that deemed the artistic and ritual creations of humankind to be fitting accompaniments to worship.[33] Yet he was still the man she knew, moving amid the protocol of his office with simplicity and candor. His own chambers he kept deliberately spare and modestly decorated. He lodged directly across the narrow street from the cathedral in the Maison Lambert, a Renaissance building which contained a suite of rented rooms. Later he was to move across town to the Hotel Favre, a lodging being vacated by his dear friend and fellow Christian humanist, Antoine Favre, Annecy official and later president of the senate of Savoy. Here, in 1606, François de Sales, with Favre, had founded the Florimontane Academy, forerunner of the French Academy.

The Savoyard village was small enough so that, except for really inclement weather, moving about from place to place could be done easily on foot. It was only a brief walk from the cathedral to the prison on the Palais de l'Isle where François used to visit the prisoners and speak with them about their concerns. It was just across a canal or two to the end of the village to the convent of the Poor Clares, a community exiled from Geneva at the same time as the bishop. This convent was a favorite of François' and he spent many hours preaching there to the nuns. Just up the rather steep hill from the Clarisses, the chateau loomed. Below the chateau was a convent of Jacobins. It was in their parochial church in 1575 that François had been confirmed and had received his First Communion. Circling back toward the cathedral one came upon the Church of Notre

Dame de Liesse, a medieval pilgrimage site famed for its icon of the
Virgin. In this sanctuary in 1566 Francois' young mother, married
and as yet childless, had prayed fervently before the Holy Shroud
then venerated in Annecy that she might give birth to a son. The
next year her first born—François—entered the world.

Not only the city itself but the terrain surrounding Lake
Annecy claimed the bishop's affection. Across the lake on its north-
eastern shores was the hamlet of Talloires which François restored
as a pilgrimage center, moving the neglected relics of St. Germaine,
an eleventh century abbott and hermit, into a small church on the
mountainside. The quiet hillside with its magnificent view moved
François. He nourished the hope that someday he would retire from
the burdens of episcopal responsibilities to the solitude of the hilltop
retreat in order to spend his last years writing.

This was the small, familiar world of her friend into which
Jeanne stepped in the summer of 1607. She remained in Annecy for
three weeks, visiting the women of local society with Madame de
Boisy and listening to François preach in his own cathedral. After
Mass on Sunday, June 4, the two friends returned to his episcopal
apartments in the Maison Lambert. Gravely François de Sales
explained to Jeanne that he had been deliberating on the matter of
her future. But he had not merely been calculating the pros and cons
of whether or not Madame de Chantal should leave the world. For
some time he had been cherishing an idea of great audacity and nov-
elty. Apparently, he had some inkling of this idea before he had met
the Dijonnaise widow, but the contours of his dream had become
clearer to him as their friendship had progressed. He dreamed of
starting a congregation for women that would be different from the
traditional relaxed women's religious orders as well as from the
newly emerging or newly reformed women's orders which made
severe physical austerity so central to their practice. He had had
some idea of such a new women's community, but it was not until
he met Jeanne that he began to feel that the concept could become
a reality. Together they would be its co-founders. He had waited a
long while before determining that this new institute was indeed
meant to be and that Jeanne was indeed being prepared to lead it.
His meeting with Jeanne, the subsequent development of their relationship, the trajectory of events, all combined to give him sufficient
surety that a divine will was behind the project.

When her director told her of his intention to speak of her future, the baroness knelt on the ground before him. Her biographer reports the memorable scene:

> The Blessed One let her stay kneeling; he remained standing about two feet from her. "Yes," he commenced, "it is time to begin. You are meant to enter the Poor Clares."—"My father," she replied, "I am ready."—"No," he responded, "you are not strong enough; you should be a sister at the hospital in Beaune."—"As you please."—"That still is not what I mean," he said; "you should be a Carmelite."—"I am prepared to obey," she answered. Then he suggested several others in order to test her. He found that she was like wax softened by the divine heat and disposed to accept any form of religious life that he might suggest to her. Finally, he told her that what God wished for her was not to be found in any one of these ways of life that he had named. With that he explained in detail the plan that he had for our little Institute. "At this proposal," our Blessed Mother recounted, "I suddenly felt an interior resonance along with a sweet satisfaction and an insight that assured me that this was the will of God. I had not felt this at all at the other suggestions although my soul was completely resigned to them."[34]

The Salesian view of the spiritual life rests upon the assumption that one must be utterly emptied of self-will in order for the will of God to become manifest in one's life. This exchange between the two friends in the bishop's chambers in the Maison Lambert demonstrates how seriously that assumption was taken by them both.

The new women's community that François envisioned was, for its day, unusual in intent and design. He wished to institute a foundation for women who were deeply drawn to the life of devotion yet who were not robust enough, or were too young or too old, or who simply had no taste for physical rigor, to join the reformed contemplative orders. Widows and the infirm whose handicaps did not prevent them from carrying out the basic activities of the rule were to be accepted along with the unmarried and physically sound. The life was to be, to an extent, mixed. Contemplation and action in the prelate's mind were the two principal exercises, the two arms, of love—the one embracing God, the other one's neighbor. The central focus of the life was to be the surrender of one's self to the love and will of God. This was to be effected principally through prayer. But the senior sisters (those out of the novitiate) were to go out periodically in small groups to visit and attend to the sick and the poor. François was aware of other women's communities in Italy that were fashioned along these lines.[35] It was to be a simple congregation, not a formal order. That is, members would not take solemn vows of entrance that would, in the eyes of both civil and canon law, effectively divest them of the right to own or inherit money and property or to marry. They would merely make a simple vow of chastity and generously offer themselves to God to be used in His honor through the observance of the rules of the congregation. The community would be under the direct jurisdiction of the bishop of the diocese, distinguishing the future institute further from existing women's orders that generally fell under the legislation and government of male religious communities. Thus it would have a life and spirit all its own and be afforded a large degree of self-determination.

This was the framework of the life that the Savoyard and his Burgundian friend were to build. Its spirit was to be its own—very, very simple. Its members were to be daughters of prayer, given in self-surrender to God's will. There was to be no particular charism, no distinguishing occupation of the life. Like a single candle consuming itself in its own fire, offering its very substance in its ascent, the women of the community were to be given over to the fire of love of God that had brought them together. Their asceticism was to be markedly interior. The externals of observance, though disciplined, were not to be harsh. Of this Jeanne was to write:

> Our Institute . . . is based entirely upon the interior life . . . its aim is to give to God daughters of prayer and souls so interior that they will be found worthy of serving and adoring His infinite majesty in spirit and truth, leaving the great orders to honor Our Lord by outstanding devotional practices and the exercise of the heroic virtues.[36]

The women who would be drawn to the group were not to be the ascetic elite of Christendom. Moreover, from its very beginning the congregation was to open its doors to lay women who wished to withdraw from their usual duties for short periods to intensify their own lives of prayer. In this the institute was very novel, for by accepting lay women within cloister walls it further blurred the distinctions between monastic and non-monastic spirituality.

To the casual observer these women would not be occupied with any outstanding undertakings. (In fact, François de Sales was roundly criticized for establishing what seemed to some a rest-home.) But within their house, as individuals and as a group, they were to cultivate the "hidden way" of spiritual maturity that Jeanne and François had been practicing now for so long. One of the hallmarks of this way was the "douceur" for which the bishop was so famed. Extended to an entire community this disposition became a gracious cordiality and regard for one another. In symbiotic harmony the women were to practice the presence of God in the most ordinary of everyday routines. The life of the nascent congregation could be easily stated: simplicity, humility, the life of the humble Jesus. But a wealth of meaning and symbolic richness was contained in this life.

It was agreed by the two principals that the foundation should be in the city of Annecy so that François might be near the infant congregation. But it was certainly not time yet for it to come into being. Jeanne's children were still young. Moreover, François needed time to arrange the necessary conditions for the foundation. A suitable facility must be procured and the legal mechanism for such an undertaking set in motion. Most importantly, entrants must present themselves who were called to such a life. Certainly six or seven years would have to elapse before the imagined institute could become a reality.

What was required of Jeanne now was that she return to her widow's life in Burgundy and give herself to it with a renewed sense of devotion. Certainly, all the patient waiting and surrender to the sacrament of the present moment that she had been practicing had a new meaning now that she could see in what direction she was headed. There were innumerable obstacles that had yet to be removed as well as a multitude of details to take care of before her new way of life could be established. But she was confident that these would, in one way or another, take care of themselves. Through the many discouraging and painful events that lay ahead of her before the congregation could be established, she retained a sense that her destiny rightfully lay with this particular project. This and the great ease with which Jeanne decisively oriented her life in this new direction would seem to indicate that, although François was the one to articulate the plan, it was a plan formed from their respective longings and made possible by the exchange of shared values.

They did not inform anyone of the proposed alteration in Jeanne's life. No doubt her family would strenuously object. The specifics of the change in all its multi-layered complexity would have to be well thought out before there could be any hope of effectively persuading those whose legal as well as emotional approval was crucial to the execution of the plan. Nonetheless, and quite quickly, several dramatic events within their families' spheres hastened the project's realization along. François' mother, Madame de Boisy, began to nurture the hope that her son, Bernard de Sales, Baron of Thorens, might marry Jeanne's eldest daughter Marie-Aymée. She urged her first born to press the case. To both friends it seemed a rather difficult matter to arrange. The prospective bride was as yet only nine years old. Moreover, she was the favorite of her maternal grandfather. To deprive him of her company by removing her from Burgundy was something to which he could scarcely be expected to agree. For several months they let the suggestion remain unexplored.

Then an event occurred which made the marriage a viable possibility. Jeanne de Sales, François' fifteen year old sister who was in France in the charge of Jeanne de Chantal, fell gravely ill in October. She was a much-loved child, and especially dear to her bishop brother. The widow de Chantal was beside herself. Despite her unflagging and knowledgeable ministrations at the sickbed, her young charge swiftly succumbed to a savage fever and dysentery. Her grief over the loss of the girl was compounded by her painful sense of responsibility to the family who had entrusted their child to her care. Although she felt that nothing could replace the loss they had suffered, she impulsively made a vow before God that the house of Sales should be recompensed for the loss of its daughter through the offer of one of her own daughters to their line. She notified François of the sad news and of her vow.

The response she received from him was characteristic. His resignation to his sister's death was swift and complete. Not that he did not grieve. He did, deeply. But his grief was pure and unimpeded by any resistance to the fact of what had happened. His love for his sister was quite genuinely within the context of greater and more resilient love—his love of God. As her spiritual guide, François was concerned that Jeanne's response lacked the resignation that could transform her grief. He suggested that she reflect upon this fact.

> My daughter, you must not merely acknowledge that God has affected us, you must accept the fact that He does so in a way that pleases Him. I see you with your vigourous heart which loves and wills so powerfully—and I am grateful for it—for what good are the hearts of the half-dead? Once a week each week you should take upon yourself the specific task of loving the will of God above everything else. And this should be done not only on bearable occasions but on those which are unbearable.[37]

Jeanne understood well the meaning of his words. With characteristic decisiveness she wrote out for herself this little prayer, to be reread each day in the morning and evening.

> Lord Jesus, I don't want options any more! Pluck whatever string of my lute that you wish—it will play this one harmony alone for ever and ever. Yes, Lord Jesus! Without ifs or buts or exceptions may your will be done to fathers, children, everything, even myself.[38]

The unification of her entire person into one continual act of loving surrender was the object of her struggle. Her passion for this simplicity of person was overwhelming: one place to stand from which to view all events, one immeasurable love to enrich all loves. To be simple implied a mental and emotional attitude of vast resilience and flexibility that nonetheless radiated from one focus—the love of God. All events, exterior or interior, would be interpreted, modulated and given priority in relationship to this central focus. But the process of gathering the disparate experiences and impulses of a richly endowed individual like Jeanne was a long and, especially at first, a complicated task.

As a result of the vow made in tears over the body of Jeanne de Sales, the baroness began negotiations that would in the next few years link her family with the house of Sales by the marriage of

Marie-Aymée and Bernard. Gradually she won over the resistance
of the two grandfathers. In the fall of 1608 the prospective groom,
with his elder brother, François, who was in the process of carrying
out a papal commission, journeyed to Burgundy to meet Jeanne's
daughter. A marriage contract was drawn up. It would be October
of the following year before the union would be sacramentally
blessed, the legal age for consummating a marriage by then having
been achieved.[39]

The successful negotiations served only temporarily to offer
Jeanne any unruffled sense of joy, for very soon she was assailed by
new doubts about her vocation. The change must at times have
seemed utterly unthinkable, especially since none but she and the
bishop shared the secret of their as yet unborn plans. Her anxiety
was made more poignant when the unrelenting housekeeper at
Monthelon launched a scandal-monger's campaign to discredit
Jeanne and cause Marie-Aymée's marriage plans with Bernard to
collapse. Apparently this vitriolic woman had in mind another match
for the young girl and hoped, by discrediting the mother in the eyes
of the elder Baron de Chantal, that the old man might renege on his
agreement that the daughter be allowed to marry into the Sales' family. The baroness was deeply wounded by the assault but was soon
exonerated when her own father in Dijon, hearing the scandalous
tales, asked his daughter to explain. It was then that the long-stand-
ing unhappy situation at Monthelon was revealed to the elder Frémyot. He, chagrined by his blindness to his favored daughter's
plight, insisted that the family be permanently removed from Monthelon. But Jeanne was aware that any move that they made at this
point could be temporary. She suggested instead another trip to
Annecy for herself and her children.

The impending convergence of the two families made this possible. The entourage, including Charlotte de Bréchard, a family
friend under the direction of François, arrived in Annecy the first
week of Lent in 1609. The mother would be able to once again hear
the bishop preach a series of Lenten sermons and the daughter
would have a chance to become familiar with the new country which
would be her home and to meet her prospective mother-in-law
under whose affectionate tutelage she would begin her life as a baroness. Annecy at this time was aglow with the praise and attention
that its own bishop's book, *The Introduction to the Devout Life,* was

receiving not only in Savoy but in France as well. The Chantal contingent was once again graciously received by society, and it was with a special delight that the ladies and gentlemen of the Savoyard town wished them welcome, for a wedding was cause for delight. But the bride's mother, concerned as she was for her daughter's future, did not view the marriage as an end in itself. For her it was part of a larger picture: the gradual provision for her children of new networks of support and, therefore, provision for her own more independent future.

What lay in the back of her thoughts as she circulated deftly through the conventions of social interchange that spring in Annecy was the image of the new congregation that she and François held to be the culmination of their dreams. He had told her on her last visit that he wished the congregation to be named for Saint Martha, that often overlooked character in the gospel account of Luke. Like Martha, the sisters of the new congregation would be helpful—they were to visit the sick and the poor. Like Martha, they would be the unobtrusive, uncelebrated women who opened the doors of their homes and lives to Christ.

Still, the name of the congregation had not been settled once and for all. As a name is symbolic of the intent of its bearer, so the vision of the new foundation had not yet been formalized in its creators' minds. Jeanne had never really been content with the patronage of St. Martha. She had long had a deep devotion to the Virgin Mary and somehow felt that whatever direction her own life were to take must certainly be under her auspices. As a young girl, motherless for as long as she could remember, she had adopted the gentle Virgin as her own maternal protectress. It was natural that she should feel the necessity of Marian patronage for the budding institute. But she refrained from countering François' enthusiasm. She merely entrusted to God her petition that the Virgin become her patron. Her biographer recounts that some time after the actual foundation, when Jeanne did not have the subject at all in mind, François arrived early one morning with a happy, excited face and announced that he had been thinking and had changed his opinion. Perhaps they should name their little band the *Daughters of the Visitation* after that event in the liturgical calendar which celebrated the visit of the pregnant Virgin to her cousin Elizabeth who was also with child. François felt that it represented a particularly hidden mystery and that it was not solemnly celebrated in the church. The new congregation could take upon itself the responsibility for observing the feast with loving devotion. Jeanne was overjoyed.

The image of the Visitation of the Virgin Mary was more than a pious ensignia for the envisioned congregation. It was expressive of both the structure and the inner meaning of the life the two friends intended to initiate. For them, love of God and love of neighbor together represented the fullest response of the individual to the call from God. In the image of the Visitation the two were exquisitely expressed. The first edition of the rules and constitutions of the congregation contained the following passage:

> Now, this congregation, having two principal exercises—one, contemplation and prayer which are practiced primarily within the house, the other, service to the poor and sick, especially of the same sex—has appropriately chosen for its Patron Our Lady of the Visitation because in this mystery the most glorious Virgin performed the solemn act of charity toward her neighbor by visiting and ministering to holy Elizabeth during her confinement while at the same time she composed the *Magnificat*, the sweetest, most elevated, spiritual and contemplative canticle ever written.[40]

Like Mary, the Daughters of the Visitation would hide within themselves a most profound event—the birth of God in the human being. Like Mary they would unobtrusively, under the guise of the most ordinary activities, be gestating, giving the very substance of their lives over to the mysterious incarnation of God in the world.

Jeanne herself was already deeply immersed in the process to which the mystery of the Visitation pointed. Her director had said that she was pregnant with God. And the movement within was now strong and independent enough that she had little choice but to witness it through to the moment of birth. After that, the realized dream would have a name and face and would offer to her its own challenges. Yet she still suffered attacks of doubt. She was very close to her own father and felt keenly her maternal responsibility toward her children. In carefully determining the specific details of her children's fates she, as it were, had emotionally to encounter her feelings about each one of them and let go of the present way in which they were tied to her.

Marie-Aymée was not the only child for whom she had lovingly and prudently been providing. The two younger girls, Françoise and Charlotte, it was envisioned, could be brought to the convent to stay with their mother and the community until they were older and their long-range futures could be determined. It was common for women's monastic houses to have a few young female boarders. The Visitation was not intended primarily as a school, as were some foundations, but it would be possible to accommodate the baroness' two girls.[41] Her eldest child and only son, Celse-Bénigne, who was thirteen in 1609, was already lodged in Dijon with his maternal grandfather so that he could undertake an uninterrupted course of studies. It seemed to his mother that he was in an ideal situation, and their separation, though painful, would not be without his interests in mind. Besides, the envisioned congregation was not to be cloistered in the manner of an ordinary contemplative order. If circumstances necessitated, Jeanne could return to Burgundy to take care of family affairs. She had considered her children's financial needs, too. Most of her estate would be made over to her children. Her brother was to administer for her a small amount held in reserve out of which her dowry (generally a pre-condition of entry into a seventeenth century women's monastery) could be apportioned.[42]

Jeanne de Chantal mused on these issues during the Lenten season of 1609. It had all begun during Lent five years earlier. From the nebulous impulses that had propelled her to seek the confidence of the preacher to whom she once again so attentively listened, a real vision of life lived solely for the Lord she loved had been formed. Her director had given her confidence in her own inner longings. He had listened carefully with her, helping her to discern the authentic direction that her life should take. He had showed her ways to discipline the qualities she possessed that worked against her own best interests and by his gentle encouragement had enabled her many personal strengths to mature. She was becoming her new self. The central fact of her being was to be her love of God. She knew her God's face in the Christ she had been so long adoring, consuming and creating. Once again in the liturgical year she had arrived at the time in which she ritually prepared herself to die once again to self and be raised up once more into an ever deepening life with God. Five years ago she had been in Dijon, the town of her birth, for the Lenten observance. Now she was in Annecy, the little village where her new life would be born, where she and François would found the Congregation of the Visitation. Holy Thursday, the night on which the Last Supper is celebrated and the Eucharist reserved for adoration on church altars until Good Friday, Jeanne joined Charlotte de Bréchard and other members of a confraternity of the Holy Cross on a city-wide procession to visit all the altars where the sacrament was exposed. She donned the white habit of the group and, secretly slipping off her shoes as an act of identification with the obedient Jesus, walked the rough cobblestone streets of the Alpine village and stood silently upon the chill stone floors of the dimly-lit churches of Annecy. The rhythm of liturgical observances created a rite of passage through which, day by day, year by year, she was moving. On Good Friday she knelt before François and renewed her vows of chastity and obedience.

III

It remained for her to make her hidden growth known. What she had been considering for two years must be told. Her father must be the first to know, and he must give his unreserved blessing to the project in order for it to be a success. Jeanne returned to Dijon after Easter. President Frémyot had always had a great affection for his daughter, and now that he happily presumed she would be spending more time with him after the unpleasantness at Monthelon, Jeanne had little heart to broach the subject of her permanent leavetaking. But it had to be done. She kept waiting for a suitable opportunity. Finally in late June, she seized the moment.

> "When I saw that my father was alone [she recounted to her biographer] I felt that entering his room would be like entering a torture chamber since I knew how painful it would be for him to hear what I was going to suggest. I knelt down and asked for divine aid from the bottom of my heart." She went on little by little preparing her father for what she had to say, beginning: "Would he be very offended if the girls were moved from their paternal grandfather's home since the affairs in that house had never been conducted in the way she thought they should be?" The prudent president responded immediately, "She should not be overly concerned about that. As soon as her eldest daughter

was married to the baron of Thorens, she would be entrusted into Madame de Boisy's care seeing as how the older woman so greatly desired it. It was time for the two younger ones to be placed with the Ursulines to prepare a cloister for their hearts (if God disposed their hearts for the cloister). As for her son the baron de Chantal, he was already taken care of." "Seeing that celestial Providence had made my father speak in this way," our blessed Mother said, "I responded to him, my heart beating wildly: 'Sir, my dear father, do not find fault with me if I tell you that by this careful provision for my children I find myself free to follow the divine vocation to which God has been so long calling me—to leave the world and consecrate myself utterly to his divine service.'"[43]

At these words, her father burst into tears. His misery and gentle remonstrances went straight to her heart. But, in the shared intimacy of his sorrow she could open herself to him at last. She explained that what she was sharing with him was a confidence, one that she and the bishop of Geneva had harbored now for several years. President Frémyot knew and respected François de Sales. His authority behind the plan did put the issue in a new light. Sorrowfully the father came to some sense of his daughter's sincerity and the rightfulness of her vision.

It remained for her brother André, the archbishop of Bourges, to agree. His response, when the plan was put to him some time later, was a definite no. Apparently her father, once at leisure to reflect on her removal, pleaded with André to convince Jeanne that she should be satisfied with the retirement and devotion to which her widowed state entitled her. Jeanne was now openly faced with the pressure, applied this time without reservation, that her family was able to levy against her vocation. Here was her own affectionate father, through her brother, urging her with legitimate motives that she could only painfully resist, to give up the dream that was her most authentic self-expression.

She stood her ground, gently but firmly reminding herself as she explained to her brother that she really did believe that her retirement was the will of God. She had not given herself over thoughtlessly to the idea the moment it entered her mind. For four years now she had wrestled with her own impatience. In the process she had learned what it was she was wrestling for. She was learning

to discern her own will from the will of God. She was learning the
lesson of obedience, and with no little difficulty. True obedience,
she had found, was a listening, an attentive waiting on the part of
the self that does not know the answers, that perhaps did not even
know the questions to be asked. Obedience was a willingness to be
surprised or disappointed, a willingness to die to one's own judgment about the way all things should be. She had not listened alone.
She had with her a friend who also knew the practice of true obedience, who was willing to wait with her, to listen, to aid in the
process of discernment. She spoke without fear to her brother.

> ... as I dared to speak to him as a sister and not as a daughter,
> I told him clearly that I could not deceive my own soul making
> it believe that what truly came from God was all imagination,
> that I was not confusing the Shepherd's voice with the Merce-
> nary's, and, finally, that I was only seeking the will of God.
> However much I might desire my withdrawal, if the Monseig-
> neur of Geneva had directed me to remain in the world as a
> widow, I would do it. Likewise, if he had commanded me to sit
> atop a column for the rest of my days like Saint Simon Stylites,
> I would be content. I was not seeking any situation or way of
> life but obedience to the will of God.[44]

André was impressed. The brother and the father agreed to
wait until they all three could meet together with the bishop before
any final decision could be made. The occasion would be the wedding of Marie-Aymée and Bernard to be held in October at
Monthelon.

The arranged match was a good one—as Jeanne's own marriage
had been. François performed the ceremony in the parish church in
the village. Two days after the celebration, on October 15, Jeanne
and the three principal men in her life met together to discuss her
future. It was her day. She was eloquent, self-assured and convinc-
ing. As she spoke her father and brother frequently broke in to voice
one objection or another. Her responses were measured, well-con-
sidered, and gracefully stated. During the entire long exchange
François de Sales did not utter a single word but sat by "admiring
the wisdom and generosity of the saintly woman."[45] When she finished the two Frémyots did not merely consent but were enthusias-

tic about the proposed congregation, declaring their delight in and respect for the envisioned plan.

There was one minor objection. The president hoped that the new institute could be founded in Dijon, while the archbishop wished it to be in Autun, each so that he could have Jeanne and the community near him. But Annecy was finally agreed upon. The new baroness of Thorens was so young, it would be much better for her mother to be in the vicinity. The other girls could easily stay for a few more years within the community itself, and the lifestyle envisioned made it possible for Jeanne to have the time to attend to their rearing. Her two male relatives, being so amiably disposed by now to Jeanne's new life, were judged ready to agree to an actual date for her removal from Burgundy. Jeanne pressed François to announce a time. He made a decision: six weeks to two months. That would give her adequate opportunity to close all the accounts on her former life. President Frémyot was charged with telling the elderly Baron de Chantal who up until now had not been consulted in the negotiations. The baron's response, perhaps surprisingly, was, like her own father's, to weep. Despite his irascible temper and his weakness in being so influenced by his housekeeper, he had a genuine affection and respect for his daughter-in-law. The president wavered, thinking that perhaps a year or two's delay would soften the blow for the old man. But Jeanne was ready. She took care to win her father-in-law over as she had done the others. Finally it was settled. She could go.

The new congregation was waiting for her. For its part, it could not delay either. François had always attracted to himself women with a receptivity to the devout life. Now he had several of these who had confessed to him they wished a life in religion. Charlotte de Bréchard was the first of these. When the prelate had honored her call to a vocation, he told her of the new group being formed. Joyfully she committed herself to a life under the direction of her dear friend Jeanne. In Annecy, the daughter of François' friend Antoine Favre, Jacqueline, was experiencing a conversion of life under her bishop's direction. Other Savoyard young women of his acquaintance were likely discovering a call to a celibate life. Each of these women had recently come into contact with the Genevan bishop and had, in his mind, been singled out for a particular relationship to the nascent Visitation.

It was the end of an era. The winter cold closed around Burgundy. After the wedding and the various negotiations at Monthelon, Jeanne accompanied her friend south to Beaune and attended the Mass he celebrated at the hospital there. They bid each other goodbye. Shortly afterward François wrote her a letter.

> I have just come from prayer, where I was considering the reason we are in this world. I have learned that we are here only to receive and carry the gentle Jesus: on our tongue by proclaiming him; in our arms by doing good works; on our shoulders by supporting the yoke of dryness and sterility in both the interior and exterior senses. Happy are those who carry him gently and with constancy. . . . Courage, my daughter, stay close to the side of your holy abbess and constantly ask her that we might live, die and be reborn in the love of her dear child.[46]

She was being more and more incorporated into the reality of Christ through all that she said and did. Always she was aware of the curious paradox of the burden she lifted—it was liberating. François had been teaching her the liberty of the children of God— that interior flexibility and expansiveness that was allowing her to become her insistently emerging new self. In the end the process would result in peace, the peace that would come from her total surrender to a will outside her own. Her mentor, in a letter dated the end of November, likened her state to the state of the beloved apostle John at the Last Supper.

> So, there you are, utterly given over into our Saviour's hands by the abandonment of your entire being to his pleasure and holy providence. Oh God, what happiness to be thus in the arms and against the breast of Him of whom the Sacred Spouse said: "Your breasts are incomparably better than wine." Remain this way, dear daughter, like another little Saint John, while the others eat a variety of foods at the Saviour's table, rest and lean your head, your soul, your spirit, by means of a simple confidence, on the loving breast of the dear Lord. Because, it is better to sleep on this sacred pillow than to be awake in any other posture.[47]

She, like the saint her director had likened her to, would need the memory of those comforting arms to make the passage to her new life bearable. It would not be a painless one. In February 1610 when preparations for the removal were well under way, Jeanne's youngest daughter, Charlotte, then just eight years old, fell suddenly ill with a fever similar to the one that had claimed Jeanne de Sales. She died within a few hours. Jeanne wept piteously. There was nothing else to do. She wrote of her sorrow to François. Unbeknownst to her, he too was suffering the loss of a loved one. His mother Madame de Boisy had been stricken suddenly and succumbed. News of this death intensified Jeanne's own mourning. The only favorable issue of this sad passing was that now Jeanne would certainly have to go to Savoy to be near the young bride. The wagging tongues of society had already caught wind of what was planned and there was much unfavorable opinion about Jeanne's leaving. The tongues would have less reason to wag now.

She said goodbye at Monthelon. A sizable crowd assembled to see her go. In the front of it her father-in-law, tears streaming down his face, awkwardly accepted her embrace and acknowledged her final words asking for his pardon for whatever ways she might have offended him. Behind the eighty year old man swarmed the poor and outcast of the vicinity, those to whom Jeanne had ministered so faithfully for so many years. "Their baroness" was going. Torn by their grief at their own loss, they tearfully embraced her one by one.

In two days, taking time to visit all the local pilgrimage sites and bid farewell to others, she arrived in Dijon. For several weeks of Lent she stayed in the city of her birth, concluding the details of the final arrangements that would once and for all mark an end to the only way of life she had, until this time, known.

On May 29, 1610 she and the little band that was to accompany her to Savoy—including Charlotte de Bréchard, Marie-Aymée, Bernard, and Françoise—gathered at her father's home. The household as well as local friends were there to witness her parting. Her father, fearful that his tears might pain his daughter too much, for now he was wholeheartedly behind her departure, remained in his chambers until the last moment. Leave-taking was a formal occasion in seventeenth century France; a rite was needed for a passage. There were many tears. Jeanne herself, eyes brimming, nonetheless moved with dignity through the rite. But she was not to be allowed a gracious exit from her former world. Celse-Bénigne, her oldest child

and only son, who was at the time just fifteen, at the last moment
flung himself down on his knees and implored her not to leave with
a speech (her biographer recounts) that was so polished that it might
have been memorized. The assembled witnesses redoubled their
tears. Jeanne hesitated but, presumably not knowing how in the circumstances to respond to the display except to follow through with
the leave-taking, moved toward the doorway beyond which her
father was now waiting to take his final goodbyes. Celse-Bénigne
thereupon threw himself down across the threshold and cried out,
"Well, mother, I am too weak and unlucky to hold you back but at
least it will be said that you trampled you own child underfoot!"[48]

The tears that had been threatening to descend now spilled
down Jeanne's cheeks. She stepped over Celse-Bénigne's prostrate
form, paused and let the tears fall, still struggling to retain her com-
posure. To add insult to injury, two ecclesiastics, who had been
privy to the scene and had up until that moment admired the widow's poise, took the opportunity to uncharitably and rather archly
comment: "What, Madame, can the tears of a young boy create a
breach in your perseverance?" "No," Jeanne replied simply to them,
"but what would you have? I am a mother. . . . "[49]

The boy's curse on his mother proved true. Through all the
centuries since its occurrence, this parting scenario has been
remembered and marveled at by persons who might know nothing
else about Jeanne de Chantal. It has proved to some that she was
really a heartless woman, to others that she was a paragon of
detached fortitude. Neither is expressive of the truth of the matter.[50]
Celse-Bénigne was a handsome, volatile young man with a flair for
the dramatic (he was known to be a dueler in later days). There is
no reason to believe that he had expressed such resistance to his
mother's leaving before the day of the actual departure. That his
speech to prevent her removal appeared to those present to be memorized indicates that he had probably been secretly brooding on the
event for some time. Jeanne was very devoted to her only son. But
he was of an age to go off to school, perhaps to Paris. He would
have begun to have an independent life even if she had not left. It
was apparently the idea that she was leaving him rather than he leaving her that was hard for the boy to take. His anger was launched at
her in the way in which it would most wound her, and wound her
it did, but she had a clearer view than he of the overall issues

involved. She silently received the blow and moved on to bid her father goodbye.

The elder Frémyot and his daughter stood together in tearful conversation for some time. Then she knelt to receive his final blessing. He gave it with great dignity and assurance, telling his daughter by his demeanor that he recognized the rightness of her actions and that he supported her totally. With a renewed sense of calm she climbed into the carriage that awaited her. As the carriage passed through the gates of Dijon she and Charlotte de Bréchard began to sing psalms. "How lovely is your dwelling place, O Lord of Hosts. . . . Blessed are those who dwell in Your house, ever singing Your praise" (Psalm 83). Despite the anguish of the rite, the passage was complete. Jeanne de Chantal was to begin her new life.

3.

Friendship
(1610–1614)

I

The carriage bearing Jeanne-Françoise Frémyot, Baronne de Chantal, and her small company toward Savoy carried in it the remnant of her Burgundian family life. It also carried aspirations for a new self-identity that she had been secretly nourishing since that Lent in 1604 when, at the ancient ducal chapel in Dijon, she had met François de Sales. It had taken great resolve on her part and great fidelity to the integrity of her emergent new self to find herself on that road twisting southeast out of Dijon. She had been urged on by some impulse within. But this was not all. At the end of the road was François whose friendship had acted as the magnet that had drawn her own desires. Something existed between them that went far beyond mutual encouragement and appreciation. Nor was their relationship explainable solely on the grounds that they loved the same things or shared the same values. Several weeks before she set out on the definitive journey, her friend wrote to her from Annecy, where he was waiting.

> O God, my dearest Daughter, how tenderly and ardently I feel the sacred bond and the good of our holy unity! I preached a sermon full of flames this morning I was so aware of it. I must tell you how much I wish for blessings for you! You cannot imagine how I was impelled at the altar to commend you to Our Lord for ever and ever.[1]

The passion that the bishop expressed here and the surprising convergence of that passion with the most central and profound of

102

religious activities in the Catholic faith, the celebration of Mass, begins to give some insight into the nature of the friendship that Jeanne and François shared. Theirs was a relationship in which the powerful dynamics of the interaction between male and female were experienced simultaneously with the profound human search for ultimate meaning and identity.

Until this point in the narrative it has not seemed opportune to speak more specifically about the language and conception of friendship with which the bishop and the widow thus far understood their relationship. For his part, François from the very beginning was sensitive to the nature of the bond growing between them. Moreover, he was able to give a voice to what was transpiring between them. This was not only because he was responsive to the moods that were being evoked but because he was equipped with a theoretical framework and a vocabulary with which to describe and explore those moods.

He, like Jeanne, sensed from its inception that their friendship would be unique. "God has given me to you,"[2] he had written on the brief message passed to her as he left the town gates of Dijon at the conclusion of his 1604 visit. Within the week she had received a letter that made his meaning more explicit:

> The farther I am from you in terms of physical distance, the more I feel myself connected and united to you in an interior way.[3]

The relationship had as its basis the sense that it was ordained, that it was part of a larger process of self-definition in which they both were engaged. François felt the potential weight of the union very early. There was a mutual recognition that their deepest hopes and widest capacities as human beings were mirrored in the other. He identified and named the phenomenon: Christian friendship. In June 1604, in one of his most insightful letters designed to direct Jeanne toward the clear perception of her confusing inner motives, he wrote:

> I have never intended for there to be any connection between us that carries any obligation except that of love and true Christian friendship, whose binding force Saint Paul calls "the bond

of perfection." And truly it is just that, for it is indissoluble and will not slacken. All other bonds are temporary, even that of vows of obedience which are broken by death and other occurrences. But the bond of love grows in time and takes on new power by enduring. It is exempt from the severance of death whose scythe cuts down everything except love: "Love is as strong as death and more powerful than hell," Solomon says. . . . This is our bond, these are our chains which, the more they restrain and press upon us, the more they give us ease and liberty. Their power is only sweetness, their force only gentleness, nothing is so pliable, nothing so solid as they are. Therefore, consider me intimately linked with you and do not be anxious to understand more about it except that this bond is not contrary to any other bond, whether it be of a vow or of marriage.[4]

To be a Christian was, for François de Sales, to be a fully realized human being, for in living out his or her call to a devout life, a man or woman was becoming the lover of God that he or she was created to be. A Christian friendship was a bond with another person cultivated within the context of the ultimate vocation of becoming fully human. The bond itself became part of the vocation. The key to comprehending what François de Sales meant is to be found in his equation of friendship with love. It can thus be part of the total process of becoming the pure lover of God that humankind, in the Salesian view, is intended to be. But this is a more complex assertion than it may seem on the surface, for the concepts of friendship and love have long histories in the Christian world. To understand more clearly their meaning for the two friends in question, it will be helpful to chart briefly the development of the terms.[5]

As with so many ideas, the Christian understanding of friendship had its roots in the classical world. Friendship was a topic that many of the major Greek and Roman philosophers touched upon. Among the Greeks there were varied understandings of the concept but still basic themes emerged from their philosophical ruminations.[6] Plato laid out the basic questions to be posed: Is there mutuality in friendship or not? Is the bond forged by likeness or unlikeness? Must both parties be virtuous? Are friends chosen for utility or benefit?[7] The Stoics and the Epicureans each gave a different emphasis to the debate, the former asserting that friendship requires virtue to be held by the friends, the latter seeing utility or the need for help as the basis of the relationship.[8] Aristotle proposed that the essence of friendship is to be found in the similarity and equality of the parties, especially in terms of virtue. The Peripatetic master also identified types of friendships which he distinguished by the reason for which they were formed. Bonds could be created for the sake of utility, pleasure or virtue, the last mentioned being the most perfect. Aristotle also conceived of a friendship of unequals. This he found in marriage, a relationship which he felt was based on the difference between the sexes and made viable by each of the two parties making up for the deficiencies of the other. These friendships, because they were not based on equality, were never of the perfect variety.[9] In conclusion, the Greek legacy supplied several basic assumptions to the theories of friendship that were to come from the Christian world: friendship assumes a similarity of natures, of interests and of pursuits as well as an equality among persons.

Of the Romans, it was Cicero's treatise *On Friendship* that was to be of greatest importance for Christianity. For Cicero, the essence of friendship was complete sympathy in all matters of importance, good will and affection.[10] In its true form it could exist only between men and it had to be based upon the quest for virtue. In the Roman orator's mind, the impulse to acquire friendship was natural; something innate compelled men to seek it so that they might be aided in their pursuit of the higher life. Cicero also rejected the notion that a friend could be valued as much as oneself or that friendship was an exchange of duty or kindness. For him, friendship had its limits, and if the bond caused one to leave the path of virtue it should be forsaken. Thus, the idea of false friendship, also explored by Aristotle, was present in Cicero's treatise. It has been observed that Cicero's concept of friendship distinguished him from other practitioners in the Roman world, and that, on the whole, classical friendship was a juridical and almost ritual bond, forged to promote the political and social interests of the partners.[11]

With the stage thus set, the Christian era opened. The new religion at one and the same time incorporated and transformed the concept of friendship handed on from the classical world. The Christian contribution was twofold. First, friendship was inserted into the spiritual life as a form of love, and, second, the invitation to friendship was extended to all people of good will.[12] The language of the biblical text enjoined love of God and of neighbor as the

essential acts of the Christian life, and so the possibility for the cultivation of friendships as part of the Christian path to perfection was
open to all. Yet the Scripture also revealed another dimension of the
Christian conception of neighborly love. A more world-eschewing
temperament is summed up in James 4:4 with the words: "Do you
not know that friendship with the world is enmity with God?
Therefore whoever wishes to be a friend of the world makes himself
an enemy of God." The crucial word here is, of course, "world,"
and depending upon the interpretation of that word, friendship with
others either was or was not an aid to salvation.

In the patristic era Christian thinkers wrestled with the tension
and/or relationship between love of God and love of other persons.[13] Jerome, though producing no unified statement about friendship, did speak of it as a work of Christ and as a love that could
serve to unite friends in the pursuit of the Christian life.[14] Among
other church fathers, Ambrose, Basil and Chrysostom wrote about
the sometimes conflicting claims that love of God posed to the love
between friends.[15] Friendships could cause problems as both Jerome
and Chrysostom discovered,[16] and it was not always clear in the
thought of the period whether ties of love with others detracted
from or aided in the quest for personal salvation. It was an issue that
was never to be resolved and that forms the subject of whatever
Christian discussions there have been about friendship. On the one
hand, the tradition affirms that friendship falls under the aegis of
love and can be part of the personal and collective journey of salvation. On the other hand, there remains a vivid fear that too much
attachment to anything other than the divine will may serve as an
obstacle to advancement.

Augustine of Hippo, as he does with most of the concepts central to the church, stands in a prominent place in relation to the idea
of friendship. In his early writings Augustine wrote of friendship as
companionship in the pursuit of wisdom. His mature works show a
developing concept of friendship informed by his growing concerns
with the church as the body of Christ in the world. He saw Christian society, the city of God, as a society of friends united by their
love of God and dedicated to living out that love in relationship with
one another. The city of God was to be a universal friendship in
which all individual spirits are present to each other in knowledge
and love of their Creator.[17] Besides this extension of the concept of

friendship beyond the individual, Augustine revealed a tendency to the spiritualization of ancient ideas. The Platonic assumption that friendship is based on likeness was amplified and Christianized. Similarly, the love between friends and God became located in the *imago dei* present in the soul of humankind, so that the likeness of friends was then found in their shared likeness to God and their friendship became inextricably bound up with their quest to recover that image in its pristine state through the perfection of love.

Thus friendship was in Augustine inseparably linked to the Christian way of being as first of all a cultivation of love. What is important to be aware of here is that love, in the Christian past, was not a one-dimensional ideal. In its classical formulation that was taken over and modified by Christian thinkers, love was a richly-textured phenomenon that had four major manifestations: *epithemia* (what we would call libido or lust, the drive toward the satisfaction of sexual desire), *eros* (the desire or longing to be united with the beloved, or with the true, the beautiful and the good), *philia* (friendship) and *agape* (charity or the sacrificial love for God and humans as well as the redeeming love of God shown in Jesus Christ).[18] The Greek language allows for four terms to express the complex phenomenon. Generally, in the Christian view, three of the four loves would be considered as having their origin in the natural order of things, the fourth, *agape*, as being uniquely a gift of grace, a love springing from a supernatural source.[19] Yet despite their varied origins (and despite theorists who would assert otherwise),[20] the four named loves are for much of the Christian tradition not discrete realities but four interacting modalities of one reality.

Love as a pivotal and many layered concept in Christian thought has a scriptural basis. The Gospel of John and the Johannine letters lay the theological groundwork for the centrality of love in the Christian schema.[21] In these writings love (*agape* is the focus here) constitutes the essential nature of God. The animation of love in the person of Jesus Christ is seen as God's redemptive activity in the world. Participating in the love that is shown in that salvation, the Christian lives so that the spirit of love of God and neighbor can be seen in all his or her other actions.

St. Paul does much to fuse the imagery of divine and human love when he likens the relationship of Christ and the Church to a marriage.[22] Moreover, Paul seems not merely to provide a mundane analogy for a spiritual reality—the union of Christ and church; he seems (in 1 Corinthians) to assume a holistic view of the fact of human love. For him, human love, even in its most physical form, is linked to the reality of divine love. While there is in Paul an ascetic tendency, an impulse to distinguish between "flesh" and "spirit," the distinction is not primarily between the body and the quest for divine things but between attitudes or actions that render a person either spiritual or worldly. The experience of human love is not then isolated from the experience of divine love.

The patristic world demonstrated how love, with its interdependent modalities, was incorporated into the theology of the church. It was Augustine who gave to the concept an orientation that was to remain normative for generations. Blending the emanation theories of his Neo-Platonic predecessors with the scriptural concepts of a God who is love, he envisioned a Creator who formed the human soul in His own image and who endowed it with the capacity to love Him.[23] By loving, the soul is drawn back to the source of its origin. For Augustine all human loves are related to the love of God. But because of the woundedness of human nature, human loves are not rightly perceived. They are sought as ends in themselves, not as yielding to a higher, more spiritual love—the love of God. So Augustine preached both the integrated quality of all loves along with his belief that the forms of loves are corrupt without a true knowledge of their goal and end and that individuals must seek the redemption of these loves in the *agape* exhibited by Christ.

There is then, for Augustine, a hierarchy of loves, the most perfect of which is the love of God, *agape,* or *caritas.* Humankind's true end is the realization of the apotheosis of love. The Christian must experience the re-creation of the image of God within the soul and must be remade in that divine image. In this process, the human heart and its actions are of crucial importance, for the bishop of Hippo made the heart the realm of Christian interiority. Drawing upon rich biblical imagery in which the heart represents the inmost self as well as the seat of all the forces and functions of the soul, Augustine described the heart as the beginning of the spiritual journey and the special action of the heart—*desiderium* or desire—as the soul's dynamic that leads to God.[24] It is into this framework of the reformation of the soul through the properly directed desire of the heart that Augustine's positive evaluation of friendship should be placed.

The Augustinian notion of friendship is countered in Christian thought by the other more skeptical evaluation of friendship that emerges very clearly in the writings of the fathers of western monasticism. Christians seeking a radical expression of their faith came more and more to live together in community during the fourth and fifth centuries of the Christian era, but they did not necessarily come seeking friendship. They came seeking individual salvation and a school in which they could learn obedience from their saving Lord.[25] Thus the evaluations of friendship in both *The Rule of St. Benedict* and the works of John Cassian are complex and ambivalent.[26]

Benedict of Nursia's *Rule*, though it provides a fraternal context for Christian perfection, does not dwell upon the relationship between brother monks but upon their relationship with their superior, the abbot.[27] The Benedictine monk, moreover, does not primarily see himself through the eyes of his neighbor (i.e., how his actions affect his neighbor or how his neighbor's actions affect him) as much as through the eyes of God.[28] The focus is individual, not social, and the cultivation of friendship is not a central method in the service of the Lord.

Likewise, in the view of that other pivotal figure in the history of western monasticism, John Cassian, friendship is an ambivalent topic. In his *Institutions*[29] Cassian clearly warns against the dangers of individual friendships, especially for the young. Yet in his *Conferences*[30] a more positive evaluation of friendship is found. The communal life appears here as an ideal nursery for deep and lasting friendships between men who have renounced the world. What is clear is that Cassian is speaking in the *Conferences* of a highly refined type of friendship between persons already well advanced in the Christian life whose friendship is based on their mutual and selfless love of God. The advice in the *Institutions* reflects the author's opinion about friendships formed among those less advanced and therefore prone to attach themselves to others for motives that might be more a hindrance than an aid to personal advancement.[31]

The tension between the view of friendship as a work of love appropriate to the search for God and the view that distrusts unions between individuals continued through the western monastic tradition until the present day.[32] Theoretically, it is affirmed that such relationships can be mutually salvific and edifying, but in fact a deep skepticism remains about the actual possibility of achieving such elevated unions. More often than not, monastic literature warns against the formation of "particular friendships" and fears the disruption of community and the establishment of cliques.

Yet despite the myriad warnings against them, friendships did flower, encouraged by another strong current of thought and imagery in the monastic mileu. In the late sixth century, Gregory the Great developed a language of the Christian interior life that was to have a long and lasting influence on the subsequent development of Christian friendship as theory and as living phenomenon. The contribution that Gregory made has not been extensively studied.[33] Yet he seems to have given to the medieval and subsequent monastic world not only a theology but a psychology of the spiritual life that, though endlessly enriched, would never be supplanted. He saw the pilgrimage of the Christian as primarily an experience of desire.

The idea that desire is intrinsic to the spiritual life was not novel, but the intensity and the nuance of its development in Gregory was. He located the essence of the Christian experience in a desire that was at one and the same time both divine and human. Humankind desires its fulfillment, its homecoming in God. But God is encountered on the earthly pilgrimage "along the road": in persons, love, desire and words.[34] The pursuit of God is thus for Gregory both individual and profoundly social. As a result of hearing the words of life and encountering other fellow pilgrims along the way, the heart's desire is rekindled and a glimpse of the divine love seen.

Gregory developed the psychology of desire as a dialectic of presence and absence, possession and non-possession, certainty and uncertainty, light and darkness, faith and eternal life. Desire was much more than a simple yearning. It was the refusal, by the heart, to resolve the tension implicit in the paradox of being both mortal and destined for immortality. It is not simply that Gregory used images derived from the human experience of love to metaphorically posit divine truths but that he described the essence of the spiritual life as an experience that was also human. What seems to be important here is to recall that the Christian tradition understood love in a multi-dimensional fashion. Because God is seen in persons, desire, words and love, if Gregorian assertions are carried to their logical conclusion, friendship becomes not only possible but an essential component of the Christian life.

Gregory the Great, along with Benedict of Nursia, provided monastic culture of the later centuries with its essential ingredients. It was a homogeneous culture, despite its geographical diffusion, because it possessed a homogeneous language.[35] The monastic world anticipated in both practice and theory what the Christian faith believed the kingdom of God to be. Thus its language was based on worship that sought to possess, increase and communicate the desire for God. It was the language of a pilgrim people whose journey through life would lead them to a celestial homeland. Along the way they could have a foretaste of what they sought through human contact. God was found, if only darkly, in these others and the essence of the finding was the experience of desire. In desire itself humankind possessed God.

Under the aegis of the leaders of the Carolingian Renaissance of the later eighth and early ninth century, monastic culture acquired a definitive shape that left its stamp on the entire Christian world. For the language of monasticism was not simply a language of a cloistered elite but a much wider phenomenon. Because the early medieval monastery was both the preserver and disseminator of literacy and cultural values, and because the monks were often in positions of secular responsibility, the language of the monastic life became the language of literate Christendom. By this means, Gregorian patterns of thought had, by the ninth century, supplied the vocabulary with which Christendom understood itself and answered the fundamental human questions: Who am I, where am I going and what should I do?

The extent to which Gregorian formulations permeated the thought of individuals in the Middle Ages is indicated by the presence of this language of desire in letters of friendship.[36] The writings of Isidore of Seville, Alcuin, Anselm, Herveus, and Peter of Blois have been shown to reveal the extent to which these men could understand their relationships as unions of desire.[37] The pure friendship expressed in these letter is formulaic and patterned without being merely cliché. They speak of friendship with the affective imagery of the heart, and depict the anxiety of separation and the

longing of the friends to bridge the distance between themselves. It
is Gregorian desire that is present here, that dialectic tension
between separation and union in which pilgrims know a foretaste of
the celestial home.[38]

This positive evaluation of the role of friendship in the spiritual
life, which runs counter to the distrust found in most monastic literature, seems to have found its fullest expression in the twelfth
century among writers belonging to the Cistercian Order newly
founded by Bernard of Clairvaux. Cistercian spirituality of this
period was remarkably introspective and self-consciously aware of
the psychological motivations and development of the contemplative
life. This was in part because of contemporary tension resulting
from a newly emerging concept of the apostolic life which con-
flicted with the traditional values of monasticism. This was also in
part because the recruits for the new order were adults: they did not
adhere to the traditional practice of accepting child oblates into the
monastery.[39] Experience gained "in the world" was now part of the
experience brought to the contemplative life. In this atmosphere the
Gregorian language of desire, already part of the contemplative
vision, was given a fresh impulse for expression.

Much of the specific vocabulary that has been referred to as the
"Gregorian language of desire" came from Scripture, as has been
suggested. Most particularly, the poetry of the Song of Songs had
become part of Christian liturgy and devotion. This poem from the
canon of the Hebrew bible, with its erotic vocabulary of the courtship of a man and woman, attracted the exegetical energy of centuries of religious writers and produced a variety of differing interpretations.[40] Not all of these treatments found favor in all historical
periods. The mystical one—which is of significance here—was only
fully developed in the twelfth century by Bernard of Clairvaux and
his contemporaries.[41]

With the Cistercian founder the courtship drama between
bride and bridegroom became internalized as the story of the coming
and going of God in the human soul. What this suggests is not simply the fact that a traditional language of worship that had been
developed in the monastic world became newly popular, perhaps as
a result of the interests and psychological orientation of the new
monks. It also points once again to the fact that, in the contemplative
tradition, love, in its several modalities, was the source of spiritual

imagery and self-understanding. In the erotic scriptural poem the Song of Songs, the interdependent nature of the four loves is made particularly explicit. Love, for the mystical troubadors of the Song of Songs, was a richly textured blend of *epithemia, eros, philia* and *agape*. In using the Song of Songs as their poetic vocabulary, Bernard and his contempories revealed their intuition that human union and divine union are part of one reality that is brought to its fullest expression in the gradual divinization of all human activities and capacities. The transformation of human love into love of God is made possible precisely because of the employment of the language of desire, for in this language all modalities of love are present. It is one of these modalities that itself is the binding force that relates all the loves to one another. This is *eros*. *Eros* is desire, the yearning to be united to the beloved. It is *eros* that seeks to become part of something beyond itself, whether it be another person, the true, good and beautiful or the divine. The Song of Songs evokes the presence of *eros*, the dynamic relational quality of love. Hence the Song of Songs is an artistic (or inspired) expression of the desire for union with another person and the desire for union with God at one and the same time.

The Song of Songs portrays the transfiguration of the human into the divine. The transformation of love is central to this process. But the raw vitality of human love does not become divinized without passing through the fires of purgation. The lover of God must gather up all the potential energy of his or her capacity for love and discipline it, purge it of its self-seeking motives and direct it to its proper end. Love then is liberated from the raw instinct to gratify self and becomes conscious of the implications of self-gratification. The transformation of love becomes first a matter of perceiving the motives that underlie all loves, and then a matter of directing love to its proper end which is also its source: God. The key is *eros*, for it is desire that draws love out, that expands its capacity, that passionately rushes toward divinization. It is *eros*, when properly directed, that transforms human loves into *caritas*. As love comes from God, so love returns humankind to Him. As an abbot and director of souls, Bernard knew this well.[42]

The transformation of human love through friendship figures largely in Cistercian writing. As has been suggested, the new communities of white monks put a heightened value on human relation-

ship in the spiritual life.[43] Bernard wrote to his friends William of
St. Thierry and Peter the Venerable as well as to others in the language of desire and mutual love that we have seen was implicit in
the tradition.[44] The Cistercian world likewise produced what is perhaps Christianity's most sublime expression of friendship, the treatise *On Spiritual Friendship* by Aelred of Rievaulx.[45] Inspired by
Cicero's treatise, Aelred took the classical dialogue form and created
a work that stands as the Christian world's most complete and positive statement on friendship.[46] Friendship was, in his mind, well
defined by his classical predecessor's phrase: agreement on matters
human and divine, with charity and good will. The Cistercian felt
that friendship came directly from God who in His love created
human beings to share that love by loving each other and Himself.
The human heart has in it an inclination to bind itself to other
hearts; this it does rightly and lawfully, for God had built love into
human nature. Yet, friends must be aware of the possibility of false
bonds that spring from the desire for carnal pleasure, material gain
or self-seeking. True friendship seeks none of these but instead
seeks the mutual perfection of the friends through greater love of
God. So essential is this true friendship to the person pursuing the
life of the spirit that Aelred goes as far as to state (paraphrasing St.
John) that "he who abides in friendship abides in God and God in
him" and "God is friendship."[47] The life of the just *is* the life of
spiritual friendship, for the true relationship of two fellow pilgrims
is not only virtuous but the practical expression of love as it ought
to be between all people.

Aelred's treatise was contemporary with another treatment of
friendship, *The Treatise on Christian Friendship and Love of God and
Neighbor* by Peter of Blois.[48] This theologian and member of the
humanist circle that included John of Salisbury and Peter of Celles
gave to posterity a glowing presentation of friendship. In his eyes it
was no less than "a divine gift whose value we can never appreciate
too much."[49] For him the bond between friends is found in their
mutual perfection in love, for love is the context in which the theologian sets his evaluation of friendship. More scholastic in tone
than Aelred's dialogue, Peter of Blois' treatment of the subject is no
less positive and affirmative about the God-given possibilities in
genuine spiritual friendship.

With the deaths of the twelfth century luminaries an era ends.
Although the language of love and desire continued with remarkable

intensity in the church's devotion, it came to be used less to describe love between fellow pilgrims than love between the soul and God. Following Bernard, a long line of mystics found their most profound experiences of God reflected in the mirror of the Song of Songs: the German visionaries Hadewijch, Mechthild of Magdeberg and Gertrude the Great, the Franciscan spiritual Francisco de Osuna, the Spaniard Raymond Lull, the English anchorite Julian of Norwich, the Carmelites Teresa of Avila and John of the Cross, all belong to a long line of Christian mystics whose language of ultimate encounter is the language of love. What we have termed the Gregorian language of desire found new variations as well as beauty in the visionary raptures of some of these great figures. Moreover, the devotional imagery that gained ascendancy from the thirteenth century onward was the imagery derived from the language of desire: the Sacred Heart and Christ as bridegroom to the soul-bride. What seems to have disappeared from the Christian experience of desire is the very Gregorian insistence that deity is encountered in persons and words as well as in love and desire.

Love was the road to perfection for the late medieval and early modern world, but friendship as a God-given means to attain the heights of that perfection was, in general, suspect and questionable. The current of thought prominent in monastic literature, which warned of more than simple friendship, overtook the tradition. There were some authors who spoke in moderately appreciative terms of the phenomenon, for, in theory at least, friendship was considered a form of love. The hermit Richard Rolle in the fourteenth century admitted that friendships could be good as well as bad when they were loved for God and not for fleshly reasons, but in the end he reiterated the typical reservation—that friendship should be found mainly between God and the individual soul.[50] The general opinion on the topic is well expressed by Teresa of Avila, who in her *Way of Perfection* stated:

> For the love of the Lord, refrain from making individual friendships, however holy, for even among brothers and sisters such things are apt to be poisonous and I can see no advantage in them.[51]

In religious literature generally, friendship was not seen as central to the religious quest. If admitted at all it was seen as auxiliary.

This does not mean that there were not friendships nor that the post-medieval centuries did not see the rise of many lay and religious communities dedicated to the Christian communal ideal. Certainly the mendicant orders, though producing no theoretical statement on friendship, found in their imitation of the poverty and apostolic preaching of Jesus that friends, like disciples, were essential companions along the way.[52] One has only to read the fourteenth century Franciscan Bernardino of Sienna's eulogy for his friend Vincent to discover how deep the bonds of friendship could go among the friars.

> He was always so closely united to me and loved me with all his soul. In religion he was an older brother to me; in love he was another self. When I was weak of heart, he encouraged me. I was lazy and neglected God's ways and he spurred me on. I was improvident and forgetful and he reminded me.[53]

On the other hand the great work of the *devotio moderna*, the *Imitation of Christ*, does not suggest any loving relationships for those dedicated to the life of spirit other than the love of Jesus Christ.[54] It appears as though the positive evaluation of friendship had for the most part receded into the background for those who had occasion to write of friendship in a theoretical way.

Most of the explicit religious statements about friendship that emerge from the late sixteenth and early seventeenth century, the period which is of greatest importance here, assume to greater or lesser degree that particular friendships are incompatible with perfect love of neighbor. The writings of Jules Negrone, Jean-Jacques Surin, Vincent de Paul, M. Tronson, Francis Suarez and others attest to that assumption.[55] Surin, for instance, felt obliged to broach the question in one chapter in his book on the love of God, "Can those who have achieved the state of pure love of God, and who seek only to please Him, love and be affectionately united with anyone in a close friendship?" His answer amounts to a very tepid and highly qualified maybe.[56]

Similarly, the opinions held by Vincent de Paul indicate to what an extent both love of neighbor was affirmed and yet individual liaisons frowned upon. In the view of the founder of the Daughters of Charity, the organization of women dedicated to love of neighbor through service to the poor and infirm, particular friendships were "more dangerous than they might seem to be." They could cause division in community and act against Christian love which should extend to all equally.[57]

It is into this general climate that we should place François de Sales' injunctions about the obligation to indifferent love that those vowed to a religious life should observe. In his *Conversations*, he advised cloistered women:

> . . . we must strive to love (everyone) equally since Our Lord did not say: "Love those who are more virtuous" but (spoke) indifferently: "Love one another as I have loved you" without excluding anyone, imperfect though they might be.[58]

Jeanne de Chantal too, echoing his concerns, stressed the obligation of religious to love neighbor and warned against friendships that arise within community that are not based solely upon love of God.

> . . . the great Saint Augustine very succinctly and well tells us how we must love our Sisters: "Now, there must not be any carnal affection, only spiritual." In other words, you must not have human, sensual friendships which are based on frivolous qualities such as birth, family, attainments, connections, congeniality, similarity, temperament and a thousand other chimeras conjured up by the human mind—like natural beauty and social graces. We must not love anyone, no matter how close they may be, except in God, for God and according to God. To love our Sisters in God is the only means to prevent the impurities which sometimes slip unto the most spiritual of friendships.[59]

Similarly, François de Sales warned of the possible dangers of friendship for lay people as well as religious although he felt that outside of a supportive community, a true friend might be more a benefit than a hindrance to spiritual growth, for a friend could encourage the practice of the devout life. In the same work in which he holds that "friendship is the most dangerous love of all"[60] and skillfully delineates the vanity and sensuality that can give rise to questionable liaisons, he also writes:

> Many people may perhaps claim that they should not have any kind of particular affection or friendship, that this would occupy

the heart, distract the mind and cause envy. But they are mis-
taken in their advice. . . . Those who are in religion do not have
need of particular friendships but those who are in the world
need them in order to secure and assist one another amid the
many dangerous passages through which they must pass.[61]

The two friends in their exhortations to those in religious life
did exhibit the contemporary distrust of particular frienships but
their understanding of personal relationship did not end there. On
the one hand, François saw in such unions the potential for mutual
perfection. He wrote of friendship in this way for those outside
vowed religious life. Moreover, both he and Jeanne sought and cultivated friendships of an intense nature, most particularly with one
another both before and after taking vows. In the actual lives of the
two friends both the negative and the positive interpretations of
friendship found in the Christian tradition interacted and played off
one another, producing a situation in which the sense of mistrust
and the cautionary advice about friendship was heeded while specific relationships were cultivated.

For the idea that friendship was one modality of love had not
disappeared from the Christian ideological repertoire entirely. François himself was magnificently explicit about this. For him, friendship as a form of love could spur one on or direct one to the ultimate
love of God. Friendship, in his formulation, was a particular type of
love: it was a *mutual* love in which both parties had to be aware of
their reciprocal affection and in which there was communication
between the two. Thus friendship was unlike other loves which can
exist without mutual interaction. For the bishop there were grada-
tions of friendships ranging from evil liaisons, reprehensible for
their motives and aims, to true friendships, that is to say, spiritual
friendships. For like love, friendships were classified according to
the extent to which they, as natural relationships, were informed by
and assisted the love of God. True friendships were thus characterized by the content of the communication that transpired between
the friends.

The more exquisite the virtues . . . the more perfect your friendship will be. . . . Should your mutual and reciprocal communi-
cations relate to charity, devotion and Christian perfection, oh
God, how precious will this friendship be![62]

François de Sales may have been writing specifically for lay persons in this passage, but it could be applied as appropriately to his own relationship with Jeanne de Chantal. Like John Cassian many centuries before, François de Sales was called upon to give advice to those seeking a life of perfection. His advice to these was to avoid exclusive unions that could disrupt community and impede the growth of charity. Yet he recognized the importance of and recommended the practice of friendship when the friends in question were sufficiently mature and grounded in their quest to keep the love of God central to the love between them. The same is true of Jeanne de Chantal. At the same time, as will be shown in Jeanne and François' own relationship, the traditional tension between love of God and love of other was very present in the actual experience of their friendship.

One suspects that this renewed expansive attitude toward friendship that is found in Salesian thought alongside the caution about attachments was in part made possible because of the general cultural climate of the time. The last half of the sixteenth century delighted in love and in relationships (both between people and between God and humankind). In France as well as in Italy and Spain there was an effusion of amorous literature that filled its audience with sentiments of passion. Everywhere "love reigned like a despot in minds and often in bodies."[63] The French voraciously consumed this literature, of which *Astraea* by Honore d'Urfé was the principal achievement. Moreover, the preoccupation with love was not merely a popular, literary phenomenon. Sixteenth and early seventeenth century philosophy was imbued with the Platonism revived by Ficino and busied itself pondering the nature of beauty and love.[64]

Love was in the air, and Christian writers did not lose the opportunity to capitalize on the burning interest by turning their contemporaries from worldly to other worldly desire. François de Sales, in his *Treatise on the Love God*, mentions a number of his contemporaries or recent predecessors who had turned their pens to the task of describing and celebrating divine love.[65] Among these was his own teacher at Paris, Genebrard, who wrote an exposition on the Song of Songs. But François was chief among those who found in the taste of the time an opportunity in which to revise the timeless teachings of his faith. It was very much in the tradition of Christian humanism to find in the concerns of society an entry into divine concerns. The bishop himself at one time remarked:

> It is very important to consider the historical era in which one writes.[66]

It had been possible in the Christian past to articulate the dynamics of a spiritual relationship in the vocabulary drawn from the human experiences of desire and union. At the turn of the seventeenth century it was once again possible and probable that such language would occur. It was, in a sense, a conventional language. But its utterance was absolutely new and unique, for the use of a traditional pattern of literary images in the hands of a master never produces convention. François and Jeanne did not merely place their experience into the framework of a traditional vocabulary, for the relation between language and experience is more complex than this would imply. The experience itself was in part formed and shaped by the patterns of meaning and relationship implicit in the language available to the two friends.[67] For them the purpose of human life was to become a perfect lover of God.[68] Love, in all its human and divine complexity, was the stuff of which life was made.

François de Sales, like his predecessors in the tradition of desire, did not leave an explicit analytical treatment of the different modalities of love and their relationship to one another. But he did, like them, conceive of the kinds of love as gradated.[69] Less cynical than Augustine of Hippo about the exercise of the human forms of loves, he did teach that *all* loves were possible points of departure on the journey to the full actualization of love of God.

His *Introduction to the Devout Life* is a meditative exercise designed to trace the way one moves from the small spark of desire to lead a devout life to the full embrace of that life. Similarly, his later voluminous work, the *Treatise on the Love of God,* casts the entire theology of creation and salvation in the drama of God's loving relationship with the world and humankind's return to God through love. The book is concerned with the development of the mystical state, the realization of the pure love of God.

Throughout both of these works the author is preoccupied with the modalities of love. Love is "means and end at one and the same time, the vehicle and the destination, the way to go to itself."[70]

God extends Himself to creation as love, and humankind responds through the natural endowment of love, which is gradually transformed and perfected by grace into a love which resembles God's own love. The point is that humankind's experience of love, whether of God or of other persons, is one love, for human beings do not have two natures but one alone

> ... "composed of body and soul" which has need of sensual pleasures whether it be for the particular conservation of each person or for the conservation of the species and the human race.[71]

This makes the human being a profoundly relational creature. The person achieving the selfhood apportioned to him or her by divine design will be one who loves to his or her fullest capacity. The exercise of this full capacity implies the utilization of the energies latent in the four modalities of love in the service of the Christian vocation.

Unlike some in the theological tradition, the Savoyard did not regard the marital bond simply as a necessary outlet for the human urge toward sexual gratification.[72] His theory of marriage is based upon a more humane evaluation of the nature of male and female interaction. One end of marriage, at least in terms of the salvific plan of creation, is the propagation of the species. The exercise of sexual desire is part of God's design but, as with all loves, lust must not be exercised without reference to its transformation under the aegis of *caritas*. Thus while the marriage debt is "holy, just and commendable in itself," and affection is legitimately a part of marriage, like other bodily pleasures it must be steered away from self-preoccupied exercise.[73]

Most importantly, marriage was for François de Sales a type of friendship. The effect of marital love is first a union of hearts, not of body.[74] Husband and wife are to be friends, to enjoy a mutual love that results in the reciprocal perfection of both parties realized day by day over the course of a lifetime. This was possible because in François de Sales' eyes any love could bring the human heart to God, provided it was not a love contrary to the will of God.

In his own personal experience of spiritual friendship François de Sales makes clear the rich fabric and texture of human relationship that derives from the interaction between the modalities of love. His friendship with Jeanne de Chantal was one in which the powerful dynamics of the interaction between male and female were experienced simultaneously with the most profound love of God. The key is *eros*, for it was the language of desire made accessible to him through the tradition that provided their friendship with a vocabulary and that gave their love a voice. And it was *eros*, experienced as the binding force that draws a man and woman together that supplied the momentum for their mutual passionate desire for God.

Only seven months after their initial encounter François wrote to Jeanne about the way in which he felt they were bound together.

> . . . from the first time that you consulted me about your interior life, God granted me a great love for your spirit. When you confessed to me in greater detail, a remarkable bond was forged in my soul that caused me to cherish your soul more and more. This made me write to you that God had given me to you, not thinking that it would ever be possible for the affection that I felt in my spirit to be increased—especially by praying to God for you. But now, my dear Daughter, a certain new quality has emerged which it seems I cannot describe, only its effect is a great interior sweetness that I have to wish for you a perfect love of God and other spiritual blessings. No, I am not exaggerating the truth in the least, I speak before "my heart's God" and yours. Each affection is different from others. The one I have for you has a certain quality which consoles me infinitely and, if all were known, is extremely profitable to me. Consider this an absolute truth and have no more doubts about it.[75]

The prelate here articulates his heightened sense that their specific relationship is of special importance in the unfolding of his life's story. It is not just that in some general way God meant them to be together. His own understanding of who he is is aided by their intimacy. This self-understanding is irrevocably linked to his vocation as a priest in the service of the church. In his sacerdotal function, he understood himself to be presiding over the sacramental entry of divine grace into the world. It was particularly in the celebration of the Mass that this was so. That he experienced Jeanne as present to him during this sacred mystery is striking. It points to the merging of his own most profound sense of self and his relationship with her.

> After all, I never say the Holy Mass without you and whatever concerns you most deeply. I do not receive the sacrament at all without you. In the end, I am as much yours as you could ever wish.[76]

There was also the recognition that not only his self-definition but hers was bound up in their shared love. He began to speak of "our" heart, "our" love, "our" soul. This single union of persons then sought the same attainments.

> I salute you, you small and great crosses, be you spiritual, temporal, exterior or interior. . . . You ask why I do this? But it is fitting, my dearest daughter, because I adore your crosses with the same affection I have for my own and I hope (at least I ask it of you) that you would love mine with a heart likewise disposed.[77]

Similarly:

> . . . it is true, my dear daughter, our unity is utterly consecrated to the highest unity and each day I sense more vividly the truth of our sincere connection which will not let me ever forget you even long, long after I have forgotten myself in order to better attach myself to the Cross.[78]

The ultimate meaning of the liaison is experienced by them both as an onslaught of love, an overwhelming desire to rush into the arms of and be united with their divine lover. Likewise, the liaison itself participates in the quality of love between lover and beloved. François admits that he belongs to Jeanne, despite separations of time and space. Their love has created a reciprocal bond that cannot be forgotten or effaced.

> You well know, seeing as how I have written to you about it, that I go to you by following the spirit and it is true. No, it will be impossible for anything to ever separate me from your soul.

The bond is too strong. Death itself would not have the power to dissolve it because it is of a quality that lasts forever.[79]

He further describes the love he holds for her. The occasion is his reflection upon their mutual commitment to institute the new women's religious congregation.

You would not believe how much my heart was strengthened by our resolutions and by everything that contributed to their establishment. I feel an extraordinary sweetness about them as likewise I feel for the love I bear you. Because I love that love incomparably. It is strong, resilient, measureless and unreserved yet gentle, pliant, completely pure and tranquil. In short, if I am not deceived, it is completely in God.[80]

Not only are the ecstatic flights of desire evidenced in François' letters but also the more mundane emotions of love like tenderness, mutual care, and anxiety over the other's well-being. Perhaps most touching of all is the anticipation the eminent bishop feels while awaiting each new communication from his friend.

I had gone ten whole weeks without receiving a single scrap of news about you, my dear, I should say my dearest daughter. Your last letters were from the beginning of the past November. But the good of it is that my heart's patience almost ran out and I believe that it would have been completely lost if I had not forced myself to remember that I must conserve it in order to be genuinely able to preach it to others. Now, finally, my dearest daughter, yesterday, there was a packet which came for me, like a ship from India, rich with letters and spiritual songs. Oh, how welcome they were and how I carressed them![81]

He even shows nostalgia for the events and sites that provided the plot and scenery for the budding relationship. The Savoyard wrote to his Burgundian friend of a visit to St. Claude five years after their decisive encounter there.

We have made a very successful voyage through the country. How ardently I prayed to God for you during my contemplation of the Holy Shroud which was being publicly venerated as well as before the Blessed Sacrament and before our dear Saint Claude where I stayed in the lodgings where you had stayed. I took pleasure in seeing the place where I heard your confession and I was consoled to be able to once again present that heart which, as its father, I presented for the first time on the altar at St. Claude.[82]

That his avowals should not be misconstrued in any way, François on occasion qualified his ardent expressions. He assured Jeanne that his affection for her was "whiter than snow and purer than the sun" and that his ardor to hear from her was "paternal and more than paternal."[83] His concern was slight that she would misinterpret his meanings, but he was aware that others might fail to understand the nature of the passionate bond between them. For this reason he early on counseled her to let no one see the correspondence he sent her.

I am willing that you would communicate the advice I have given you about your conscience to your confessor. But not the letters which are a little too unguarded and cordial to be seen by other than the simplest eyes and which express my utterly frank and open intentions in your regard.[84]

This last solicitation is enough to indicate that the language that passed between the bishop and the widow, while influenced in tone by the love vocabulary available to them through the Christian contemplative tradition, was not a language very commonly used to convey the sentiments of relationships between chaste men and women. He was aware, though not afraid, of the fact that their passionate interchange could be misconstrued. The letters that he sent to her, although utilizing images familiar to the tradition, were not formulaic. Nor did he write in quite the same manner to others he knew.[85] For her alone was reserved the language of union. For her alone the language of the heart was given full sway.

In François' most deep desires he found Jeanne. More than that, when ordinary language failed him, he appealed to her secret knowledge of the communion between hearts.

The other day . . . I was meditating on the grandeur of the love that Our Lady bears us. . . . It seemed to me that, if we confi-

dently place our hearts and affections on Our Lady's lap and
breast, they will no longer be ours, but hers. This consoled me
greatly. At the end, I set about entrusting to her not only my
own heart's children, but also the hearts of my children and the
children of my heart. You know, my dear daughter, that you are
part of this company and in what place among them I put you.
Oh God! I had such a burning sweetness to lodge you in that
sacred breast and say to Our Lady: "Here is your daughter
whose heart is utterly given up to you!" I don't know how to
express what my heart spoke, because, as you know, hearts have
a secret language which only they themselves understand.[86]

The focus of much of the above discussion has been on François de Sales' employment of the language of love in the early years
of his friendship with Jeanne de Chantal. What of his friend? It will
be remembered that Jeanne burned much of her own correspondence after the bishop's death so that no letters survive from these
first years of the relationship when she was still a widow. Yet there
are oblique references to her initial posture toward her spiritual
friend to be found in his correspondence. One gets the impression
that, particularly in the beginning, her attitude toward the bishop
was in part one of admiration, even veneration. After all, he was a
powerful and holy figure in the religious and social world of the
time. And, while Jeanne was not one to be overly intimidated by the
robes of religious office (her own younger brother was an archbishop), still she met him first in his vocation as priest. In the world
of Counter-Reformation Catholicism, the priestly role was highly
respected. In these first years while she still retained her widow's
lifestyle, Jeanne seems to have experienced in her love for François
a certain measure of simple gratitude, dependence and even worship.
Indeed, the Savoyard occasionally complained about what he considered her over-evaluation of him.

My daughter, I am nothing but vanity, yet I do not esteem
myself as much as you do. How I wish that you really knew me.
You would not cease having such absolute confidence in me, but
you would hardly esteem me at all. You would say: Here is a
cane on which God wishes me to lean. I am confident of it
because this is what God wishes but the cane itself is worth
nothing.[87]

Still, her veneration was merely part of her response to him. He was first and foremost her confidant, the one other person in the world who was intimate to her heartfelt aspirations. François comments frequently on her openness with him. It was her unbounded love for François, her sense that she had genuinely met a spiritual friend, that gave her the boldness to reveal herself so openly. She, too, certainly sensed the ordained quality of their friendship. She had not forgotten the preternatural vision received in the meadow at Bourbilly. She looked to the Savoyard as one sent to her from God, through whose instruction and shared love she would come fully to incarnate the divine will in her own life.

It is impossible to know how much the erotic locutions that characterize his correspondence were employed by her during the early years of friendship. While it is present in the emotional tonality of her correspondence, in her later writings the language of desire is less verbally explicit than in his writings. This is perhaps because her literary style differed markedly from his. It was less adorned with metaphor and the elegant turn of phrase. Her letters were extremely expressive, but this is because they were so direct and unselfconscious and not because of their rhetorical artifice.

What is clear in these early years is that his love gave her the eagle's wings she needed to span the psychological and spiritual chasm that separated her old self from the new. They were friends, spiritual companions whose mutual love compelled them together to the personal expanses of which they were capable. Her attentiveness to his direction, the bold vision of her future sustained by him that ran so counter to her family's expectations for her, her longings to be in his presence, her willingness to journey to wherever she could meet him, the extraordinary responsiveness, pliancy and receptivity that she displayed toward him and his suggestions all point to her more than willing embrace of the love of which her friend so beautifully wrote.

II

The little Burgundian band arrived in Annecy about a week after setting out from Dijon. Monseigneur François de Sales and a collection of attendants came to meet them on a hillside pass in order to escort them into town. They were lodged at the home of Antoine Favre, the bishop's dear friend and father of one of the intended founding members of the new institute. It was Holy Week, so their first order of business was to attend to the observance of that most sacred period of the Christian liturgical year. After Easter, diligent preparations for the establishment of the congregation began.

A community house had been promised to the bishop by a donor who hoped to join the nascent congregation. At the last minute, her offers of both house and self fell through. This meant that a new site had to be procured and plans to found the community on Pentecost shelved. A modest house was for sale on the outskirts of the town. It was called "la Galerie" because of the gallery that ran along one entire side of the dwelling and looked out over the fields that led down to the shore of Lake Annecy. It was an extremely simple habitation by seventeenth century aristocratic standards but it served the community's needs. Downstairs, in a large room below street level that had been a cellar, they prepared a chapel. Upstairs were a few spare rooms to be used for dining and sleeping chambers. Jeanne and her first companions themselves furnished the house with a modest collection of beds, chairs and tables brought from their respective homes.

However, the widow de Chantal was not only concerned with the preparations for the new foundation; Marie-Aymée had to be installed in her new home. Mother and daughter (as well as the rest of their entourage) spent a month at the Castle of Thorens, the bridegroom's residence. Jeanne wanted to make sure that the young wife was established in her environment and that the necessary operations of the household were well under way before she returned to Annecy. She was conscientious in her duty, so that it was May before she and Charlotte de Bréchard saw the shores of Lake Annecy again.

Then the final preparations that would lead to the beginning of a new life went into full sway. Trinity Sunday (in 1610 it fell on June 6) was set for installation in "la Galerie." To accompany Jeanne were two women, Charlotte de Bréchard and Jacqueline Favre. Anne-Jacqueline Coste would enter with these three as outsister. They were an unusual assembly.[88] Jeanne was by then thirty-eight years old, a widow with three underage children with no previous formal experience in vowed religious life. She was to be the mother superior. Charlotte de Bréchard, Jeanne's family friend and godmother of her deceased youngest daughter, had herself an unusual and circuitous route to the convent. She was of noble birth but had endured a brutal childhood. The youngest child of a baron of Burgundy, she was an unwanted family member who after her mother's early death was cruelly neglected. She seems to have culled her deep religious sensitivities out of the agonies of her past and to have found meaning in ministering to the needs of the sick and poor. It was while doing this in Burgundy that she met Jeanne, who was engaged in the same pursuits. In 1607 she was invited to stay with the Chantal family at Monthelon. During her stay she professed an interest in religious life. She even spent a trial period with the Carmelites of Dijon, but the physical rigor of the life was too much for her. In 1608 she met François de Sales at Monthelon and put herself under his direction. The bishop assessed the qualities of this woman and agreed with her that she had a genuine vocation. His confidence in her is attested to by his encouraging her to enter the new congregation.

The third and youngest member of that tiny band preparing for Trinity Sunday in 1610 was Jacqueline Favre. The beautiful, vivacious daughter of Annecy's leading citizen had a very different upbringing from her future sister in religion. Jacqueline had all the love and attention that a stable, well-to-do family life could offer. She had known François de Sales since childhood, he being often at the family home. She had read the *Introduction to the Devout Life* and at the bishop's unpressured suggestion had tried a few minutes of prayer a day. But she was an irrepressible socializer and fiercely independent. Yet there was a streak in her that the bishop had recognized early on, though he did nothing overt to encourage its emergence. One evening at Chambery in the midst of an elegant ball, dancing with the guest of honor, she had a vision of human transience. At that moment she decided to give herself to God. But she told no one of her plan until her father revealed that her hand had been asked for in marriage (by Louis de Sales, François' younger brother). She was forced to decline and, putting away her fine dresses with some regret, she began to pray in earnest and to visit the poor. When Madame de Chantal came to Annecy in the winter of 1610, Jacqueline was ready to enter "la Galerie" with her.

These three founding members of the congregation were to be assisted in their undertakings by Anne-Jacqueline Coste who had been designated out-sister. It was the practice at the time for women's communities to have members, often from the peasant and illiterate classes, who would act as the primary contact between the community and the outside world and whose responsibilities would be domestic rather than liturgical. Anne was to play this role in the new foundation. She was the oldest of the company and had known François de Sales from the days when he was provost of the diocese. Born a Savoyard, she had been forced by famine as a young woman to seek employment in Geneva. There she worked as a servant in one of the town inns and operated something of an underground network for the aid and edification of those who were forced to profess their Catholic faith secretly.

When the young provost François de Sales arrived in the Geneva inn for dialogues with the noted Reformer Theodore Beza, he was cornered by Anne who fervently asked his opinion whether she ought to remain in the city and continue her work or return to Savoy where she could more openly practice her religion. He advised her to delay a decision and asked her if she wished to receive Communion. At a makeshift altar she received the consecrated host that the provost carried with him on a silver chain around his neck. Eight years later, Anne-Jacqueline returned to Savoy. The year was 1604 and François was now a bishop. She assumed he would have forgotten her, but one day, while preaching, François spotted her in the crowd and, making a gesture toward the silver case suspended around his neck, indicated to her that he recognized her. When the time came for the inauguration of the new community, Anne-Jacqueline Coste with her simple but unshakable faith was designated by the founder to be among its number.

Trinity Sunday neared. Jeanne had anticipated the day for six long years. She had seen her inchoate longings to dedicate herself totally to God crystalize into a definitive form. For the last three years much of her energy had been directed toward arranging the varied elements of her life to accommodate the plans that were to be realized on that day. Her joy should have been immense, yet on the eve of her rite of passage she was gripped by a terrible anxiety.

My soul felt as though it were in its death-throes. I felt myself surrounded on all sides without knowing where to escape. I was instantly stripped of the joy I had in my retirement which had become my support during all my other troubles. I seemed to see my father and father-in-law, weighed down with the sorrows of age, crying out to God for vengeance against me. On the other side my children were doing the same. It was as if a multitude of voices were speaking in my mind, accusing me of having committed a great fault. And what made me more miserable was that it was a reproach drawn from the Scriptures— that in the Church of God I would be taken for an infidel, since I had abandoned my children and no doubt had deceived the Holy Bishop. Consequently, the counsel he had given me to leave my family was against the will of God.[89]

For three hours in the middle of the night, Jeanne remained panic-struck by the ferocity of the assault on her vocation. She was tempted to call for François but "the modesty of the silence of night"[90] restrained her. Soon, laying her hand upon the scars on her breast that spelled out the name of Jesus, she gave herself over to her beloved in the way that the bishop had always instructed her. Realizing that to confront her panic with the powers of reason was useless, she made "an act of perfect abandonment of herself and all else into the hands of God."[91] Her words of surrender dispelled the tempest, not only restoring her previous calm but invigorating her with a new strength and buoyant sense of joy.

Trinity Sunday brought with it the dawn of new beginnings. The three fledgling sisters of this audacious vocational experiment assembled together in the evening at the bishop's house for supper after having made a pilgrimage of all the churches in Annecy. Around eight o'clock they met in François' oratory and received from him a copy of the rules and constitutions he had written for them. Then they each received the arm of one of François' brothers who were to escort them out into the night to make the brief promenade from Favre's residence to the shores of the lake and the waiting figure of Anne-Jacqueline Coste at the doors of "la Galerie." All the town turned out to cheer them on, waving enthusiastically at each turn in the way, following the trio even into the cramped confines of their little chapel. There they said their final farewells. After the well-wishers had departed, the new mother superior and her assistants knelt to pray. "This is the place of our delight and rest," she assured them.[92] Then she read to them the rule that their founder had composed.

During the first few years the young congregation rapidly expanded its numbers. A few of the recruits were more mature women like Jeanne and Charlotte, but the majority were young.[93] The life that they entered was very simple.[94] They were to be daughters of prayer, surrendered to the love of God. The structure that supported that life was likewise very simple. Under the rules and constitutions that had been drawn up for them, the sisters of the Visitation were to spend their days in the most ordinary pursuits. Rising at five in the morning they were allowed a period of private prayer before participating in the divine office. They assembled to recite the Little Office of Our Lady rather than the complex and long office required of most monastic orders.[95] They were to say it in Latin, the sacred language of the Catholic tradition. For this, instruction had to be given. For, though they were literate, these wives and daughters of the French aristocracy were not versed in the tongue of the church. Not all of the sisters of the congregation would be destined to recite the entire office daily. Their founder envisioned them ordered into three ranks with varied but overlapping duties, some being more occupied with the liturgy, others more focused upon the domestic maintenance of the house.[96]

The shared prayer punctuated the day at intervals in the true rhythm of monastic time. Other segments of time were given over to eating (twice a day, at 10 A.M. and 6 P.M.), simple work[97] (mostly of a domestic nature intended for the running of the house), spiritual reading, recreation (there were two periods a day for this common friendly interaction), assembly (a time given for the ongoing formation of community), and obedience (a formal opportunity for the cultivation of personal growth and instruction in spiritual formation). All of the life was to be undertaken in a spirit of silence and reflection. Indeed, a good deal of the day was actually spent in solitude, Jeanne feeling that the true spirit of interior prayer needed physical solitude as well as shared silence to flourish. There was provision for individual retreats to be taken away from community (but on the property) as well as community retreats from the round of daily life.

The aim of this simply structured life was the realization of the love of God. For the Savoyard, that love had two arms, one stretching out to neighbor, one reaching up to the divine. Thus, the original life of the congregation was to allow for the extension of these two arms. After the first year, when all of them were in fact novices, the practice was for the professed sisters to go out periodically to minister to the poor and sick in the community. Novices were to remain strictly enclosed. This going out was closely integrated into the prayerful atmosphere of life within community, for all activity, in or out, was to be one avenue to the realization of the single love. The members were to die to themselves and self-love in order to be filled with God.

> ... the congregation is a school of self-abnegation, of mortification of the senses and of the resignation of all human will. In short, it brings into being a Mount Calvary where, with Jesus Christ, his chaste brides will be spiritually crucified.[98]

The methods of this death to self were interior rather than exterior. Exercises of piety, moderate bodily mortifications and fasts had only a small place in the observance. The interior practice of the presence of God took the place of long prayers, detachment from things supplanted absolute poverty, mortification of spirit and will replaced bodily penance, charity modified radical solitude, and obedience to small observances stood in place of obvious austerity. Theirs was to be a hidden life of perfection acquired through the practice of the little virtues of humility, simplicity, gentleness, charity and resignation.

At the center of the community was Jeanne herself. For the previous six years she had been faithfully practicing the spiritual disciplines necessary for such a life. It would be her understanding, her embodiment of François' direction that would make of his personal vision a communal way of life. The Congregation in its theoretical structure and spirit was his creation. It was due to Jeanne that the life took on flesh and became a possible, practical reality. The two friends together created and nurtured a life that owed its unique being to each of them equally.

It is the bishop's contributions that strike one straightaway. His concept to found a community for women was itself uncommon.

Most of the existent religious communities of women had been founded as offshoots of men's orders and were subordinate to them. François specifically arranged for the new group to be accountable to the bishop of the diocese. This effectively removed any possibility of the women losing their right of self-determination to a more influential male order. The nuns would be aided by the Jesuits who early on were designated the primary confessors and priests for the Visitation as it grew beyond the confines of the little town of Annecy.[99]

That the Savoyard wished to found a women's community, especially a community composed of the widowed, fragile, elderly or infirm, may be startling but it is not out of character. François de Sales insisted that the source of the Christian life is the inner person, not the outer. In his pastoral dealings he had had many occasions to minister to persons not deemed heroic material in the eyes of the world. Many of these were women. Yet he discovered vast springs of devotion, of love, of willingness to be surrendered to God in the most unlikely individuals. For these he wished to create a formal place within the body of the church.

Moreover, the bishop had a certain gift for directing women. It was not merely his graceful language, amiable to the sensibilities of French aristocratic womanhood, that made this so. He understood women and possessed insight into their perceptions of things. In all of his writing he made abundant use of metaphors drawn from feminine experience. Pregnancy, birth, lactation, child-rearing, all of these he utilized in his descriptions of the devout life. And his usage suggests not an abstract comprehension of these female experiences, but an intimate familiarity and sympathy with them. After all, he was the eldest of a large family. His mother, with whom he was very close, had until he was an adult a baby at breast or a toddler at her knee. There is great tenderness in the way he takes the ordinary events of a woman's life and speaks to her of the spiritual dimension which they can reveal.

> See the little child to whom the mother presents her breast; it throws itself into her arms, gathering and folding its tiny body in this bosom and on this loving breast. See also the mother, how, receiving it, she holds it to her and, as it were, glues it to her bosom and kissing it joins its mouth to hers. . . . Thus our

Savior shows his most lovable bosom of divine love to the devout soul.[100]

He actually seemed to have preferred women as his literary subjects because they more than men seemed to embody the spiritual qualities he most valued. He especially cherished them for the hiddenness of their lives. For him, who taught the "common way" of devotion, a woman's life could be a sterling example of sanctity.

At the same time, the prelate from Annecy exhibited a remarkable insight into the spiritual struggles unique to women. Something of this has been shown in his dealings with Jeanne. While he encouraged what might be called her feminine flexibility and capacity for surrender, at the same time he installed in her a firm sense of her own self-direction and her capacity for independent thought and action. This he seemed to do quite instinctively, drawing out the qualities, both "feminine" and "masculine," necessary for her authentic realization of the spiritual life. For women more generally he possessed a feeling for the habitual dispositions that could hinder them in devotion.[101] The chief of these was vanity. Certainly other spiritual writers had dealt with women's vanity as a hindrance to the inner life. But in general the perspective taken was that women, by indulging their vanity, became temptresses, forcing men's attention away from things of the spirit. A common response to vanity seen in this light would be to disfigure or veil any beauty a woman might have. The hagiographic archives are filled with stories of saintly women who one way or another sacrificed their beauty to the betterment of their own and others' souls.

François de Sales approached the issue from a different vantage point. His formulation stems from his philosophy of beauty. As has been shown, he was steeped in the thought of his day which made beauty not an end in itself but the conduit by which one is led to a superior good.[102] He understood the harmonious proportion of the created order, including the beauty of women, to have an evocative force that draws human attention to the eternal beauty to which its earthly counterpart points. In practical terms, François de Sales used this understanding of beauty in his direction of women. A woman's beauty was not to be despised but known as a conduit which points to a higher beauty. Thus if she sees *herself* as an end in herself, if she fails to perceive the more profound meaning of her human existence, she will give herself up to vanity, adorning the outward husk of self for its own sake. Her task, in the bishop's mind, should be instead to adorn the inner part. The exterior then will begin to reflect the inner true beauty being cultivated and become an evocation of the divine.[103] Women are thus not to make themselves ugly to combat vanity but to shift attention from outer to inner.

> I would have my devout men and women, always the best dressed of the company, but the least pompous and affected. As the proverb says, I would have them adorned with gracefulness, decency and dignity.[104]

Women should be appropriately attired depending upon their station in life. Girls especially, he felt, should be attractive if for no other reason than to interest a prospective husband. But one gets the feeling that the bishop did not begrudge young women the flower of their youth as long as their enjoyment of it was unselfconscious and innocent. In later years, writing to Jeanne about her grown but unmarried daughter Françoise (who thoroughly enjoyed the fineries of aristocratic living), François remonstrated with her for her somewhat prudish concern about the girl's stylishness. "Girls should be a little bit pretty," he gently told her.[105] Widows and religious he believed should be more reserved in their style of dress. Still, they were not to counter vanity with disfigurement or deliberate unattractiveness. The focus of attention would still be wrongly directed to the outer person. Soon after entering "la Galerie" the Visitation sisters were faced with the task of designing for themselves a costume reflective of their new life. The veil that they designed was not merely functional, it was ugly. Sometime later the bishop himself suggested a new model, simple but not unflattering and, with Charlotte as mannequin, the little group constructed one from material cut from Jeanne's traveling dress. François made the final round with the scissors, shaping the black drape himself.

Vanity was chief among the spiritual problems of women. Because of it, women stood in the way of their own development. The issue, in François' opinion, was that women have a tendency to see themselves through the eyes of others, their own self-perception being colored or even determined by the cues given by those outside themselves. A woman seeing herself solely through the eyes of another becomes absorbed in her own reflection. She ceases to see herself as anything but that reflection. This fiction of self is maintained only as long as the other continues to regard the woman appreciatively. Thus all her efforts must be expended to maintain the attraction she exerts. Externally, she costumes and paints herself to appear beautiful to the beholder. Interiorly she is concerned only with seeing herself as she wishes to be seen. She becomes an object even to herself.[106]

The Salesian response to this dilemma was twofold. His response on the practical level has been shown. On a more subtle plane, François de Sales counseled his women protégées to cease looking at themselves as either physical or spiritual objects. They were not to judge themselves through others' eyes. The course of Jeanne's early spiritual journey provides insights into her director's counsel. She was, to use the traditional term, over-scrupulous in her inner life. On the one hand, she was overly anxious in her relationship with God. On the other, she was overly dependent upon the literal instructions of her director. Her task, so beautifully described by her friend, was to learn the liberty of the children of God. A certain boldness was required as well as (paradoxically) a profound humility. She was not to see herself as seen by God and man but to make a naked act of surrender to the will and mercy of God. The history so far recounted shows how Jeanne learned to use this technique for the flowering of her own more mature self. The bishop's words of advice to his friend were straightforward:

> Do not philosophize about your trials nor respond to them but proceed boldly.[107]

Perhaps a clue to the disposition that François wishes to inculcate in his women followers is found in the distinction between nakedness and nudity.[108] To be nude is to present oneself in such a way that one creates a particular desired effect. One becomes attractive because of an arrangement of features and gestures in a conventional manner, the intent being to stimulate an appreciative response in the viewer. Nudity implies that the nude is conscious of the self as being seen. Nakedness, in contrast, is unselfconscious. It is simply being without clothes, without disguise. Nakedness, as an admirable spiritual disposition, has a long history in western Christian thought. The image of Christ upon the cross, literally stripped of His garments as well as spiritually stripped of any consolation of assurance, informed religious writers for centuries. For François de Sales, in the context of his direction of women, nakedness was an essential element of a relationship with God. One's posture was not to be that of the nude, self-consciously arranging one's interior self as one wished to be seen. One was to be naked, to be, very simply, one's true and whole self before God. His emphasis upon the "little" virtues, upon the "hidden" life of the Visitation, is but an extension of this fundamental theme.

The feminine compulsion to adorn self extended, in François' mind, to the adornment of the environment. Once again, the bishop was not opposed to the cultivation or creation of beauty, but he was insistent that this not be done for its own sake but for the sake of the inner beauty the outer was meant to express. Charlotte had a particular knack for dressing things up. It was natural, according to the tastes of the time, to want to ornament the altar and chapel where the little community worshiped. But the bishop had to be firm about the elaborate and even rococo decorations that from time to time appeared at "la Galerie." Simplicity was to be the key to all decor. Yet the impulse to adorn the sacred space sumptuously was strong. On the eve of the community's profession into religious life in 1611, exactly one year after its installation in the modest house at the edge of Lake Annecy, an incident occurred that was painful to both François and Jeanne.

Jacqueline's father had promised the women a special ornament for the altar for the important day. It did not come. Jacqueline and Charlotte, concerned that the setting was lacking for the occasion, asked Jeanne if they could borrow some money to buy some hangings. The resources of the group were meager. All that was available was a few gold coins that the bishop had given them with the express instruction that they were to be used only for absolute necessities or for the care of the sick. The intent of the two was merely to use the coins to buy the decorations and then to replace the sum once Monsieur Favre's gift arrived. Jeanne agreed. Later she had second thoughts. The maneuver had seemed natural enough, but its hidden meaning soon became clear to her. She sent François a boldly worded letter describing what had taken place. They both spent a fitful night. François arrived the next morning, troubled and grave.

He was displeased, saddened. She wept. This was very unlike their usual exchanges. They understood that what she had allowed constituted a breach of obedience. It was not simply that the letter of the injunction had been disobeyed—but its spirit had been violated. Jeanne had chosen for exterior show, for beautification for its own sake. She had failed to make the crucial distinction between what was genuinely needed for the occasion and what was simply desired. The life of the Visitation was intended to be a life of attention to the inner significance of the smallest and most mundane of events and acts. The response of the bishop and the new mother superior to this single violation of that spirit indicates how completely they understood its importance and how faithfully they wished to live out their ideal. As soon as the matter was perceived, François was quick to move on optimistically to something else. Jeanne had a much more difficult time divesting herself of the emotional difficulty of the incident.

Aligned with the feminine tendency to ornament was a similarly subtle tendency to become attached to small personal belongings. The founder intended that the Visitation strive for a radical interior detachment. To facilitate this he inaugurated the practice of yearly rotation of personal effects. Each year the sisters exchanged the crosses that they had received on profession as well as other articles.[109] Similarly, seating in the refectory was not done in order of length of time in the community (as it would be in most monasteries) but was drawn by lots. This was to act as a spiritual lesson. On the last day of the year 1613, François wrote to Jeanne:

> The will of God must be loved in both great and small events. . . . You must carry out your great and small changes as perfectly as you possibly can. Having considered this issue well before God, I am resolved that Our Congregation should establish the custom of making these changes on the day on which God makes his, causing us all to pass from one year to the other, and giving us an annual lesson about our instability, our changeableness, the reversals and destruction of the years which lead us to eternity.[110]

Similar consideration was given to the governance of the house. Once the group grew and there was more than one community house, the position of superior became an elected position, tenable for a period of three years renewable for only one successive term.[111] Unlike so many religious communities where superiors often ruled autocratically for a lifetime, the governing of the Visitation was to be shared and no one person would be allowed to maintain a position of authority over the others for an unlimited period of time.

In the prelate's mind, the one end of the congregation was the realization of the love of God. Love was to govern the relationships between the women as well as, once the group grew, between the various houses. No formal structure of alliance bound the separate Visitation communities together. Annecy, while it had the authority of tradition, could exercise no formal control over the other groups of sisters. They were to be made one through the faithful observance of the rule and the spirit of love animating them.

> . . . not having a great many austerities nor permanent vows like the formal orders and regular congregations, it is necessary that the fervor of charity and the strength of inward resolve supplement these and take the place of laws, vows and jurisdiction so that the saying of the Apostle which affirms that the bond of charity is the bond of perfection might be confirmed in this congregation.[112]

The flavor of Salesian spirituality was to permeate the congregation. In their exchange with each other, the Visitation sisters were to exhibit all the "douceur" and the cordiality that the bishop himself embodied. They were to be true friends, aiding each other in their lives consecrated to Christian love of God and neighbor. A number of years later, Jeanne would write to her spiritual daughters concerning their union.

> Ah, my dear sisters, our beloved Visitation is a tiny kingdom of charity. If union and holy cherishing do not reign, it will soon be divided and consequently, laid waste, losing the luster which all the ingenuity of human effort could never regain. . . . Let us therefore all pray that the Spirit of Love, uniter of hearts, grant us this close and living union with God by the total dependence of our will to His and between us by a perfect cherishing and reciprocal union of heart and spirit: and in our little Institute by

a mutual and exact conformity of life and affection without talk of "yours" and "mine" ever occurring among us, and with our amiably serving each other to the greater Glory of God and the benefit of each monastery.[113]

François de Sales' personal stamp was clearly upon the new community. In its structure, its disciplines and its aims it reflected his unique view of the Christian life. It has often been said that Jeanne's spirituality was essentially Salesian and that it was her work in the community simply to bring into being what her friend envisioned.[114] This is not incorrect but it does not give a full picture of Madame de Chantal's contribution to the Visitation and represents her role in its creation insufficiently.[115] The monastic foundation is indeed in the style of François de Sales but at its center it belongs to Jeanne de Chantal. It is in the prayer of the community, the particular way in which as a group it tended to be drawn to God, that Jeanne's imprint is strikingly evident. It has already been suggested that there were influences in Jeanne' spiritual development other than the Genevan bishop. It is also true that, though united in hope and vision, the two friends were very different personalities. The differences manifested themselves not only in their manners and patterns of response but in their spiritual histories as well.

It is difficult accurately to characterize any person's spiritual state over the course of a lifetime but it is possible to make a few broad generalizations. The geography of François' ongoing relationship with the divine and the vistas of self that he experienced in pursuing that relationship were, on the whole, like broad plateaus and open prairies. There is a certain sense of freedom and spaciousness, a view of wide horizons and the feel of light about him. For Jeanne, the relationship with the divine was mapped with deep valleys and cavernous places; the darkness of her inner landscape with its trials, temptations, anguish and uncertainity seems to be punctuated only by periodic emergences into the fresh air and light of mountain heights. Yet there is the warmth of passion and the sweet beauty of ecstasy to temper the chill of her dark pilgrimage. Her love of God was like her love for the other close relationships in her life: intense, emotional, heroically balanced between necessary detachment and loving surrender.

The form of prayer she was drawn to reflects the particular modalities of her inner life. She found herself most called to the prayer she termed "simple attentiveness" and "simple surrender."[116] It has been shown how François, from an early date, confirmed her in the practice of this type of prayer. It was not identical to his own prayer which appears to have been on the one hand more ratiocinative, and, on the other, more characterized by a general disposition of detachment from the situations that confronted him. It was Jeanne's quiet waiting, her surrender amid the inner confusion and shadows that was distinctively her own. When she came as mother superior and novice mistress to the burgeoning community she brought with her not only her knowledge of her director's teaching but, more importantly, her own experience of the life of prayer. This she communicated both directly and indirectly to her companions. She, even more than François, had the responsibility for directing the sisters. While he maintained a remarkable amount of contact with them during the initial year—he came to the house to preach, to discuss, to hear confessions, to advise—yet it was Jeanne who day by day molded and shaped their daughters. She felt herself true to the principles of Salesian direction, but she embodied those principles in a different way than did he. And the mode of prayer that was hers became the characteristic devotional attitude of the majority of the women under her direction. She was to advise her novices:

> Resting in the spirit in God is the most important vocation for the daughters of the Visitation to have. They must not be at all concerned about formal reflections, ideas, notions or speculation about other matters, although they should honor these as gifts of God capable of leading to God himself.[117]

Elsewhere she is more explicit about the practice of this kind of prayer.

> Those who are led by this path are obligated to a great purity of heart, humility, submission and total dependence on God. They must greatly simplify their spirit in every way, suppressing each reflection on the past, the present and the future. And instead of looking to what they are doing or will do, they must look to God, forgetting themselves as much as possible in all things in favor of this continual remembrance, uniting their spirits with

his goodness, in everything that happens to them from moment to moment. This should be done very simply.

What often happens to souls on this path is that they are troubled by many distractions and that they continue without any support from the senses. Our Lord withdraws the feeling of his sweet presence from them as well as all sort of interior consolations and lights so that they remain in total impotence and insensitivity, although sometimes this is more true than others.

This somewhat surprises souls who are as yet inexperienced. But they must remain firm and rest in God above every thought and feeling, suffering, receiving and cherishing equally all the ways and works that God is pleased to perform in them, sacrificing themselves and unreservedly abandoning any of these works to the discretion of his love and very holy will, without seeing or wishing to see what they are doing or should do. But completely above their own sight and self-knowledge they must be joined to God in the supreme part of their spirit and be utterly lost in him. They will find, by this means, peace in the midst of war and rest in work. Simply put, we must remain in the state where God puts us: in pain, we must have patience, in suffering, we must endure.[118]

After a number of years it became evident that this prayer suited the temperaments and devotional gifts of the community.

... I have recognized that the almost universal attraction of the daughters of the Visitation is to a very simple practice of the presence of God effected by a total abandonment of themselves to Holy Providence. ... Several are attracted this way from the beginning and it seems as though God avails Himself of this one means to cause us to achieve our end, and the perfect union of our soul with Him. In short, I believe that this manner of prayer is essential to our little Congregation, that it is a great gift of God which requires infinite gratitude.[119]

It was Jeanne's presence in the community that sowed the seeds of contemplation which were to flower so exquisitely in the years to come.[120] The Visitation nuns were to be daughters of prayer, and Jeanne was chief among them. How definitely Jeanne's spiritual experience and not François' marked the early years is clear from the correspondence that passed between them about the writing of

his latest and most ambitious book, *The Treatise on the Love of God*.
From 1606 to 1616 he labored over this voluminous project. In the
chapters on prayer François was much influenced by his reading of
Teresa of Avila. But he was as much, if not more, influenced in his
thought by his contact with the little community at "la Galerie." It
was his custom to come and visit the house, frequently settling in
for a discussion of spiritual matters (if the weather was nice) in the
small garden studded with fruit trees that lay nestled in the back of
the house. It was in this unostentatious garden, as well as in the
confessional, that François de Sales became intimate to the life of
prayer existing at the south shore of Lake Annecy.

His vision of the panorama of prayer was widened by these
conversations. He artfully recorded his observations in the treatise
he was working on. Book nine can be said to be a portrait (at least
in part) of Jeanne's own spiritual life.[121]

> I am working on your book number nine of *The Love of God*, and
> today, praying before my crucifix, God showed me your soul
> and your (inner) state by the metaphor of an accomplished musi-
> cian, born subject to a prince who loved him perfectly and who
> had expressed to him how wonderfully pleasing the sweet mel-
> ody of his lute and voice were. This unfortunate singer, like
> you, became deaf and could no longer hear his own music. His
> master was often absent but he did not cease to sing because he
> knew that his master retained him to sing.[122]

The artfully drawn analogy was developed and used in Book
nine of the treatise. It was not an isolated instance. The segments of
this classic work of Christian spirituality that deal with prayer are
permeated with Visitation devotion. This devotion bore the mark
of Jeanne's imprint. More closely related to her sisters in religion
through their shared life and their intimate contact when she served
as both mother superior and novice mistress in these early years,
she, more than her friend, mapped out for them the specific direction in which their devotional lives were to go.

Moreover, it was Jeanne's tender and maternal handling of the
community that made sisterly love a reality. She had raised her own
four children and, for periods of time, had been in charge of other
youngsters. The maternal insight that she carried away from her past
served her well in the monastery. One finds in her writings, espe-

cially those to the other women serving as superiors of Visitation houses, a remarkable sensitivity for dealing with the various personalities struggling to live a communal vocation of love. At the foundation of her insight was the knowledge that self-knowledge and authenticity is the most important quality a superior can have.

> First, I assure you, my dearest sister, that you could not do better in order to succeed in your governance and direction than to keep yourself closely united to God by perfect obedience as you live out your Rule. Because, if your good example does not speak along with you, the remonstrances you make will be fruitless. One cannot give to others what one does not have oneself. So you must be zealous about your own perfection and closely united to God so that your good example will attract your sisters to their own duty.[123]

Her maternal solicitude as well as her sense of the sacredness of the trust given to superiors of the community is also clearly seen in her instructions.

> Know, my dear sister, that the chief responsibility of our office is to guide the souls that the Son of God has redeemed by His precious blood, not like a mistress of a household or a governess but like a mother and one entrusted with the care of the brides and servants of God. These must be treated with respect and special love, for God alone, equally and without exception, without the expectation of any other reward than the honor and happiness of rendering so worthy a service to the divine majesty.[124]

Christian charity was to be extended equally to all even though not all were equal, and individual differences of ability and temperament were to be taken into account.

> As for girls who are a little weak, one must not push or urge upon them things greater than they can bear. Otherwise they may become exhausted. One must expect from each personality only what can be obtained with gentleness. All the girls do not have equal capacity yet often the same things are expected from them. This upsets both mothers and daughters. All must run the same course of external observance but do not have the dispo-

sitions for the same interior conduct nor equal capacity for perfection. Ignorance of this fact causes much difficulty. I pray therefore that you be attentive to this and guide each personality according to its own ability and attraction in prayer as well as everything else. This is the great method of keeping our sisters in that holy and desirable liberty of spirit which is so useful for religious souls and without which they cannot make any advancement.[125]

Her unusual sensitivity to relational dynamics served her well in her new life. She was able to advise other superiors that they should never be surprised or repulsed by a sister's faults nor should they make these known to the larger community. Discretion and gentle correction are called for when failings occur. Jeanne did not approve of severe correction or frequent correction in the case of small faults of little importance. She was concerned that her charges be drawn into spiritual maturity not through fear or servile duty but through love. "To win their hearts" has been called the leit motif of her direction.[126]

This is not all. Although François de Sales initially provided the legal and practical framework for the life of the Visitation, it was up to Jeanne and the early initiates to clarify and amplify the purposely loosely-worded regulations that he had set down.[127] Between 1628 and 1642 several versions of a custom book which provided the bases for uniformity of observance among the houses of the Visitation was published. Moreover, over the course of her lifetime, Jeanne gave innumerable oral commentaries on the rules, constitutions, and custom book as well as sharing with her sisters her valuable insights into the life of prayer and surrender to the will of God. Her talks were taken down, some being corrected and annotated by her own hand. They appear in her collected works and make clear her individual legacy to the Order of the Visitation, a community that owes its special genius to the combined yet distinct gifts given it by both its founder and its foundress.

III

The year of Jeanne's novitiate passed swiftly and joyfully, its optimistic rhythm broken only once by a serious and mysterious illness that befell her. Aided by the bishop's prayers she recovered and the anniversary of the entry into the "la Galerie" soon came around. With it came the ceremony of oblation that was to formally mark the transition from one life to another.[128] Jeanne anticipated the day with all the ardor of which she was capable.

> "When will the happy day come," she wrote to François earlier in the year, "when I will make and renew the irrevocable offering of myself to God? His goodness has filled me with such an extraordinary and powerful feeling of grace of what it is like to be utterly His own that, if the feeling remains in its fullness, it will consume me."[129]

By the time of the oblation there were over a dozen women in the community. They and a crowd of visitors pressed into the flower-filled chapel that had been hung with white fabric in keeping with the intentional bridal symbolism of the ceremony. The evening before, François had heard his friend's confession and the renewal of her obedience to him. The next day, June 6, her face "aflame" with the love that the nuptial ceremony bespoke, Jeanne took her vows.

The closure in Jeanne's life represented by her entry into the congregation of the Vistiation was permanent. Never again would she be completely outside of the institutional and emotional structure provided by the little community gathered on the banks of Lake Annecy. Yet despite this fact, the closure was not complete. A few brief months after the oblation, she was back in Burgundy. Her father had died. The sad event was made more poignant by her knowledge that she had not been present during the last days of this man she loved so dearly. She was needed after the event to attend to the household affairs. The extended family, particularly on her late husband's side, had never been enthusiastic about her withdrawal from society. Now they took the opportunity to press her to stay in Burgundy. After all, they argued, she was not under solemn vows; the temporary vows of the Visitation could allow her a freedom of movement that would make a relocation (advisable for her children, they suggested) possible. When she demurred, they tried to insist that she remain at least a year. One woman among them, apparently as put off by Jeanne's inelegant new apparel as by her inelegant new life, did not hesitate to tell her that "it was disgraceful to see her hidden beneath two lengths of bolting cloth" and that "her veil ought to be torn into a thousand pieces."[130] The widow de Chantal's calm response, "Whoever loves his crown more than his head could never lose the one without the other,"[131] indicated her unshakable commitment to the path she had chosen.

Her decision had been made. She would return to Annecy as soon as her father's estate was settled. As if to confirm her resistance to the demands of her relatives, she had an experience in Burgundy that profoundly marked her spiritual orientation from that time onward. She had gone with a few others to a small parish church to hear Mass. While on her knees she was seized by what she many years later described as a "ravishment" during which time she remained totally absorbed in her ecstatic state, losing consciousness of all that was going on outside her. She remained like this well after the Mass had ended. Her son-in-law Bernard, who had been waiting to escort her home to dinner, after some time inquired of Jacqueline Favre whether Mother de Chantal wished to pray longer. Her companion replied that she did not know, for when she had spoken quietly to Jeanne, she had not answered. Bernard approached her then and, speaking more forcefully, managed to rouse her. Jeanne was startled at the interruption and the query about being ready to go. She had not yet heard the Mass, she exclaimed. Her son-in-law replied that the Mass had long been finished. She spoke no more and, reflecting upon the incident, remained pensive for the rest of the day.

She did not speak immediately to anyone about her "ravishment." A Jesuit friend she consulted soon confirmed her sense that she had had an authentic encounter with the divine. But she kept quiet about it, revealing the incident to her close companion Jacqueline Favre only twenty-four years later. It seems that the principal effect of the experience was to impress upon its recipient an acute sense of

> ... the pleasure that God takes in a pure and perfect soul. Then she was inspired to vow that she would always do whatever was the most perfect and agreeable to God.[132]

This desire for perfection was never to leave her. It became an almost urgent motivation against which she would measure her own growth and development in the years to come. Now she was sustained by a remarkable sense of the presence of God and a burning desire to abandon herself perfectly to that presence. Her friend François de Sales was uniquely linked to that desire in her mind.

> I recall, my father, that it was seven years ago today that Our Lord filled your spirit with a thousand holy affections for the well-being and perfection of my poor soul. I should tell you that, since yesterday, it has been filled with such an extraordinary feeling for perfection that, if it remains, it will consume me. My God! My only father, through your prayers and direction surrender me utterly to the Lord that we adore, revere and love so perfectly. Oh! How much I want to be faithful! It is impossible to express what I feel, besides I might only lessen it with my words—it is a work created by God's hand. Each day we see His graces for us abound more clearly; that is why each day we must become more faithful. So I consecrate my soul once more to obedience and to your will.[133]

What Jeanne now felt, joined with the exhilaration of the effort of establishing the new congregation, had its effect upon her relationship with François. During the first five years of the Visitation's existence the correspondence that passed between the two friends was as ardent and intense as it would ever be. They saw each other a great deal as the congregation's operation required much attention. On occasions when he was unable to make the short trip to "la Galerie," he suffered, as the following missive makes clear.

> Oh God! my dearest daughter, I protest, but I protest with my whole heart, which is more yours than mine, that I feel keenly the privation of not having seen you today. Tomorrow with God's help, I will come and speak with you a good hour before the sermon and we will speak of our challenge, which, my dear Daughter, you will find very agreeable and worthy of our heart which is so indivisible.

> And so, good night, my very own daughter. I wish that you could experience the feelings that I had today, while taking Communion, of our precious unity because it was immense, perfect, sweet, powerful and almost like a vow or consecration.[134]

An almost tangible warmth flows from the pages of the bishop's letters during these years. From the beginning he had been articulate about their mutual love but now the intensity of the experience colors virtually every note that he writes. During Jeanne's sojourn in Burgundy François likewise had occasion to be away from their dear Annecy.

> I have been here in Thonon for three days, my dearest daughter, where I came happily and without any feelings of weariness. Oh God, my dearest daughter, I don't know which road I took, the one to Thonon or the one to Burgundy but I know very well that I am more in Burgundy than I am here. Yes, my daughter, as it pleases the divine Goodness, I am inseparable from your heart and, speaking with the words of the Holy Spirit, we now have only one heart and one soul, because I find that what is said of all the Christians of the early Church is, thanks to God, now true of us.[135]

The effusion of affection, they both knew, pointed to their mutual passion for God. The vigor and intensity of this passion bound them firmly in their shared quest for perfection. When Jeanne confessed to her friend her overwhelming desire for this evangelical perfection, François responded:

> I am impatient, my dear daughter, that this heart that God has given us is uniquely and inseparably given to and linked to its God by this holy unifying love which is stronger than death and all else. My God! my dearest daughter, let us fill our heart with courage and from now on let us perform miracles for our heart's advancement in this celestial love. And let us note that Our Lord never gives you intense aspirations for the absolute perfection of your heart unless He gives me the same will. For He wishes us to know that it is but one single aspiration for the same thing by the same heart and that, through unity of aspiration we will know that the Sovereign Providence wants us to be one single soul in pursuit of the same goal for the purity of our perfection.[136]

One heart. One soul. These are the words the bishop used to describe their relationship. Jeanne too experienced this. Although the literary evidence on her side is not as abundant as it is for her friend, still her similar understanding of their friendship is evident in what we do have from this era.

> "Alas," she wrote to Charlotte de Bréchard in Annecy when she was in Lyon several years later, "you should have pity on me when you speak to me of seeing me again in our poor little retreat in Annecy. It is the place of all my sweetness and rest because it contains my heart's one treasure, indeed, and I can say this to you, all my spiritual well-being in Jesus Christ in the person of our honored Lord and Father. Yet, I am content to stay here . . . to suffer the privation of a good which is so precious to me. . . ."[137]

Her use of affectionate language to him is seen in a remark he makes to her when she is on a later trip to Lyon. A number of the sisters at the Visitation and others in town wished for news from her, and François desired to share her letters with them, but he found it awkward.

> In your covering letters, when you write to me you should not call me "My father, my dear love" because I want to be able to show them to those to whom you send greetings in order to comfort them. . . .

> Now, as for my niece de Bréchard,[138] she well knows that I am wholly yours, because she has seen the notes that contain that truth. However, I have not wanted to show her the last three letters, either in whole or in part. . . . [139]

The remarkable ardor Jeanne de Chantal and François de Sales now shared was given intention and direction through the imagery of the liturgical calendar. During her years as a widow, Jeanne had been initiated into the daily experience of prayer and Catholic observance. But now in the Visitation she was immersed in the symbolic world of her religion and her day was punctuated with prayers appropriate to the particular time of day and the liturgical season of the year. Encoded in the images of the liturgy as they had been developed through centuries of tradition were spiritual teachings to guide the aspirant. In their mutual quest for perfection, the bishop and his friend utilized these images to shape their desires. François wrote to Jeanne in 1610 on the feast of John the Baptist:

> Oh God! What a great saint is here presented to the eyes of our soul! When I consider him in those deserts I don't know if he is an Angel who takes the shape of a man or a man who aspires to become an Angel. What contemplations! What flights of spirit occurred within him!

> His food is admirable because the honey represents the sweetness of the contemplative life, all gathered together in the flowers of the sacred mysteries. The locusts represent the active life because locusts never walk on the earth nor do they ever fly in the air but, by a curious mixture of the two, they are sometimes seen to sail above and sometimes to rest upon the ground only to take to the air once again. Those who lead an active life alternately sail above and rest upon the earth. . . . My dear daughter, even though, because of our mortal condition, we must rest upon the earth to order the necessities of life, yet our heart must only savor the roses of God's good pleasure while doing this and must bring it all back to God in praise.[140]

On the feast of the Visitation in 1611 he wrote the following exultant note about the pregnant Virgin Mary:

> I will leave you to imagine, my dear daughter, what a sweet odor this beautiful fleur-de-lis spread about Zachary's house the three months she spent there. Imagine how they were all busy about the place and how she, with few but fine words, poured out precious balm and honey on them with her sacred lips. What could she do but overflow from what she was filled with. She was full of Jesus.

> My God, my daughter I admire myself so much that I am still full of myself, even after having taken Communion so many times! Oh, dear Jesus, be the child of our wombs, so that we will not breathe or feel anything but you.[141]

The observances of the religious calendar became for them a way of marking off important occurences along the spiritual journey. Thus on December 8, 1610, Jeanne began to take Communion daily, a practice approved by her friend and director and which for her represented a more total absorption into the mystery of death and resurrection present in the Eucharist.

The day became a memorable one. Each year the event and its significance were once again pondered. A full thirty-one years later on December 8, 1641, very ill and knowing that her death was near, Jeanne asked to be allowed to get out of bed to attend Mass.

> "Alas!" she pleaded with her physicians, "let me have the contentment of taking Communion with the community. This day is of special importance to me for it was thirty-one years ago today that, under the instruction of our Blessed Father, I began to communicate daily, unworthy as I am of this grace."[142]

The pair not only utilized the images of tradition in the direct and well-known way of culling spiritual meaning from specific passages and observances. The larger themes inherent in the tradition could also become the basis of an entirely new understanding of the Christian vocation. Jeanne had always had a special affinity for the martyrs of the church. They were her favorite saints. The martyr, in her perception, had given everything for his or her faith. This total, selfless gift of person appealed to her. It seemed to her expressive of her own relationship with God.

This attraction to these heroes of the church became the basis for her own understanding of her life in religion as well as the basis for the spirituality which she imparted to the entire community. The daughters of the Visitation, whose lives were surrendered to the love of God, were, in her imagery, "martyrs of love." Jeanne internalized the dramatic sacrifice undergone by the Christians of the early church as an interior state of absolute sacrifice. As the martyrs felt themselves incorporated in Christ through their physical deaths accomplished in imitation of their Lord, so a Visitation sister became incorporated into Christ's reality through the loving martyrdom of her own self-will. In one of the most expressive passages of her *Life,* her biographer recounts the episode that evoked from Jeanne thoughts about the martyrdom of love.

> On St. Basil's day 1632 our Blessed Mother experienced an intense assault of divine love which made it impossible for her

to speak during recreation. She remained with her eyes closed and her face all aflame. She tried to divert herself by spinning but had to stop when her spindle was only half full. When she realized she could not do anything about it, she got us to sing a song that our honorable Mother de Bréchard had written some time before and she tried to join in the singing herself. . . . The song diverted her a little and, attempting to hide the grace she was receiving, she tried to talk to us. She spoke with words of fire which were faithfully recorded then and there.

"My dear daughters, Saint Basil and most of the fathers and pillars of the church were not martyred. Why do you think this was so?" After each of us had tried to answer, the Blessed Mother continued, "For myself, I believe that there is a martyrdom called the martyrdom of love in which God preserves the lives of His servants so that they might work for His glory. This makes them martyrs and confessors at the same time. I know," she added, "that this is the martyrdom to which the Daughters of the Visitation are called and which God will allow them to suffer if they are fortunate enough to wish for it."

A sister asked how this martyrdom would be realized. "Give your absolute consent to God and you will experience it. What happens," she continued, "is that divine love thrusts its sword into the most intimate and secret parts of the soul and separates us from our very selves. I know one soul," she added, "whom love had severed in this way who felt it more keenly than if a tyrant with his sword had separated her body from her soul." We knew very well that she was speaking of herself. One sister wanted to know how long this martyrdom might last. "From the moment," she responded, "when we have given ourselves up unreservedly to God until the moment when we die. But this is intended for generous hearts who, without holding themselves back, are faithful to love. Hearts that are weak and capable of only a little love and constancy are not martyred by Our Lord. He is content to let them go on in their little way so they won't fall by the wayside. God never violates free will." She was asked if this martyrdom of love was ever equal to physical martyrdom. "Don't concern yourself with their equality," she said, "although I think there is little difference between them because 'love is as strong as death,' and martyrs of love suffer a thousand times more by staying alive to do God's will than if they had to give a thousand lives in witness of their faith, love and fidelity."[143]

The martyrdom of which Jeanne was to speak so eloquently in 1632 was not fashioned simply from the fine imagery of tradition. It corresponded to her own interior experience. She was subject not only to the excesses of divine love but to the desolations with which the interior life is replete. The theme is recurrent in François' letters of direction to her throughout these years: she has no sense of divine consolation or warmth; all is dryness, emptiness and absence. In a letter of 1612 he advises her on the meaning of this phenomenon.

> Let us go on to the interior practice about which you have written to me. It is nothing other than true insensitivity that deprives you of the pleasure, not only of consolations and inspirations but of faith, hope and charity. Yet you have them—and in good measure—but you do not enjoy them.

> It is the height of holy resignation to be content with naked dry and insensible acts carried out by the superior will alone. . . . you have expressed your suffering well to me and there is nothing to do to remedy it but what you are doing: affirming to Our Lord, sometimes aloud and other times in song, that you even will to live and to eat as the dead do, without taste, feeling or knowledge. In the end, the Savior wants us to be his so perfectly that nothing else remains for us, and to abandon ourselves entirely to the mercy of his providence without reservation.[144]

Her interior struggles were compounded by the bouts of ill health she was to suffer on and off throughout the years. Yet the recurring maladies that she suffered had the effect of rendering her compassionate to the plight of her sisters who, as a consequence of their own physical weaknesses and infirmities, had been drawn to the Visitation. It also, her biographer comments, kept her from imposing corporal penances and fasting upon both herself and the community at large.

Yet through it all the accounts insist that an onlooker would never have guessed that the serene woman they observed was subject to such painful spiritual and physical trials. The insistence seems not to be merely hagiographic posturing, for Jeanne's own correspondence to her most intimate friend, François, reveals her as struggling to endure her terrible pain by placing it in a context that gave it meaning. A poignant letter written in 1614 to François lays bare the emotional reality of Jeanne's inner desolation.

> I am not able to restrain myself from writing to you this morning because I find that I am more an impediment to myself than usual. . . . God's presence, which otherwise would give me unspeakable content, now makes me tremble and shudder with fear. I feel as though the divine eye, which I adore with all my heart's submission, sees right through my soul and views all my deeds, thoughts and words with indignation. This keeps my spirit in such distress that death itself would not be so hard to bear. And everything seems to have the power to destroy me. I am afraid of everything, apprehensive of everything. Not that I am frightened that I will be destroyed, for my own sake, but I am fearful of displeasing God.

> Ah, his help seems so far away from me. I passed the night in terrible grief unable to say anything but "My God, my God, alas, why have you forsaken me? I am yours, do with me as you choose."

> At daybreak, God ever so imperceptibly let me taste a little light in the very highest point of my spirit. All the rest of my soul and its faculties did not experience it at all. But this lasted only about half an *Ave Maria;* then my desperate trouble descended on me once again and I was lost in the darkness and confusion.

> Despite the length of this trial, my dearest Lord, I said, but without any feeling, "Yes, Lord, do whatever you please, I wish it: annihilate me, I am content to have it happen; overwhelm me, I consent; uproot me, strike me down, burn me as you will. Yes, I am yours!"

> God has taught me that it is not necessarily a great faith that is experienced through the senses and feelings. That is why, amid my difficulties, I do not wish to have feelings. No, I do not wish them at all because God is enough for me. In spite of my infinite

misery, I hope in him. I hope that he will sustain me still, so that his will can be done.

I place my weak heart in your hands, my true Father and Lord; please give it the medicine it must take.[145]

The tonic of François' calm and steady friendship as well as her own courage sustained Jeanne through her interior difficulties of the Visitation's early years. Externally, all was hard work but much gratification. The little family was growing by leaps and bounds and soon "la Galerie" was too small to contain its growing numbers. In 1614, a new community site was sought and found within Annecy's stone walls just a short walk to the south of "la Galerie." The move to the new house was a natural response to the changes taking place within the Visitation, but the move meant something of a change in the spirit of the community. A bit of the first intimacy and the first simplicity was lost in the process. The ideals of the congregation had not altered, but with more entrants to accommodate and a larger facility to care for, the Visitation became a more complex phenomenon. The realities of its administration came to rest upon Jeanne's shoulders. She had a genius for it. And she was particularly practiced in financial organization, for she had recently put not only her own deceased father's financial holdings in order but her father-in-law's as well. The elderly baron had died in 1613, making another trip to Burgundy necessary for Jeanne. His finances, too, were in a confused state and she was called on to set them right.

The two friends were thrilled to see their small community becoming popular. But the sheer effort of administration was burdensome for Jeanne. A decade later, she was to confide in another friend, Vincent de Paul, how difficult the pressures of governing could be for her.

I am increasingly wearied by my responsibilities because I have a strong temperamental dislike of action. And by forcing myself to act out of necessity my body and spirit are continually oppressed.[146]

Yet despite the cost, she applied herself diligently to the Visitation. Vocations in Annecy were flourishing. And Jeanne de Chantal was living the life she had dreamed of for so long. It was a life surrendered to the will of God, a life enlivened by the knowledge that the surrender was an act of perfect love. Whatever the difficulties might be, she was sustained by that love and her friendship with François to whom she was bound by that love's strength.

"I am overwhelmed with things to do," she wrote to him in 1614, "but I do believe that everything will be all right. I have a great desire to fulfill God's will. That is why I ask you once again to let me know what I should do to realize this. I have impulses I cannot describe and a joy which say to my soul that this great God is leading me and making me capable of his love even while I am aware of my soul's incapacity. Pray to him that he will give me the strength to do whatever is required of me. . . . "[147]

4.

Bond of Perfection
(1615–1622)

I

News of the little community quickly spread beyond Savoy. In France, where François de Sales' *Introduction to the Devout Life* was gaining popularity, interest was keen. There were queries from several quarters about starting new foundations on Gallic soil. In Lyon, two women, aspiring to the love of God, conceived the idea of founding a house of the Visitation in their town. After some initial floundering, during which time an alternate congregation headed by the women came into existence and quickly succumbed, Mother de Chantal was called to Lyon. There she and two companions stayed nine months carefully nourishing the new community for a mature and independent life. When she returned she left her cherished companion Jacqueline Favre as the superior of the new house.

The foundation at Lyon marked the first excursion of the little community beyond the shores of Lake Annecy, and this change profoundly affected the Visitation from that time on. For not only was the founding a sign that the little cluster of women was destined to become a widespread organization of women's communities bearing the name of the Visitation, it was also an event that forever changed the institutional status and organization of the congregation. The local bishop, Denis de Marquemont supported the foundation but, as the congregation was intended to come directly under episcopal jurisdiction, his few misgivings about the project had to be taken into account. De Marquemont soon began to feel that a simple congregation of women free from binding vows and without a fixed cloister could not long survive on French soil. He was not simply being conservative but was responding to the instructions laid out by the council of Trent regarding women's communities that were being implemented at the time.[1] His objections, if acted upon, meant that the Visitation would become a full-fledged religious order observing solemn vows and that the active life of the sisters who presently went out into the community would be curtailed.

The two bishops exchanged a lively correspondence, each arguing his side of the case convincingly. In the end, François assented to the changes. Despite scholarly interpretations to the contrary,[2] this alteration in the Visitation did not, in the eyes of its founders, alter the primary intention of the community. True, François had envisioned a congregation whose love would have two explicit expressions, love of God and of neighbor, and he had warmed to the flexibility and simplicity that temporary vows implied. Yet the end of the institute was in no way changed. It would still admit widows, the frail and laywomen on retreat; it would still recite the Little Office of Our Lady instead of the Great Divine Office said in other orders, and it would still consider the hidden cultivation of the humble virtues as its chief asceticism. In fact, the change seems not to have been resisted by the community itself. Jeanne in later years wrote that after the first years of works of charity:

> ... suddenly we found ourselves differently inclined and with a great desire for cloister such as our Blessed Father had resolved in favor of. ...[3]

Jeanne herself, throughout her very active life, continually yearned for more seclusion and more time for prayer. Whatever the modification in the original visage of the institute, its heart remained fixed on the same simple goal. They were to be daughters of prayer in whatever circumstance. It would take three years and a tremendous volume of correspondence for the Visitation to become officially, in 1618, a religious order.

In the meantime, the life of the Visitation continued in "dear Nessy" and the relationship between the bishop and the mother superior deepened. The friendship that François had several years before declared to be a "bond of perfection" was ripening into maturity. This bond was the linking of the two of them with the imperishable power of their love. It was a love of a particular kind, a love that strove toward the image of perfection that Christianity had developed over the centuries. In the seventeenth century, the image of the perfect follower of Christ was that of a lover. Yet love in this context implies not simply the desire for unity with the beloved and its achievement but the death of self-love in order for that union to take place.

The language of desire which the contemplative tradition had so long cultivated could never be fully realized in the present life. For humankind, love of God could only occur through a glass darkly, His presence known as much through absence as possession. The struggle to clarify spiritual vision and to facilitate the longed-for unity was part of the dynamic of desire and brought with it experiences and self-perceptions that were in contrast to the experience of desire that the language of tradition proposed. Death as well as love, separation as well as union, alienation as well as comfort were part of the complexity of the Christian love of God.

This could not fail to have a profound effect upon the friend-ship that Jeanne and François enjoyed. Both in their own personal development strove to follow the crucified as well as the bridegroom Christ, and the radical interior asceticism they practiced made them each intimates of the Jesus of Calvary. They knew, through the sym-bols of their faith, that love and death were inseparable and that in order to rise again to new life with the figure they followed, they must die with him as well. At the closing of his great and passionate *Treatise on the Love of God*, François had written:

> ... Mount Calvary is the mountain of lovers. All love that does not begin with Our Savior's Passion is frivolous and dangerous. How unhappy death is without the love of the Saviour and how unhappy love is without the Saviour's death. Love and death are so mingled in Our Saviour's Passion that we cannot have one in our heart without the other. On Calvary one cannot have life without love, nor love without the death of our Redeemer. But, except there, it is either eternal death or eternal love. All Chris-tian wisdom consists in choosing rightly. . . .[4]

The choice for the two friends was the choice of love as defined by tradition. They thus chose a love that required them to die to self. For perfect love of God in Salesian thought, although it did not eschew love of other people, did require an austere detachment from all that was not God Himself. The friendship that Jeanne and François shared was founded on their shared desire to love God perfectly. Both terms—love and perfect—are important here, for perfect love implied that between the two of them not only would the dynamics of love and desire be operative but the dynamics of perfection and its corollary, detachment. Jeanne had for some time experienced a deep inward attraction to the idea for perfection. Since she underwent her "ravishment" in the country church in Burgundy and gained the insight that perfection was infinitely pleasing to God, she had dwelt upon this impulse.

Perfect love, in her eyes, was embodied by the naked Jesus hanging upon the cross. The psychological and spiritual vulnerability of the image, the complete surrender and utter poverty (both inner and outer) that it suggested, the paradoxical dependency and ultimate trust encoded there, all this she was drawn to and strove to emulate in her own life. It was the same for François. Together they felt the appeal of the imagery and assisted each other in realizing it in their own lives. The richly modulated experience of love had led them deeply into their mutual quest. Now the dynamics of their shared quest drew them into a new relational phase in which detachment would bring new poignancy to their love. In May 1616, Jeanne was preparing to take her annual retreat. As always, it would be a time of reflection and of renewed commitment to the path she had chosen. This time, the retreat would mark a turning point both in her own spiritual orientation and in her relationship with François de Sales.

She had chosen detachment as her theme for prayerful consideration. It was a theme that had often preoccupied her and one which she found difficult to grasp. Her natural tendency, particularly in painful situations, was to fly to the comforting presence of her friend, François, and be healed by his affectionate warmth. This was a role he gladly played for her for many years. Yet he was convinced, as was she, that the true source of healing was not to be found in human love but in the divine love that gave life to that other love. Perfect love of God implied a growing independence from the necessity for human support. As Jeanne and François' love for each other burned brighter it paradoxically sought to focus itself upon the greater love toward which they both yearned. This meant that they must assist each other, in a subtle but fundamental way, to strip themselves of their total dependence upon one another. For her, the task was not easy, but her friend, who was perhaps more temperamentally attuned to the practice of detachment, gently but firmly led the way. A contemporary of Jeanne's recounted an incident that the mother superior had described:

> One time, after having thoroughly explained to him what was causing me pain, I was not consoled as I generally was. God did not allow this so that I might learn to look to Him for what I thought to find in the Blessed One, who, just this once, seeing that he was unable to help me, although he had spoken to me at length, got up without a word and went out, leaving me in my pain. Not knowing what to do and seeing that the Saint had not healed me, I could do nothing else but go before the Holy Sacrament to be healed by Our Lord. And there I learned what I had never before truly understood, that one must not seek all one's consolation in creatures, but in God and that the true means of being healed consists in relying upon and abandoning oneself to the divine mercy without any reservation.[5]

During the retreat of May 1616, this single focused dependence upon God was, once again, the lesson she would learn from her friend. Yet his prodding her into detachment did not signal a lessening in their friendship or a cooling of their love. One month before the event he wrote to her while he was away at Thonon:

> You yourself, my dear Mother, know very well that this holy unity that God has made is stronger than any separation and that physical distance has no power over it. So, God bless you forever with His holy love. He has made us one heart, single in its spirit and life.[6]

Around the period of the retreat Jeanne was busy preparing for the experience and wrote down for herself a series of questions that she posed to François along with his answers. The passage reveals the fact that, although it was François who guided Jeanne into a more radical detachment during the retreat, he did not force it upon her or urge it for personal motives.[7] It is fashioned in the form of a conversation that Jeanne directs to her own soul:

> First, you must ask your dearest Lord if he finds it appropriate for you, as a reconfirmation, to each year renew your vows and your general reliance and abandonment of yourself into God's hands. Could he specify in particular those things he considers will move you most to make this perfect and unconditional surrender so that I can truly say, "I live, now not I, but Jesus Christ lives in me." To have this happen, you must ask your good Lord not to spare you or to allow you to withhold anything whether it be great or small.[8]

Her friend was to honor her request. Jeanne took her retreat on the grounds of the monastery and during that time she was in contact with François by letter. Somehow, the exchange between them has come down through the centuries intact. It is the only surviving sequence of letters written by the two friends. It begins with a letter from Jeanne in which she asks about the bishop's health, which had been poor, and expresses her desire to prolong her retreat for several days.

> How are you feeling, my poor dear Father? Always better by the grace of God? Oh, please, my good Saviour, I have been praying for such a long time that my Father's precious health be restored. Well, we will talk among ourselves about that. But could you simply and briefly answer yes or no to what I have requested? The four days, during which you have indicated to me what I should do, are over and I have reported to you what has occurred in my last two brief notes. The first two contain my confession, which you may find incomprehensible. Could I remain in my precious solitude a few days longer, and continue with my latest meditation? I have had a great inclination to quiet my spirit in God a bit more. Because, to tell the truth, I have been a bit distracted these past days and if your illness has not made me anxious, it has grieved me and been a distraction. On three separate occasions, when it was spoken of to me, I was touched to the quick. When I was told that it was dangerous, you can imagine

my dearest Father, where that led. Oh! Lord, help me. May he be blessed.

Please, my dear Father, one word of news about you and if I should remain in my little retreat or not. As for the rest, it will happen in its own time. I ask for your answer provided it is not an inconvenience to anyone. If it is otherwise, my Sister Jacqueline will tell me so. Good day, my poor dearest Father; the gentle Jesus be your all.[9]

François granted her request to prolong her retreat until the feast of Pentecost and responded:

My very dear Mother,
    I am aware that I should remain in solitude and silence today and perhaps tomorrow. This being so, I will prepare my soul, as you are doing and in the way that I advised. I would like you to continue the exercise of denuding yourself and abandoning yourself to Our Lord and to me. But, my dear mother, I ask you to include some acts on your own in the form of ejaculatory prayers that accord with the denudation. For example: "I want this, Lord; pull, pull firmly from my heart all that clothes it. Oh Lord, I do not withhold anything; separate me from myself. Oh myself, I leave you forever until Monseigneur commands me to take you back." These must be asserted gently but firmly.
    Furthermore, my very dear Mother, you must not take any kind of nurse but you must leave the one who nonetheless still remains and become like a poor little pitiful creature completely naked before the throne of divine mercy, without ever asking for any act or feeling whatsoever for this creature. At the same time, you must become indifferent to everything that it pleases God to give you, without considering if it is I who serve as your nurse. Otherwise, if you took a nurse to your own liking you would not be going out of yourself but you would still have your own way which is, however, what you wish to avoid at all costs.
    These renunciations are admirable: of self-esteem, and even of the esteem of the world (which in truth is nothing except in comparison with really miserable persons), of self-will, of pleasure in all creatures and natural love, in sum, of all of your self which must be buried in an eternal abandonment so that it is never seen or known any more as we have seen and known it.

But it should be seen and known only when and in the manner that God asks it of us.

Write and tell me how you find this lesson. God wants to possess me forever. Amen. For I am his here and also where I am in you, most perfectly, as you know; for we are indivisible except in the exercise and practice of renunciation of our whole selves to God.[10]

Jeanne replied the same day:

Alas, my only Father, how this precious letter does me good! Blessed be Him who inspired it; blessed also be my Father's heart for ever and ever!

Certainly, I have a great desire and, it seems to me, a firm resolution to remain in my nakedness, by the grace of God— and I hope that he will help me. I feel that my spirit is utterly free and with I don't know what kind of infinite and profound consolation to see itself in God's hands like this. It is true that all the rest of me remains greatly astonished. But if I do well what you have asked me, my only Father, as no doubt I will with God's help, everything will be better still.

I must tell you this: if I wished to allow it, my heart would seek to reclothe itself with the feelings and expectations that it seems that Our Lord has given it. But I will not permit this, so that its motions are only perceived as if they were far away. For, in the last analysis it seems to me that I ought not to think, desire or affirm anything anymore except whatever Our Lord makes me think love and will at the same time that the superior part [of my soul] prescribes it. As for the inferior part, I am careful not to pay attention to it.

My God wishes to strengthen us with his sweet kindness and we make whatever he wishes for us happen perfectly, my very dear Father.

May Jesus make you a great saint! and I believe he will. Blessed be his goodness toward your healing and rest!

Good day, my true Father. This evening I will send word to you of how I am.[11]

This letter evoked a vivid response from the bishop:

Oh Jesus! What a blessing and a consolation to my soul to see my Mother completely naked before God! It has been a long time since I have felt such sweetness while daring to sing the response "Naked I came from my mother's womb and naked I will return. The Lord gives and the Lord takes away. Blessed be the name of the Lord."

What contentment Saint Joseph and the glorious Virgin had as they traveled to Egypt where, for most of the journey, they saw no one else except the gentle child Jesus! This is the meaning of the Transfiguration, my very dear Mother, no longer to see either Moses or Elijah but Jesus alone. This is the glory of the holy Sulamite,[12] to be able to be alone with her only King and to say to him, "My beloved is mine and I am my beloved's." So in our affections we must remain completely naked forever, my very dear Mother, even though, in effect, we reclothe ourselves. For we must have our affection so simply and absolutely united to God that nothing can attach itself to us. How blessed was the Elder Joseph who neither buttoned nor fastened his cloak so that, when someone tried to catch him by grabbing at it, it instantaneously fell from him.

How much I admire the Saviour of our souls who came naked from his mother's womb, died naked upon the cross and then, utterly naked, returned to his mother's breast to be laid in the tomb. I admire the glorious Mother who was born naked of her maternity[13] and was stripped of that maternity at the foot of the Cross and could well say, "I was naked of my greatest happiness when my Son came into my womb and I am naked as I receive him dying upon my breast. The Lord has given, the Lord has taken away. Blessed be the name of the Lord." So I say to you, my dear Mother, blessed be the Lord who has denuded you. Oh, how content my heart is to know you are in this desirable state! I say to you as it was said to Isaiah: Walk and prophesy naked for three days. Persevere in this naked resting before God. You do not need to perform any acts if you are not prompted by your heart. But you should gently sing, if you can, the canticle of our nakedness, "Naked I was born in my Mother's womb," etc.

Do not make any effort but, grounded in yesterday's resolution, go, my very dear daughter, and hear and incline your ear: forget all the tribe of your other affections "and your father's house" because "the King" has coveted your nakedness and simplicity. Remain resting there, in a spirit of simple confidence without even looking with attention or any care whatsoever.

Good day, my very dear Mother. LIVE JESUS, naked of father and mother on the cross, live his most holy nakedness! LIVE MARY, naked of her son at the foot of the cross!

Make the imperceptible surrender to your nakedness gently. Do not make any more effort; give up your body ever so sweetly. VIVE JÉSUS! Amen.[14]

The surrender on Jeanne's part was complete. This shift, at once subtle and profound, from dependence on François to dependence upon God alone signaled a new perception of their relationship. Jeanne's response to the bishop's ecstatic letter makes this clear:

My dear Father,

Monsieur Grandis[15] told me today that we must take still better care of you, that you must no longer live on such a strict diet and that you must be taken care of and watched closely because of the flux that is so fearful. I am greatly pleased with these instructions as well as the one that insists that you guard your solitude, for it will be used in the further service of your dear Spirit. I could not say "our" because it seems to me that I no longer have any part of it now that I find myself so denuded and stripped of all that was most precious to me.

My God! my true Father, how deep the razor has cut! Can I remain in this feeling long? At least our good God, if he so pleases, will hold me firm in my resolutions as I wish. Ah! How your words have given my soul strength! How it consoled and touched me where you wrote, "What blessings and consolations my soul has received to see you utterly naked before God!" Oh! May Jesus grant you to continue to be consoled by this and me to have this happiness!

I am full of hope and courage, very calm and tranquil. Thanks to God, I am not anxious to look and see what I have been divested of. I remain very simple, I see it as though it is very far away, but it does not allow me to come near, for, suddenly, I am turned away. Blessed be Him who has denuded me! May his goodness confirm and strengthen me to do his will. When Our Lord gave me the sweet thought that I sent you on Tuesday—to surrender myself completely to him—alas! I did not think that he would begin by making me put my own hand to the work. May he be blessed in everything and may he wish to strengthen me!

I have not told you that I am without much interior light and consolation. I am simply especially peaceful and it even seems that, during all these past days, Our Lord has somewhat withdrawn that small gentleness and sweetness which provides some feeling of his dear presence. Today again, there more or less remains very little to support or maintain my spirit. Perhaps the good Lord wishes to place his sacred hand upon all the parts of my heart to take everything from it and strip it of all else. May His holy will be done!

Alas! My only Father. I have been reminded today that one time when you ordered me to denude myself, I replied, "I don't know what is left," and you said to me, "Haven't I told you, my daughter, that I will strip you of everything?" Oh God! How easy it is to leave what is outside ourselves. But to leave one's skin, one's flesh, one's bones and penetrate into the deepest part of the marrow, which is, it seems to me, what we have done, is a great, difficult and impossible thing to do save for the grace of God. To him alone then glory is due and may it be given forever.

My true father, what if, lacking your permission to enjoy the consolation I take in our exchange, I do not reclothe myself at all? It seems to me that I must no longer make nor have any thought, affection or desire except those that have been pre-scribed for me.

I close by giving you a thousand good nights and by telling you what has occurred to me. It seems to me that I see the two portions of our spirit as only one abandoned and surrendered together to God. So be it, my very dear Father. May Jesus live and reign for ever! Amen. Don't be in a hurry to get up too soon. I am afraid that the coming feast day will make you do too much. God lead you in everything.[16]

The final letter of the exchange came from François.

All is going very well, my very dear Mother. It is true, you must remain in this holy nakedness until God reclothes you again. "Remain there, " our Lord told the apostles, "until you are clothed with power from on high." Your solitude must not be interrupted until tomorrow after Mass.

My very dear Mother, it is true that your imagination is wrong in trying to persuade you that you have not ridded your-self of caring about yourself and of your attachment to your spiritual state. Have you not left and forgotten everything? This evening affirm that you have renounced all the virtues, desiring them only in the measure that God gives them to you and not wanting to be concerned to acquire them except to the extent that his goodness will use you in this way according to his will.

Our Lord loves you, my Mother; he wants you to be utterly his own. You no longer have any arms to carry you except his, nor any other breast to lean on except his and his providence. Do not let your eyes look elsewhere and do not rest your spirit anywhere except in him alone. Keep your will so simply united to his in all that it pleases him to do to you, in you, by and for you and in all things ouside you, so that nothing ever comes between the two of you. Do not think anymore about the friendship nor the unity that God has created between us, nor of your children, your body, your soul, nor anything whatsoever. For you have given everything to God. "Clothe yourself in Our Crucified Saviour," love him in his suffering, offer up prayers to him. Do not do what you must do because you are inclined toward it any longer but purely because it is God's will.

I am very well, thanks to God. This morning I began my review of conscience that I will finish tomorrow. At the bottom of my heart I sense an imperceptible new confidence to better serve God "in holiness and justice, all the days" of my life. And yes, I also find myself naked, thanks to Him who died naked for us in order that we might live naked. Oh my Mother, how happy Adam and Eve were when they did not have clothes!

Live utterly happy and peaceful, my very dear Mother, and be reclothed in Jesus Christ Our Lord. Amen.[17]

In this written exchange it is possible to see the dramatic transitional phase in Jeanne's life and in her friendship with François very clearly. The shift had been long prepared: since 1611 she had been considering the theme of perfection and measuring her own ability to love against the perfect love of God that implied a death to self; in the practices and spirituality of daily life at the Visitation the equation of perfection with self-surrender had held sway especially in the images of spiritual nakedness that the bishop contrasted with the natural feminine tendency to self-adornment, as well as in the dependent and naked prayer of "simple surrender" that Jeanne taught; the outer events of Jeanne's life, particularly her familial relations, called upon her capacities to accept loss and death as necessary parts of growth and maturity.

When she went on retreat, the long preparation bore fruit. She began with a desire to surrender herself perfectly into God's hands, but her dear friend was seriously ill. Try as she might, she could not help brooding upon his condition, fearful of the possible loss of the person who was dearest to her. Her initial four days of retreat were therefore seemingly unproductive because of her concern over her friend. But the illness provided the occasion for them both to recognize that the very person who had fueled and increased her love of God was now the only barrier between her and the total surrender that she sought to achieve. Once this fact was grasped in more than a theoretical way, the exchange between the two friends quickly escalated to a crescendo of almost ecstatic realization. The affective clarity of Jeanne's description of her new nakedness indicates that she indeed had grasped the fact of her total dependence upon God with more than intellectual assent. François knew this very well, for his thrilled response to her tentative but awed independence from him makes this clear. She had not cut herself off from her real love of him. She states clearly that the "inferior part" of her soul wanted to reclothe itself in the emotional warmth of their love. But she was, very strikingly, coming to grips with the fact of her aloneness and her ultimate dependence upon God.

The exchange is extraordinary and shows the two friends, paradoxically, at the most intimate moment of their friendship. The erotic overtones of the bond between them are not absent in the retreat correspondence: the images of nakedness and surrender are powerful and emotionally charged. But this is not to suggest some repression of an aspect of their union but rather the conscious and deliberate utilization of the manifold richness of human love in the service of a love which both friends perceived as the source and end of their own unity. Moreover, as their love was first of all a love of friendship and not a married love, the dynamics of separateness and independence were as much a part of the love experience as were union and dependence. It was the heightened articulation and experience of this distance between the two friends that was made explicit and celebrated during the retreat of May 1616.

The realizations made during this time were never to be forgotten. Instead, they supplied the direction in which the relationship was to grow from that time forward. It is not the case that the love between Jeanne and François had cooled or that they ceased to think of themselves in terms of union. If the letters from May had not survived it would be very difficult for the general reader to detect, from the warmth and affection of the language of their subsequent correspondence, that anything particularly unusual had taken place between the two friends during those few days before Pentecost. But something dramatic did take place, and it meant for Jeanne particulary a new orientation to her life. She had up until this time focused upon François: he was her support, her guide, her love. Now, by her own choice, she looked to God to fill this place in her life. Ironically, her perceived experience of her new love was dim and confused and was consequently strongly mingled with the sharp pains of death. While she had loosened the ties that bound her to all other loves, she found that the love to which she surrendered herself revealed itself to her primarily as distance, even absence. From that time forward until only a few months before her death, she would experience the pain of separation, both from François and from God, with poignant intensity. It was out of this courageous maintenance of her own spiritual experience of aloneness that Jeanne forged her vision of the "martyrdom of love." It was also the loving embrace of death to self that enabled her to confront both the fact of her spiritual desolation and the facts of the physical deaths of many of those nearest to her over the next few years.

Despite the pain, Jeanne recognized the tremendous simple strength that seemed to accrue from this naked standing before God. It was this that could cause her to write to her dear friend Jacqueline Favre in October of the same year:

> Now, do not tell me any more that you are the only miserable one. We love you every bit as much with your dryness, self-loathing and insensibility of God and of all good things. Truly my own, are you not great and strong enough already to make your way without all these supports? One thing is necessary: to have God. The more nakedly and simply you possess him, the stronger you will be. So content yourself to possess him with holy and unalterable resolutions to be completely his, never knowingly to offend him, and labor with the fine point of your spirit, just as you are. Oh God! my very dear and only Sister,

one single act of virtue performed in this state is worth a hundred or even more than a thousand virtues performed with and through the sweetness of the sensible presence of God. Your road is the road of the cross, and are you not blessed, my dear soul, to travel alongside your sacred Spouse, the cross on your back and the pure love of his holy will in your heart?[18]

II

The strength she spoke of to Jacqueline Favre would soon have to sustain Jeanne in more than her altered relationship with François. She still was very much responsible for and involved in her children's lives. Neither Celse-Bénigne nor Françoise was yet married, and this was a cause for concern on Jeanne's part. Even Marie-Aymée, happily situated as she was with Bernard in the chateau of Thorens, caused Jeanne to be anxious.[19] Marie-Aymée had not yet borne a live child. She had been pregnant several times but had lost the infants before or during birth. As a consequence, the young baroness' health had been severely compromised and her frailty was a source of worry.

The general outlook for Marie-Aymée was newly dampened in 1616 when her much loved Bernard was called away to fight as a colonel in the army of the Duke of Savoy. But she was of a sturdy, if gentle, temperament and all hopes were once again high when in 1617 she found herself newly with child. She was a mere nineteen years old at the time and during the years she was baroness of Thorens she and her mother had enjoyed a growing intimate friendship. Since Bernard was away, she had decided to stay at the convent in Annecy to be with her mother and to be away from the castle which seemed too empty without her husband. Everything seemed to be going well. Then in May they received news that the baron had died in an epidemic that swept the army camp. The young wife was desolate, as was her mother, but the younger of the two of them bore her grief with a resignation that surprised all who knew her. She decided to remain near her mother and arranged for some friends in Annecy to be with her during her confinement. Then in early September, well before term, she quite unexpectedly went into labor and gave birth to a tiny baby boy. Jeanne had been wakened and had hurried to her daughter's side in time to hastily baptize the infant which died immediately. It was soon clear that Marie-Aymée herself had little time to live. In this last day of her life, Jeanne's daughter requested that she be clothed in the habit of the Visitation. François was called and officiated over the ceremony of profession and then over the sacrament of extreme unction. Marie-Aymée died in her mother's arms at midnight the following day.

The sudden and sorrowful loss of her daughter, son-in-law and grandchild weighed heavily upon Jeanne. She had, in François' words, a heart that "loved powerfully and felt things strongly,"[20] and it was cruelly battered by these three deaths. Nevertheless these losses served to incorporate Jeanne more deeply into her already powerful, single-focused dependence upon God. In her grief, the mother superior became convinced that she had failed to baptize her infant grandchild properly before his quick demise. Her thought of a tiny soul, eternally denied the sight of its maker because of her imprudence, tortured her. Finally, she sought François and tearfully confessed her fears. He asked her:

> Why should you be so intensely self-reflective, my Mother? Do you still retain some self-interest?[21]

His response had the effect of making her see that her anxiety was the result of a lack of trust and an over-scrupulous self-concern. Immediately she was at peace, and from that time forward, whenever she found herself regretful over some fault committed, either actually or in imagination, she recalled this incident as the time when François

> ... impressed upon her very deeply that one must look to God as the one against whom the offense was committed, rather than to oneself as the one committing it.[22]

Once again, she was directed away from self-reflection to focus upon a God in whom she found a judge whose compassion and wisdom dwarfed human frailty. It enabled her to face her loss with courage and gracefulness. When she next wrote to her friend this was evident in the mood of her writing. Yet, as always with Jeanne, the spiritual insight gained did not obscure the very real emotional response that she felt in her loss.

> Truly the spiritual medicine that the good Saviour has given me, together with physical medicine, has once again had its effect.
>
> But both medicines work so gently that I experience very little weariness from it. I even feel relieved of my queasiness, my only Father, and my spirit remains full of sweetness and ease in its submission and love of the divine will which today I desire to see reign even more in our holy union.
>
> But, my God! Despite this, I understand and feel how truly my daughter was the perfectly loved child of our heart. I suppose she will always be this since she so deserved it. This is an incomparable comfort to me in my grief—to sense the love you have invested in her like a drop of precious water in a great ocean.
>
> It also comforts me to be able to tell you this, my only and good Father. God be praised! I say this with my whole soul, in peace, gentleness and with the sure knowledge and recognition of the grace that his goodness has bestowed on us by giving us such a child and by drawing her back to himself so happily. . . .
>
> But for the time being, I should perhaps refrain from speaking about our poor little one so intimately for the contentment I gain from it always leaves me with sadness. My Father, my only Father and everything you know that you are to me, it would restore me to have a little talk with you because, finally, everything created on this earth is now nothing at all to me in comparison with my very dear Father, Monseigneur.[23]

Marie-Aymée was not the only child of the Chantal family in whom François had taken an interest. The young baroness had been a particular favorite of his, but the bishop had not been hesitant about entering into the lives of any of Jeanne's children. It was Celse-Bénigne who occupied him next. This strong-willed, intelligent eldest child of Madame de Chantal had been making something of a name for himself in French society. He had left his school career at the age of fifteen to try himself in another more glamorous life, that of a nobleman at the court in Paris. The life seems to have suited his taste if not his mother's. Celse-Bénigne was a favorite of the king and the darling of the court ladies, but was given to gambling and dueling, a practice which was outlawed at the time and carried stiff penalties. Celse-Bénigne's reckless exploits would torment his mother for a number of years to come. Through it all François acted as a friend and paternal influence for the boy, gently guiding him as much as he would allow. But chiefly he served as Jeanne's confidant and comfort, admonishing her when she seemed to be overly-anxious about her son and offering her advice on detachment when the situation actually warranted her distress.

His role was similar in the case of Françoise, Jeanne's youngest surviving child. Like Celse-Bénigne, she sought the gaiety and finery of aristocratic life though she lacked her brother's reckless abandon in the pursuit. Jeanne's chief concern in the years after Françoise had reached marriageable age was to find an eligible suitor for her. This turned out to be no easy task, for Françoise was constantly changing her mind, agreeing to a match and then backing out of the agreement. She would be in her early twenties before she would finally unite herself to the wealthy Burgundian Count Toulongon, a man well her senior who was very much in love with her. The match would take a number of years and a great deal of effort for Jeanne to arrange.

Over the years, Jeanne's maternal solicitude for her youngest daughter revolved around what the older woman considered the girl's too-frivolous pursuit of feminine display. In this the bishop acted as a moderating influence on both mother and daughter. When he met Françoise on the street in Annecy one time when her mother was away on the business of the institute and found her garishly decked out with ribbons and curls and displaying a generous portion of her bosom in a fashionable décolletage, he very discreetly produced a few pins from the folds of his own garments to restore the girl's modesty and made a few good-humored remarks that had the desired effect.

François did not pretend to be a surrogate father for the Chantal children but he did occupy a paternal place in their lives left vacant by their natural father's death. It was not the same place filled by Jeanne's brother André, the archbishop of Bourges, who was the solicitous uncle, especially for Celse-Bénigne. But it was a very real place nonetheless and had the effect of giving an added dimension to his relationship with Jeanne. With her, because of her children, he was not only friend but father as she was mother. This parenting aspect of their friendship was also present in their relationship within the Order of the Visitation. They very consciously spoke of themselves as Mother and Father and concerned themselves with the upbringing of their many daughters with the same zeal and investment that concerned parents would display toward their natural offspring.

The increased parental responsibility that accrued to them as the Visitation rapidly grew, simultaneous as it was with the new degree of detachment from each other that they were cultivating, had the effect of shifting their focus from the relational dynamics between the two of them to the dynamics of nurturing and shaping their spiritual offspring. Interestingly, they each brought the qualities of nurture to their task that conform to what has become the traditional and gender-differentiated understanding of male and female roles. Thus, as a spiritual parent to the order, François de Sales functioned as the parent who supplied the laws for the family—he wrote up the constitutions and rule, and while remaining somewhat distant from the day-to-day maintaining of the family, he supplied an authoritative figure whose vision of discipline and direction gave the entire family coherence. To his daughters in the order François could appear as a somewhat awesome figure, indeed so much so that at one point Jeanne had to reassure a young novice of the founder's gentle disposition.[24]

Jeanne, on the other hand, emerges as a spiritual parent with all of the traditional feminine qualities associated with mothering. Her tender solicitude, her sensitivity to differences of temperament, her insistence that her daughters must be won through love and not force of any kind are all hallmarks of her maternal governing of the order. Moreover, it was she and not her friend François who "ran the house," who supervised the day-to-day events and brought to the small details of life at the Visitation her particular touch. The manifestation of these particular parenting qualities on the part of the two friends is striking when one considers that in their own relationship, especially in the beginning, it was François who displayed qualities like gentleness and flexibility, that could be termed "feminine," and Jeanne whose disposition was marked by the "masculine" traits of rigor and zealousness. It is also interesting because it was not necessarily expected that the mother superior of a religious order would exhibit the feminine qualities associated with mothering or that a male in authority would deport himself in a "masculine" manner either in the seventeenth century or earlier in the monastic tradition of the church.[25]

What seems apparent is that both Jeanne and François had available to themselves a wide range of personal qualities which might be deemed either "masculine" or "feminine," and that, depending upon the situation, they each might exhibit more or less of these various qualities as it was appropriate or natural to do so.[26]

As parents of the Order of the Visitation they complemented one another: while François supplied the theoretical framework for the family, Jeanne put theory into concrete practice. It was this interaction between them that dominated their relationship during the years between 1616—the year of the retreat—and 1622. He was still her spiritual advisor, she still looked to him for guidance in many matters, and he still looked to her for his growing insight into the depths of contemplative prayer. Certainly, they still understood themselves through the language of lovers and within the context of a spiritual friendship whose unitive love could never die. But in their correspondence the focus shifts. There appear to have been fewer letters between them, and this despite the fact that they were often separated during these years, she busy with new foundations all over France, he occupied with the fulfillment of his various episcopal duties. There are many more letters, especially written by Jeanne, to other people, particularly to the growing number of mother superiors of the order.

To François, Jeanne writes about the enlargement of a cloister, about buying mills, about a trousseau for her daughter and about her son's adventures, about his writing projects, about his preaching ventures, about troublesome individuals in some of the houses or about news at Annecy. There are passages in which she dwells for a while on the earlier intimate personal concerns that before dominated their correspondence, but these passages are in the minority. François' notes are likewise filled with an abundance of details about the events of daily life. Always, he has some small bit of advice for her or some fond phrase, but the general impression one gets from their letters during this period is of two long-time companions whose shared and separate responsibilities take center stage in their lives.

The years following the "denuding" were indeed filled with a variety of events. The popularity of the order was overwhelming, and for five years between 1618 and 1623 Jeanne de Chantal was away from Annecy establishing new foundations in Grenoble, Bourges, Paris and Dijon. François was likewise often on the road, preaching or on diplomatic missions or concerning himself with the establishment of the Visitation. Indeed, at times it seemed to them as though the vicissitudes of managing their growing family were all-consuming, for though some of the foundations went smoothly and many of the entrants proved well adapted to the life, there were many problems. For instance, besides the ordinary difficulties with postulants who turned out to be unsuited for the community and a few girl boarders who lived unhappily among them, François and Jeanne had to deal with the remarkable antics of two women, Madame des Gouffiers and Madame de Tertre. The former of these women proved to have, in Jeanne's own words, "a dreadful spirit."[27] This religious of the Order of the Paraclete was unhappy with her choice of life. She became an ardent enthusiast of François de Sales and the nascent Visitation. Using her influence to help establish the community at Lyons, Madame des Gouffiers at first appeared to the founders to be a welcome addition to the growing family. But time did not prove their evaluation apt. After a blissful year in the novitiate at Annecy, Sister des Gouffiers was enjoined to travel to Champagne to formally divest herself of her ties with the Paraclete to which she still was bound. But instead of attending to this she traveled to Moulins where she succeeded in interesting a group of women, as well as the local bishop, in establishing a Visitation house in their town. With astonishing boldness, she sought to initiate the foundation herself, quite without the founders' consent. It was not until the Moulins community had received the official episcopal blessing in June 1616 that Jeanne and François learned of the audacious move of this self-appointed spokesperson for the community. In the ensuing confusion it was decided to send Charlotte de Bréchard to bring this bogus house under the auspices of the authentic Visitation spirit. But Madame des Gouffiers had expected the mother superior herself to come to Moulins and was piqued when this did not occur. She next moved on to Paris, again presumably to formalize her canonical status, but when next heard of she was busy once again drumming up support for a new house in the French capital. Both François and Jeanne made frequent vigorous appeals to her to take her place as one of the daughters of the community, but she was difficult to convince. Finally, she gradually lost interest in the cause of furthering the Annecy spirit and embarked on new ventures.

Madame de Tertre was another personality who figures darkly in Jeanne's and François' story. Left a widow at the age of twenty-two, this rich and frivolous young woman had involved herself in a scandalous affair and, apparently, had conceived an illegitimate child. Urged by vigorous family pressure, she appealed to the founders of the Visitation to enable her to retire from the world. She was situated at the ill-starred convent at Moulins under the kindly eye of Mother de Bréchard. But the simplicity of religious life was not to the young noblewoman's taste even though, as a foundress, she enjoyed a certain number of privileges denied the other sisters. For years Madame de Tertre, while periodically vowing her intention to observe the spirit of the order, continued to treat herself grandly, dressing and scenting herself as was the vogue in the capital, entertaining visitors in her rooms or getting exemptions from other matters of convent rule. As with Madame des Gouffiers, the two founders wrote frequently to their charge to modify her activities. But it was not only her love of luxury that was a problem for them but her strong will as well. She was very fond of Charlotte de Bréchard and, when she learned that this woman was to become superior of a new community in Nevers, she acted on her own to begin proceedings with a prominent citizen of Nevers for establishing that house herself so that, as foundress, she too would have the right to live there. Her activity, unknown to Jeanne and François, was discovered and stirred up considerable provincial rivalry, so much so that local governors and bishops came to defend the claims of their respective provinces to the presence (and money) of Madame de Tertre and the honor of Mere de Bréchard's rule. The young order's reputation was seriously compromised by the young widow's dealings. Finally, it was decided that the two women would remain in Moulins. Despite this, Madame de Tertre spent a good many unhappy years rebelling against the confines of the situation in which she found herself, going so far as to have a separate house erected for herself on the convent grounds. Remarkably, her sad history ended happily. In 1632 she had a dream so vivid that it compelled her to a dramatic conversion. She requested that she become a legitimate novice in the community she had so long resented and made a public demonstration of her good faith by tearing up the document which secured her privileges as foundress. She died fifteen months later.

These were two of the more vivid episodes that severely tried the patience and parental abilities of both Jeanne and François. But there were many more prosaic, if nonetheless equally taxing difficulties to surmount in establishing the Visitation in the many towns in France that requested its presence. The foundation at Paris proved to be one of the most exacting. Jeanne had been away from Annecy all during 1618, busy with the new communities at Grenoble and Bourges, when in the spring of 1619 she was called to the French capital. Preliminary contacts had been made with individuals who hoped to support the new venture, but still Madame de Chantal and her little band found themselves for the most part surrounded by influential people who were hostile to the encroachment of a provincial community into the devout Parisian world. The whole situation was made even more painful for Jeanne because, during this critical period when the group's reputation was being built, Celse-Bénigne who was with the court, chose this moment to agree impetuously to act as a second for a friend planning a duel. Both church and state had heavy censures against the ancient practice, which were enforced when the encounter was discovered. All parties were sentenced to be condemned by hanging (an especially ignominious punishment for noblemen who routinely had the privilege of death by the sword). Celse-Bénigne and the others managed to flee from town but the criminals were hanged in effigy in the public square and the young baron's public career seemed to come to an ignominious end. It did not reflect well upon his mother.

Nevertheless, the Paris Visitation not only survived but began to flourish. Late in 1621, two and a half years after she had arrived, Jeanne felt that the group was stable enough to continue on its own without her. She planned to head toward Dijon where a house was envisioned and from there to make her way back to her beloved Annecy and the presence of François whom she had not seen for over two years. Illness prevented her leaving right away, but in February of the following year, in spite of the rigorous cold, she headed south to the city of her birth. Dijon would be the tenth house of the Visitation to be established. It was twelve years since she had left her natal place in an atmosphere of criticism and malicious talk. The intervening time and Jeanne's growing reputation for holiness had healed all the old wounds. When she and the sisters with her entered the city, virtually the entire populace turned out for an enthusiastic welcome.

The year 1622 was, in general, one of the most rewarding of this decade of Jeanne's life. Not only was her order flourishing but she had the joy of being received back into a home town that had so sharply questioned her decision to begin the order in the first place. Moreover, she and her daughter Françoise had come full circle in their somewhat strained relationship. The young countess, having lost two infants to premature births within the previous two years and now pregnant for the third time, seemed to have begun to identify with her own mother and her maternal concerns and to see her in a new light. On the way to Dijon Jeanne and her companions had stopped at the Toulongon estates where Françoise proudly gathered together a small circle of admirers to fete them. Then, after she had successfully given birth to her first surviving child, a girl, Françoise took the baby to Dijon to receive its grandmother's official blessing.

Yet despite the successes she enjoyed, Jeanne de Chantal's inner life was still characterized by the darkness and poignant longing of the last ten years. On the feast of Sts. Peter and Paul in June of 1621, she had written to François about her inner state and about her need to see him once again.

> I have several things to tell you, my only Father, but my poor mind is so overwhelmed and distracted by a thousand worries I can't remember them all. Today's feast always revives me when I think of my only Father receiving a thousand blessings from these great and holy Apostles whom he loves and serves with such affection.
>
> Certainly I am joyful and nothing, thank God, afflicts me, for I will whatever God wills and in the fine point of my spirit there is no other desire than to accomplish his most holy will in all things. That reminds me, my dear Father, that I cannot feel my abandonment and sweet trust any longer nor am I able to make any act. Yet these virtues seem to me to be more solid and stable than ever before. My spirit, in its fine point, is in a very simple state of unity but it cannot make any act of union because when it wants to, which at certain times it too often attempts, it feels the effort and sees clearly that it cannot unite itself over again but simply remains united. My soul doesn't want to stir from where it is, it does not consider anything nor can it do

anything except form in its deepest self a deepening desire, which makes itself felt almost imperceptibly, that God will do with it and all creatures and everything whatever he pleases. . . . Sometimes my soul says the "Our Father" out loud for the whole world or for particular people or itself but without turning itself away or considering why or for whom it prays. Frequently depending upon the situation and necessity or when the desire comes without being sought, my soul glides into this unity. About this, I see very clearly that this union suffices for everything but, my only Father, I am often fearful of it, and this can be very painful. I force myself to make acts of union or adoration at morning prayer or at Mass or during thanksgiving. Tell me, please, if I am wrong about this and if this simple union does indeed suffice, in God's eyes, for all the other acts like the ones I have mentioned to which we are obligated and if it suffices during dryness when the soul has neither knowledge nor feeling of itself except in the extreme point of the spirit.

I certainly don't know how I happened to tell you all this, my only Father, because I was not intending to when I sat down to write. Still, I am very glad I have told you. I should add this: that this unity does not keep all the rest of my soul from sometimes feeling an inclination and a longing to be near you, and then I don't have any inclination, affection or feeling for anything else. However, I don't linger on this nor does it cause me any anxiety, thank God, because of the union in the fine point of my spirit. But when I happen to consider the incomparable happiness of seeing myself at your feet and receiving your blessing again, tears spring quickly to my eyes and I can't help feeling that they will flow freely when God grants me this blessing. But I always turn promptly to some other consideration. I don't have any particular wish for this, for I leave it up to God and to you to deal with me. . . .[28]

These complex yet clearly delineated self-perceptions are characteristic of Jeanne. At bottom, she perceived that her soul was intimately united to God. Or, to put it more precisely, the faculties of her soul, especially the will, were at their root surrendered to the direction of the divine life that in the Christian view is present at the core of the human person. She perceived that her own relationship to this divine life was characterized by subtlety, simplicity and non-activity. Although she sensed the appropriateness of this for herself, yet it disturbed her that it did not manifest itself more actively and affectively. At the same time that she lived in this obscure but sure knowledge that she was properly aligned with the divine, Jeanne nonetheless experienced a great deal of interior activity, most of it of a disturbing nature. Her thoughts were distracted with the thousand details of life to which she had to attend; she found herself yearning for François' presence and visualized her very emotional response to their long-awaited meeting; despite her intuitive certainty she was concerned to have her friend validate her perceived experience of God. At other times, as we have seen, she was plagued with troubling doubts of various sorts.

The portrait that emerges from this self-rendering is a classic picture of the experience of purification that is charted in Christian treatments of the process of contemplative prayer. To begin with, there is an awareness, sometimes hard won and often on a very subtle level, of a relationship with God that goes well beyond the ordinary and which informs and directs the whole life of the individual. Then there is simultaneously an experience of a process, sometimes positive and sometimes negative in its effects, that draws the individual into a more intimate relationship than he or she had enjoyed before. This process of purification has been variously depicted by different writers but its meaning is essentially simple: it is understood that the soul is being emptied of its self to make room for God.[29] The manifestations of this purgative process can be manifold: they can show themselves as dryness, as temptations, as doubts, as desolation or as the absence of any particular perception whatsoever. Jeanne is unique in the history of Christian contemplative literature in the length of the period of purification, for she suffered the vagaries of this process for nearly forty years, experiencing a lifting of her inner burden only a short time before her death.

She often sought François' reassurance that she was indeed on the right track, and despite the fact that she had consciously surrendered her interior direction and well-being to God alone, she still longed for the companionship of her friend. Just two months later in August 1621, she wrote to the Genevan bishop about leaving Paris. The letter includes a touching account of her desire and the way in which she abandoned to providence even that very natural impulse.

How fortunate those two good Israelites are to be able to see my one and only true and cherished Father! Certainly, if I am delayed here, I will remain with all the more affection and much more than you might imagine. Because it seems to me if one or the other of us dies without my having confessed to you one more time, I would be in danger of having a multitude of worries and scruples. But I have already told Our Lord very calmly that obeying his holy will I do not want to pay attention to anything that concerns me alone and I have entrusted myself to his mercy so that he might grant me once more the grace of making an honest review of my conscience before you. It's not that anything of importance has happened since I have seen you and I don't know if this isn't actually a temptation. You can judge. For I don't have anything new to tell except about my responsibilities where I feel as though I commit so many faults through my lack of prudence, charity, zeal, care and good example. However, I think about and confess only the particular faults that I am aware of. This does not cause me any anxiety but I hope some day to look thoroughly at it all with you. Meanwhile I remain in peace.

You say you have no news to send? Ah, can't you draw a few words from your heart for me? Because it's so long since you have said anything to me. Dear Jesus, what a consolation to speak heart to heart one day! May the divine Saviour grant me this grace and in the meantime, my only Father, may he make you purely and simply all his own.[30]

Jeanne spent six months of the year 1622 in the town where she had been born. It was a relatively peaceful time for the mother superior. Her long-time friend Jacqueline Favre had been sent to join her to take over the position of superior when Jeanne left Dijon. It had been seven years since the two of them had had the joy of living under the same roof together and sharing the intimacy that this could afford. It was also clear, not only from the enthusiatic response of the common people of her birthplace but from the attention Jeanne now received from others, that the personal transformation she had undergone in the past years was evident to all those who met her. On the journey from Paris she had been consulted and visited by a multitude of seekers hoping for advice or requesting a blessing. It was her holiness that drew them, for she had quite visibly become the person she had been hoping all these years to become.

III

When Jeanne left Dijon in October she headed south to Lyon to visit the convent she had established there a full seven years before. François as well found that his varied duties would take him to Lyon while his friend was in residence there. It had by now been over three years since they had spoken face to face. In Jeanne's mind the possibilities for their meeting loomed large, for not only did she have a number of important matters to discuss that concerned the Visitation, she also anticipated the review of conscience with her friend that had been postponed for so long. Moreover, François' health had been poor during the last year and this had been a continuing cause for concern. To see him once again and in good health was a desire that she cherished.

But the respective responsibilities that defined the lives of these two took precedence over any personal desire, so that, on his first brief visit in town, the bishop had only a few opportunities to see his friend and these were virtually only in passing. He was on his way to Avignon with the court of Savoy and would return again in early December. He advised Jeanne that she should visit two more of their newly founded convents, take her annual retreat and meet him in Lyon once again on his return. The city had also been chosen as the meeting place for a somewhat more regal reunion. The royal couples of France and Savoy were planning a triumphal celebration of King Louis' recent victories over the Huguenots in southern France and the Genevan bishop was to participate in the observance.

The state entourage arrived back in Lyon on December 8, the feast of the Immaculate Conception. Excusing himself from court duties, he went to preach at the church of the Visitation and, as the bishop's palace was occupied by the royal houshold, he chose to stay overnight in the gardener's cottage attached to the monastery in order to be near the community and be available to them. But his pressing responsibilities to the court could not be ignored, and François soon found his calendar filled from morning till night for the duration of his stay in Lyon. Somehow he managed to clear a space of several hours in his schedule for Jeanne alone. They had a good number of important matters to discuss that affected the administration of the Visitation: there was the question of episcopal authority and individual authority, for it had been suggested that the communities might arrange themselves under the direction of one general, either male or female, who would see to the common observance in all houses;[31] there were also some important points in the Custom Book that remained unclarified.

They met in the parlor of the monastery and François opened the conversation:

> "My Mother, we have several free hours. Which one of us should begin?"
>
> "Me, please, my Father," Jeanne quickly replied. "My heart greatly needs to be attended to."[32]

His response was more in keeping with their shared vision of perfect detachment than her request had been but it was gently put:

> "What, my dear Mother. Do you still have urgent desires and personal choices? I thought I would find you quite angelic." Then he added, "We were speaking about ourselves in Annecy; now we should attend to the business of our congregation. How much I love our little Institute because God is loved so well there."[33]

Without a word Jeanne folded up the sheet of paper on which she had made some notes for her review of conscience and unfolded the larger sheaf of papers which contained the information necessary for a discussion of the order's affairs. They spoke for four hours; then when they had finished, François asked her to leave for Grenoble to visit that foundation and then to return to Annecy by way of Valence, Belley, Chambéry and Rumilly to visit the Visitation houses in the first two cities, to see about establishing one in the third, and to visit a community of Bernardine sisters undergoing a reform under Salesian direction in the fourth. He promised to meet her again in Annecy.

With her friend's blessing, Jeanne de Chantal set out early the next morning and soon arrived in Grenoble where she arranged to take her annual retreat a few days before Christmas and then enjoy the company of her sisters for the holy day. Three days after Christmas, on the feast of the Holy Innocents, she reported that, while at prayer and bringing her intentions for François before her God, she quite distinctly heard a voice which uttered the words "He is no more." Her immediate response was to give the phrase a Pauline interpretation, for her director had often set before her his own desire for perfect abandonment to God, wishing that he should live no more but Christ alone should live in him. The experience of this locution gave her some pause but she did not dwell on it for long. She simply accepted her own interpretation and rejoiced at the knowledge that her friend was being so deeply incorporated into the mystery that they both worshiped.

In fact, François de Sales was no more. He had caught a chill Christmas eve while attending a lengthy dedication service in the damp winter air. Despite this, he had said Midnight Mass for the sisters at the Visitation, said the second Mass of Christmas for the court at a Dominican church, and then had been obliged to return to court. Finishing his business there, he had returned to the Visitation where he said the third Mass of the festive night. When day dawned he had received two new postulants into the order and preached on their behalf. Then he was expected to be at court again to bid goodbye to the queen mother who was leaving town the next day. His companions noticed that he appeared very ill the day after Christmas, yet he continued to spend himself in the service of others. He spent the evening with the Visitation sisters, giving them a conference on his favorite motto, "Ask nothing and refuse nothing." The next day he continued to keep his appointments and to say Mass although he noted that his eyesight seemed to be failing. When he returned to the convent at midday his servants noticed that he had difficulty rising after a light meal and that he found it impossible to write the letters that urgently needed attending to. As he rose from his desk chair he collapsed. The doctors were hastily summoned and they made a diagnosis of apoplexy through a rupture of the cerebral artery. For a full day the physicians used all their ingenuity to apply a truly horrible succession of remedies to their patient while friends and pious visitors clustered round the bed. François de Sales died at eight in the evening on December 28, 1622, the feast of the Holy Innocents.

Jeanne left Grenoble without hearing the sad news, and she arrived in Belley ten days after Christmas still ignorant of her friend's death. For Michel Favre, François' confessor and confidential secretary as well as chaplain of the Visitation, had made sure that no letters or information reached her while she was on the road because he wished to be the one to gently break the news to her himself. At Belley the sisters were requested not to make any display of their grief, for it was decided that the mother superior should be allowed to celebrate the feast of Epiphany, which marked the end of the joyous Christmas celebration, with serenity. Jeanne was not aware of the conspiracy of silence, but she was troubled that she had had no news of François for some time. Approaching Michel Favre, she inquired after their mutual friend. He replied that the bishop had fallen ill in Lyon and handed her a letter written by François' brother Jean who had been his assistant and now, with François' death, had become bishop of Geneva.

Jeanne's first response upon hearing that François had fallen ill was to announce that she wished to return to Lyon immediately. But she sensed the mood of her informants:

> When Monsieur Michel put the letter . . . in my hand my heart beat wildly. I drew myself close to the presence of God and his will, greatly fearing that there was something painful to be learned in this letter. In the small space of time that it took to recollect myself in God, I understood the words that I had heard in Grenoble: "He is no more," the truth of which was clarified for me by reading that blessed letter. I fell to my knees, adoring the divine Providence and embracing the holy will of God which included my incomparable affliction, as best I could.[34]

Madame de Chantal wept through most of the day and night, her tears in her own words being "abundant but very gentle." She continued with the regular round of community life but in her grief paid little attention to what was going on around her. This warm woman whose heart François had said "loved powerfully and felt things strongly"[35] was not even in this most personal of moments free from barbs of criticism thrown by her detractors. She was approached by one of the priests present at the convent for the feast. He informed her that a soul perfectly resigned to the will of God really ought to dry its tears. She answered simply:

> My dear Father, if I knew that my tears were disagreeable to God, I would not shed even a single one.[36]

She even for a while tried to suppress the gentle flow of her grief, but Michel Favre, seeing that she was actually making herself ill by the effort, had the wisdom to counter the questionable advice of the visitor by encouraging her to give free expression to her tears.

Summoning the vast reserves of courage and resilience that she had been cultivating now for so many years, Jeanne did not let her sorrow prevent her from attending to the very real duties that now awaited her. She remained at Belley for a few days, writing to the new Genevan prelate to express her condolences and to pledge her obedience, as well as to the appropriate persons in Lyon to insure that the body of her friend would be promptly returned to Annecy where he had requested burial;[37] she directed conferences with the sisters and conducted business as usual. When she left the city she followed the itinerary that François had marked out for her at their last meeting. Yet despite her refusal to collapse under the weight of her burden, Jeanne felt this most painful of all deaths with the full force of her ardent nature.

In two letters—one to the assistant superior at Annecy and one to her brother André, the archbishop of Bourges, both written from Belley—her anguish is seen through the transparent veil of her account of how she received the sorrowful news. Another letter, one to Jacqueline Favre,[38] is usually cited to describe the way in which Jeanne received the blow, and it has become commonplace to accept the mood of that missive which shows Jeanne in a state of calm resignation to the fact of what has happened. But the letters to her brother and the assistant, which were written some time before the one to Jacqueline, are remarkably revealing and in their rush of explanation and almost tangible emotion show perhaps more clearly than the other piece of correspondence the process by which this woman encountered her grief and transposed it into the loving acceptance of all life that characterized her. In the course of these letters the process can be seen to repeat itself several times: she begins to make a statement, either about the event or about something unrelated to it; suddenly she is reminded of her pain, the trail of the preceding thought having led her to it or it having rushed up unbidden by itself; she hesitates in the gripping experience of her anguish for a moment; then she gently brings her thoughts and feelings back to God by making that simple act of self-abandonment that her friend François had taught her. In her words can be seen both

Jeanne's tremendous sensitivity and her great strength, a capacity that derived from her ability to love all aspects of her experience. This she had had in potential when she had met her mentor in Dijon that Lenten season of 1604 but it had been her relationship with him that had brought that capacity into its mature realization.

> To Sister Françoise-Marguerite Favrot,
> Oh God! Dear Sister, how right it is to acquiesce to the holy decree of Providence! But to stop the pain, only the One who has caused the wound can heal it! Yet we must have courage. Don't worry about the sisters at Lyons; they are daughters of obedience. I hope that we will soon have the blessed body. Oh, my dearest daughter, what an occasion for my welcome home! But, my God, you have wished this and so I wish it too, with all my heart, even with the unspeakable anguish of it. We will leave Monday or Tuesday or later. I long to be in our blessed house more than you can imagine, but God must be served without reservation in whatever way it pleases him. May God be our only consolation! There is nothing more than that but it is enough. May he be eternally blest.[39]

To her brother André, she wrote:

> You say you want to know what my heart felt on that occasion. Ah, it seems to me that it adored God in the profound silence of its terrible anguish! Truly, I have never felt such an intense grief nor has my spirit ever received so heavy a blow. My sorrow is greater than I could ever express and it seems as though everything serves to increase my weariness and cause me to regret. The only thing that is left to console me is to know that it is my God that has done this, or, at least, has permitted this blow to fall. Alas! My heart is too weak to support this heavy burden; how it needs strength! Yes, my God, you put this beautiful soul into the world, now you have taken it back; may your holy name be blessed! I don't know any other song except "May the name of the Lord be blessed!"
> My very dear brother and dear Father, my soul is filled with grief but also full of the peace of God's will which I would never oppose with even the slightest resistance. No, my dear Father, I affirm what it has pleased Him to do—to take from us that great flame that lit up this miserable world and let it shine in His king-

dom, as we truly believe. May His name be blessed! God has
chastised me as I deserved because I am certainly too insignifi-
cant to merit such a great blessing as well as the contentment
that I had in seeing my soul held in the hands of such a great
man who was truly a man of God.

I believe that God in His supreme goodness does not want
me to take any more pleasure in this world, and I don't want to
take any more either except to hope to have the joy of seeing
my dearest Father in the bosom of His everlasting goodness. Yet
I still will to remain in this exile—yes, my dear brother, I truly
do. It's a terribly difficult exile for me, this miserable life. But I
want to stay here, as I said, as long as it is God's plan for me. I
will let Him do with me as He wishes. Remember me as well as
this little family in your holy sacrifices. They are so sorrowful
and suffer with such grace and resignation that I am consoled.
We will leave here soon to go back to poor little Annecy. My
pain will be redoubled by seeing our sisters there. God be blest
in and for everything! Long live His will! Long live His
pleasure![40]

Jeanne de Chantal returned to Annecy in mid-January. François' body had been laid out in the Cathedral of St. Peter after its
long and solemn journey across France into Savoy. There, on Jan-
uary 29, his funeral Mass was preached. On the following day Bar-
nabite priests carried the bishop's coffin across town to the Visitation convent where it was placed on the high altar, very close to the
choir grill where Madame de Chantal and the sisters were gathered.
The body was to remain there for several months until the tomb in
the crypt could be prepared.

François had promised his friend that she could speak of her
personal concerns when they met once more at the monastery on
the shores of Lake Annecy. One day, when she found herself free
from her ordinary duties, she asked the acting superior if she might
be allowed to go into the church where François' coffin lay. There
she knelt down and poured out the confession that had by now been
aching for expression for so long. She spoke to his body very simply, as if speaking to a friend who was still alive and, according to
her own report, she received a response—she heard his voice, if not
actually, at least in her heart. Tranquil and reposed she made her
peace not simply with her friend's passing but with the part of her-

self which had always remained with him even when they were apart. Kneeling there before his white-draped coffin, Jeanne de Chantal experienced a new understanding of the detachment for which her friend had been so long preparing her. He was gone, and yet in his place was the wisdom and consolation that he had always given her. The wholeness and integrity that the two of them had striven for she now realized. She was in her own mind now utterly naked and dependent on her God alone in union with the crucified Christ whom she adored.

Jeanne's story does not end with the death of François but it does enter a new phase. After François' passing and until her own death in 1641, Jeanne de Chantal was to be more and more absorbed in the business of her order. The Visitation's initial popularity grew tremendously so that by its foundress' death there were over eighty houses of the order. Because of the growing number of communities and her desire that observance among them should be uniform, she called the first general chapter meeting of superiors in 1624. At the general chapter the various superiors drew up a clearly defined version of the Custom Book that was to guide the Visitation in its effort to act as a large and diverse community joined by their union in sisterly love. Over the years the Custom Book continued to be revised and amplified in response to the changing needs of the institute.[41]

For the rest of her life Jeanne de Chantal's days remained filled with the occupations of her position: she wrote thousands of letters to innumerable persons on topics ranging from the concerns of court luminaries to the requisition of foodstuffs for the kitchen to the delicate spiritual counseling of a sister. She also traveled incessantly: by boat, by litter, by horseback and by carriage she zigzagged her way across the terrain of France and Savoy, setting up new communities, receiving visitors, or giving spiritual instruction. As her travels continued her reputation spread, and the foundress of the Visitation not only attracted those seeking wisdom but the curious and adoring throngs as well.

All this attention to the Visitation and its affairs was essential as Jeanne had known long ago when she freely embraced the life and all its consequences. But before 1622, although she had her share of the responsibility, François was still there to confirm her sense of how decisions should be made and to add his perspective to all the efforts she put forth. Now he was gone and the decisions fell to her alone. She felt very strongly that the vision of the Institute that the bishop had originated must be preserved, and to the best of her ability she led the young order through its infancy with her friend's point of view in mind. It was not always an easy task, for despite her insight into the Salesian perspective, people and forces outside her sometimes made it difficult to put forward her interpretation of a situation. One example of this was her lifelong resistance to the institution of an apostolic visitor for the congregation which she felt would compromise the autonomy that the founder had intended for his little band. Her correspondence of many years about her struggle clearly shows how insistent and clear-sighted she could be when it came to defending her interpretation of the Visitation charism.[42]

Her intention to preserve the heritage that her friend had entrusted to her extended beyond her management of the community that they had founded. Immediately after François' death, Jeanne began collecting the letters and various treatises that the bishop had written in order to organize and preserve them for posterity. It was at this time that she burned many of the letters she had written to him and which he had saved and annotated with a view to someday writing up an account of her remarkable spiritual journey. It also fell to her to write a portrait of her friend that would preserve both his memory and her sensitive impression of him for others. She had always believed that François was a saint. It was her great hope that she would see her friend François receive the official recognition of the church in canonization. She was not the only one who had perceived the remarkable nature of this man. After his death there was a spontaneous outburst of veneration for the dead man, especially in the vicinity of Annecy. Pilgrims came to worship at his tomb, and there were even accounts of miraculous healings under his protection.

Partly as a result of this, partly because of the commendable literary output that he had produced for the church, and partly because of his unflagging efforts to reconvert those who in the Church's mind had fallen away from the true faith, Rome began an inquiry into the life of François de Sales with an eye to his canonization. Depositions were taken from many hundreds of people who had known the bishop during his life, but most important of these was the deposition that Jeanne prepared.[43] She labored over it a long time, producing what is surely one of the most vivid and insightful portraits of the man ever written. The form of her account was determined by the form proper to the inquiry: the official interrogator put a series of questions to the witness which she was required to answer. The basic assumption underlying the entire testimony was that the deceased individual was being examined and judged in relation to the Christian virtues which he was to have exemplified during his life. It was required that the witness support all assertions with examples known to her at first hand.

What emerges from Jeanne's deposition is at one and the same time both a striking picture of a man deeply imbued with the spirit of the faith he lived and a clear record of her own remarkable intuitive understanding of him. The inquiry took place in the summer of 1627 at the monastery in Annecy. There, for forty hours divided into three hour segments, Jeanne sat behind the grille in the parlor across from four men: the postulator of the cause, the protonotary and two other judges who were close friends of François, her own brother André and Jean-Pierre Camus, bishop of Belley. She read from her manuscript while a scribe copied down word for word what she said; then she reread and signed her testimony. By 1627 François had been dead for nearly five years and Jeanne's grief had subsided into a cherished memory of the friend who had been so long an integral part of her life. What is clear from her account is that the vision of life that François had held and had so ardently striven to perfect in himself was a vision that she herself held dear. Her depiction of her friend reveals her as knowing his most cherished dreams and shows him as glimpsed by the eyes of someone who understood the motives behind his actions and the heroic struggle that lay behind his manifestation of sanctity.

Jeanne draws a picture of François not as a pious and archetypal holy man but as a highly individualized person who had brought his own natural endowments into a disciplined unity that gave to his life an integrity and beauty that was recognized by all. The same could be said of her. She too had been involved in a journey of self-discipline that would bring her own highly unique set of gifts to a mature and graceful fulfillment. The friendship with François had facilitated that development, given it definition and direction. Now, when she wrote of him five years after his death and she had the opportunity to reflect at a distance upon the life of the man she had known so intimately, she fashioned for the world and for herself a unified portrait of him out of the diversity of impressions that she carried with her. It was as much an image of herself as of him, for in so fully comprehending the dynamics of the inner and outer life of her friend, she reveals herself as intimate to those dynamics and as lucidly conscious both of the ideals of holiness to which he aspired and of the implementation of those ideals within the matrix of everyday life.

Madame de Chantal never had the satisfaction of seeing her friend achieve the official recognition she felt he so rightly merited. The mood of Counter-Reformation Catholicism was very much opposed to the casual standards of determining sanctity that had prevailed in previous centuries. The hierarchy was particularly wary of popular outcries and protestations of miracles performed by local figures. The canonization inquiry was suspended precisely because it was felt that there was not enough objective reporting of the man's life that was emerging from the testimony (this was not the case with Jeanne's deposition). It was not until twenty-four years after Jeanne's death, in 1665, that he was finally recognized as a saint by the official church.

Despite this profound disappointment, Jeanne continued to uphold the memory of her friend both in the administration of the order as well as in her own unfailing pursuit of the life of perfect love. Her road in that life would be a dark and painful one, her inner desolation not dissipating until a few short months before her own death. She described her inner agony to a confidant who reported:

> Her spirit was so full of all sorts of temptations and abominations that her continual exercise was to avert her attention away from her inner life, not being able to endure the sight of a soul so full of horror that she seemed to herself the image of hell.[44]

Yet this did not prevent her from conscientiously fulfilling all her varied duties with a gracefulness and compassion that was evident to all. She also continued to follow the careers of her two children. For Celse-Bénigne she arranged a very fortunate marriage with the lovely daughter of a well-appointed and pious Parisian family. The couple were married in 1623 and in 1626 a daughter, the future Madame de Sévigné, was born to them. But their story did not end joyously. The young baron, hoping to regain his reputation, volunteered for service in the west of France where Huguenot forces were making a last stand in their struggle against the French king. Jeanne's son deported himself heroically in battle and died on July 22, 1627, defending the beachhead against the landing of English forces coming to the support of the opposition troops. His young widow died only a few years later, leaving the care of their child to her parents and the Visitation in Paris. Françoise was the only one of Jeanne's children who outlived their mother; she survived to a ripe age, early widowhood and presumably her own mother's remarkable example bringing out the more mature and gracious side of her own nature. She and Jeanne remained close until the elder woman's death.

That death came in 1641, but not until she had witnessed the ravages of the great plague that swept France between 1628 and 1631 and not until she had suffered the loss of her earliest companions at "la Galerie" as well as the demise of her brother André. On the feast of the Ascension earlier that year she had once and for all laid down her responsibilities as a superior, taking her place among the rest of the sisters and refusing any special treatment or position because of either her age or her previous accomplishments. This coincided wtih a new manifestation in her interior life, the experience of a "loving and victorious peace"[45] which flooded her consciousness and for the rest of her life lifted from her the burden of the darkness she had so long endured.

Yet out of love and obedience she agreed to make another journey out of Annecy in July of that year. She planned to visit Princess Orsini, the widow of the duke of Montmorency who was hoping to enter the Moulins Visitation later in the year. The royal novice was an invalid and, through the vicissitudes of the political intrigue that had cost her late husband his life, had been for many years imprisoned in a castle near Moulins. It was through the kindness of the Visitation superior of that city that the princess had become friendly with the order's two founders and, as her own personal holiness grew and the political stain that attached to her name grew dim in the memories of all, she planned to attach herself formally to the monastery. Despite her own hopes for retirement, Jeanne granted her friend's request and set out, as it turned out, on her last journey.

As she bid her sisters goodbye, she was especially joyous and filled
with the newly acquired inner peace. She spent a number of weeks
at Moulins and then, pressured by many requests, spent some time
in Paris. There she met not only with the queen, Anne of Austria,
but with her old friend Vincent de Paul to whom she made a final
review of conscience.

By this time the damp autumn had set in and Jeanne found herself seized by one of the bronchial attacks to which she had been
subject in wet weather. The illness did not leave her and she died,
like her friend François, away from home. She succumbed at Moulins on December 13, 1641.

THE NATURE OF SPIRITUAL FRIENDSHIP

The respective histories of Jeanne de Chantal and François de Sales cannot be adequately understood without reference to the powerful and long-term relationship that they shared. This is not simply because they borrowed ideas from one another or undertook a large-scale project together. It is also because they were friends of a very special kind, spiritual friends whose single passion for Christian perfection bonded them in a nineteen year journey through self and other and brought them to the realization of their common goal.

The nature of that friendship is many-faceted. The very possibility of such an intimate relationship between a man and woman existing in European culture at all can be credited to the assumptions and vision that undergirded the Christian contemplative tradition of which Jeanne and François were a part. That tradition, throughout the Christian past, presented itself as an alternative way of being in the world which accepted as possible and even normative the counter cultural ethos of early Christianity. In the contemplative view of things, the new kingdom of God proclaimed by Jesus Christ was a present as well as a future reality, which would radically alter the lives and perceptions of those who were called to realize it. In this kingdom the distinctions and barriers between male and female were to be broken down. In fact, in the history of the contemplative life in the Christian west, the distinctions often tended to be obscured. The contemplative life continued to be an arena in which the personal and collective human quest to become filled with God was a lived reality to which both women and men gave themselves equally. For the Christian contemplative to become fully human was also to become transfigured by the divine; in the actualization of this process one came to see that the structures and distinctions observed in the untransfigured world would give way to a more unitive vision that saw likeness more than dissimilarity and commonality more than disparity.

In becoming transfigured, the individual was directed by the ideas and language of the Christian world, for the shaping of personality is always a communal as well as a singular venture. The central model for transfiguration was Jesus Christ, whose life and death and resurrection were understood to encode the very nature of God Himself and thus give humankind access to the divine life through incorporation into Christ. The dynamic of the process of incorporation, seen from the perspective of the human being, was progressive death to self corresponding to an influx of the divine. The process was both linear and cyclical: the dying to self and being raised to God was ultimately achieved only over a lifetime, but this rhythm repeated itself in discreet events during the course of a day or in the course of a liturgical year. The images and liturgical practices of the tradition facilitated this transformative process.

The Christ model presented the contemplative Christian with an image of a perfected human whose stance in the world and with the divine was profoundly relational. He taught a way of being in the world that engaged him as son, master, friend and brother. He came to both God and neighbor in love and in service. Similarly, the image of the Christian God was also a relational one. God was experienced as actively involved in the creation He had made. Thus the contemplative was challenged to become transfigured in such a way that he or she would become just such a relational being. The two aspects of this relatedness found in Christ and indeed in God Himself are the aspects of love and death. And of course the most obvious and important symbol that expresses the intimate bond between these two modes of relationship in the tradition is the crucifixion-resurrection symbol. In it the depths of both love and death are plumbed and given significance on metaphysical, historical and personal planes.

The language of the contemplative tradition, which both expresses the experience and provides the means by which the individual gives meaning to and thereby actuates the transformation in his or her self, is likewise relational in this twofold way. Love and death are the two central themes with which the contemplative actualizes the life he or she has chosen. We have observed the process by which this relational language transfigured the life of Jeanne de Chantal. Through the vocabulary and assumptions underlying what we have referred to as the "language of desire," which seems to have received its original formulation from Gregory the Great, Jeanne entered into the manifold dimensions of the love experience in Christianity. This affective language shaped her orientation to the divine as well as made possible her intimate association with François de Sales. This language of desire drew upon her own innate capacity for loving relationship; it nuanced, clarified and directed it.

Similarly, the tradition contained a language of death, of dying to self, which was operative in the transformative process. It gave to the direction of Jeanne's individual growth a particular character which, once again, deeply affected her own person, her relationship with God and her association with François. The rhythms of love and death, of dying and rising, were the framework within which all of this woman's, and indeed many Christian contemplatives', relationships were worked out. The love and death model articulated the way in which the Christian understood virtually all of reality. The model is present in the conceptions about divinity itself, in the way in which Christians understood the creation of the world, the nature of the Godhead, the purpose of humankind's existence, and the fall and redemption of all humankind. It is graphically marked upon the figure of Jesus Christ who died for perfect love of God and neighbor. Likewise, it is found in conceptions about the way in which the contemplative transformative process takes place within the human soul. Lastly, the love and death model, as we have seen in the preceding pages, is found in the very way in which human relationships are undertaken and evolved.

Spiritual friendship in a Christian context is thus a specific type of relationship between two people in which the language of love and death provides parameters and direction. It is a relationship which is understood to exist within the context of other relationships, most particularly with God. It is a relationship which exists side by side with the relationship with God as well as side by side with the unique development of the individual person. All of these progressive and changing dynamics exist simultaneously at different levels and follow essentially the same pattern: an alternating and ever shifting pattern of loving and dying, self-emptying and being filled, union and absence, intimacy and isolation. They are all related in a complex way; and though the relationship between God and the soul

is usually seen as the paramount relationship, it is not the only relationship. Though it retains priority over self and other, it does not
necessarily act to negate these relationships. Rather it serves to
bring them to a closer connection with itself and to a deeper realization of their own nature.

This study has focused upon a friendship between a man and a
woman and suggests that such associations are surprisingly frequent
in the annals of the contemplative tradition when one considers the
strong intellectual and practical obstacles presented not only by the
wider European culture but by the Christian church itself. One frequent way of interpreting these friendships is to dispose of them by
claiming for them supernatural origins and by asserting that they are
thus impossible to study as a human phenomenon.[1] The participants
themselves would avow that they experienced some large measure
of the "supernatural" in their union. But this does not negate the
reality of a very human relationship between a man and a woman.
Likewise, the recurrence of these friendships does not simply point
to the periodic anomalous intrusion of the divine into an essentially
corrupt creation but to the possibility, latent in both the ideology
and practice of the Christian faith as well as in human nature, of
cultivating a receptive human ground out of which the divine, like
a well-tended plant, emerges.

In the case of François de Sales and Jeanne de Chantal, who
most emphatically celebrated the supernatural origin and direction
of their long association, the "human" dimension was not left
behind but incorporated and transformed. It should be remembered
that the bishop had a special charism for the direction of women, a
practice that, even in his situation, was thought to be a dubious and
unnecessary undertaking. François was neither afraid of his calling
nor naive about it. As "supernaturally" directed as he was in this
venture, he never lost sight of the human dynamics of male and
female interaction. In his *Introduction to the Devout Life* he shows
himself carefully aware of the possible motives of such liaisons and
of the boundaries they should observe in order to remain the type
of friendship they were intended to be.[2] In his very insightful analysis, which is sensitive to the subtlety as well as the potential of
encounter between the sexes, François de Sales shows that he understands that the love of God is not in opposition to human love but
the source of that love and its inspiration. Similarly, in his encoun-

ters with actual women he did not see himself either as endangered or as necessarily rising above the complex tensions that can beset such encounters. He made a practice, when beginning a relationship with any woman penitent, of consigning the future of the union to the Virgin Mary with the words:

> I hope in Our Lady that never will any other fire enkindle our hearts except that of the holy love of her son.[3]

Then he entered fully into the relationship, calling upon his rich affective reserves, his empathy and his capacity for meaningful human interaction to see him through. Always, though, he was acutely conscious of the goal of any union. Deeply immersed in his own perception of God in every act and event in human life, François never lost sight of the end of that life. He believed in the necessity for the possibility of the transformation of the individual into the accurate image of God known in Christ. Each person was to become a perfect lover of God. In this process, as has been shown, the capacity for human love was not to be denied but gathered up and incorporated into the fullness of love. Love of God did imply some necessary detachment from created things in and of themselves; however this did not negate creation but gave it deep significance. Creation, and this meant particularly persons, was not to be grasped and used for one's own satisfactions or libidinous ends; persons were revelatory of the divine; they, as well as oneself, were proceeding to the actualization of their own individual integrity as well as to the perfection of their collective reality. Persons were to be met and were to aid one another in the crucial human task at hand. They were to be loved within the context of the love of God which gave a wide expansiveness to their love and created certain strictures by which the practical expressions of that love were bound. Love was understood to be the dynamic in the human soul that propelled it, as well as drew it, to its proper end. All loves, when rightly oriented, moved in the same direction.

A friendship that was also spiritual, a love between a man and a woman, could potentially engage the two partners in a manner that could have unique consequences for their development. I would like to suggest that the male/female spiritual friendship differs from friendships between members of the same sex in a significant way.

Though there are many examples of associations between men or between women that have been central in the religious maturation of the partners, there is a special quality to the male and female friendship. An intimacy between members of the opposite sex seems to have the capacity to bring into being a whole range of personal response that creates a psychological climate in which one is drawn out of his or her habitual sense of self. It has long been a seminal practice in Christian asceticism to try to create a psychological environment in which the individual's normal sense of perception and orientation to reality is altered. The motives behind fasting, solitude, silence, prolonged wakefulness, extreme poverty and other physical and mental mortifications are not simply athletic. They are spiritual. They produce a different perception of the nature of reality. This altered state may, in extreme cases, become what we might consider paranormal. Usually, however, it is a less dramatic but nonetheless radical perceptual change that is sought and achieved. The ascetic seeks a unitive and transfigured vision of all creation. He or she seeks the present reality of the promised kingdom. Stripping away the ordinary constructions of life can aid in this realization.

I would suggest that the male/female spiritual friendship has as one of its principal dynamics this stripping away of one's habituated way of being. With Jeanne de Chantal and François de Sales, the whole range of that complex phenomenon, love, was operative in their union. The pure love of God provided the overarching goal and context for their association; a fully experienced desire for each other's presence leavened and propelled them; their love for each other as equals with a shared life task bonded them more deeply; the conscious recognition of the other expressions that a man and woman's love might take was present but not acted upon. All these modalities of love existed in their friendship. Like two skillful dancers threading their way artfully through the intricate patterns of several simultaneous dances, François and Jeanne lived out the full range of human and divine love of which the Christian tradition knew. Love took these two out of themselves. It created between them not simply a place in which they felt "at home" or affirmed in their perception of how things are and should be. It also created a place of a certain tension. It was a place in which complacency could be startled into insight, in which the person, ordinarily safely contained and invulnerable in a discreet self, could be vaulted into sudden vulnerability. It was a place in which the boundaries between self and other merged and confused the habituated sense of perception. Like the time-honored practices of asceticism, the intimate contact between a man and woman could produce a state in which the perceived self was disturbed. A certain death to this perceived self occurred, and in the occurrence a breach was created into which God could enter.

The man-woman friendship was also a place in which the totally other was encountered, and this could have a profound effect on personal development. Although neither Jeanne nor François was likely to transgress their vows of chastity, they were nonetheless aware of the very powerful human dynamics that can engage men and women. This is clear from François practice of petitioning to the Virgin Mary as well as from Jeanne's account in her *Deposition* that she knew that her friend's vows had been tested on several occasions in his career.[4] They were not oblivious to the possible tension existing with the "other" on this level, and this no doubt had the effect of causing a certain amount of creative tension in the relationship, causing reflection upon the nature of love and catalyzing the entire spectrum of the love experience which they perceived as both human and divine.

Nor were they unmoved by their respective otherness in different ways. Modern research has suggested that men and women's psychological development may be quite different—men exhibiting greater concern for autonomy and achievement, women being oriented toward relationships of interdependence.[5] This would suggest that the sexes bring to the life-cycle a different moral point of view and set of priorities. In François' and Jeanne's relationship this certainly seems to have been the case. What their shared friendship added to their lives was an intense experience of "the other," an actual interior encounter with the heart of the opposite sex to the enrichment of each of them. We have seen how insightful François was when it came to the direction of women. He seems to have had a certain empathetic yet distanced perspective on the "feminine" pitfalls in the spiritual life as well as such strengths. He brought this perspective to his friendship with Jeanne and gently molded her inner life to compensate for its weaknesses and develop its strengths. Likewise, Jeanne brought an otherness to her intimacy with François. Her deep affective life, nurtured and enriched by her marriage and by her years of motherhood, gave to her love, and this extended to both François and God, a unique depth, warmth and resiliency that was her own. She was thus not simply a woman by gender but through her assimilation and embodiment of the womanly roles she had played. Always the two of them seemed to play off each other and to receive insight and strength from what was complementary in the other. What on one level was undoubtedly simply a complement of personality factors was heightened and richly nuanced by the otherness of their respective maleness and femaleness.

The male and female spiritual friendship also provides a unique context in which both the symbolism embodied in the Christian marriage relationship and the symbolism acted out in the religious celibate state are given full opportunity for simultaneous expression. Marriage is a human relationship in which the images of union and creativity are explicit. The man and woman come together and are made one; that union results in the creation of new life. Marriage is a celebration of the relatedness and dependency of the person in relationship both to God and to fellow persons. In marriage one does not belong to oneself but to the other. Celibacy on the other hand celebrates the essential solitude of the person. It is a state of life that bespeaks not the multiplicity of being in the world that marriage does, but the singularity of that being. Just as marriage as a symbol proclaims the rightness of love in the God-created world, so celibacy proclaims the rightness of the death experienced in self-denial and self-emptying. In a spiritual friendship such as the one Jeanne and François enjoyed, both of these realities, love and death, are equally present both symbolically and in practice. Their presence allows for a wide range of human interaction in which the transformation of the person into the image of God in Christ is easily facilitated. This is not to suggest that in either marriage or celibacy the presence of both love and death as individual and interpersonal dynamics is not operative. It is simply to say that there is a more explicit mix of the two in a male and female spiritual friendship as well as to point out that in Christian marriage the issue of solitary and individual development has perhaps been traditionally understressed while in the celibate world the value of human relationships and their cultivation has likewise traditionally been slighted.

In Jeanne's and François' friendship one finds both trium-
phantly celebrated. The creativity and reproductivity latent in any
encounter between members of the opposite sex and made explicit
in Christian marriage springs to life in their interchange. They gave
birth, as it were, to each other. This we have seen clearly in her case.
Jeanne de Chantal began as a gifted but as yet unrealized lover of
God and through the tempering of her contact with François de
Sales came to the mature realization of both her own personal potential as well as the vast human potential signaled by the religious tradition she embraced. Moreover, this friendship was creative of an
entirely new entity as well, the "us" that transcended them singly,
and this new entity was present in many ways in the Order of the
Visitation that they founded. Each gave to their progeny their
unique gifts and each served in its nurturing in distinctive ways. The
result was not merely an institution that outlived them but a particular spirit or way of being in the world. It had his features: an unobtrusive yet infinitely gracious exterior coupled with a self-effacing
taste for total interior denudement. But it had her temperament: a
passionate fidelity to love reflected in a simple and utterly abandoned
life of prayer.

Coupled with this creativity their friendship also exhibited the
singleness of purpose and vision so aptly symbolized in the celibate
state. They knew a deeply human love, a love that made full use of
all the dynamics inherent in itself, but their love did not become an
end in itself. The energies of their love were gathered up into an
exquisitely actualized pure love of God, a love all the more pure, in
this author's mind, because it did not turn its back on the "lower"
forms of love but incorporated and transformed those "lower"
forms into itself. All the radical solitude and the single focused
dependence upon God alone found in religious celibacy was theirs.

This friendship that Jeanne de Chantal and François de Sales
shared was known to their contemporaries, at least in its outlines. It
was one of these, Vincent de Paul, himself steeped in the contemplative tradition and a close companion to both of the friends, who
in symbolic form seems to have grasped the nature of the friendship
they experienced. It was a relationship at one and the same time
honoring their separate integrities and their intimate union and
which bore them together to the full human actualization to which
they aspired. In 1641 while Jeanne was dying in Moulins, Vincent

de Paul was in Paris praying for this woman he so admired. He
reported that at that time he was the recipient of a vision which gave
him insight into the remarkable soul whose passing was imminent
and into her relationship with François and of their relationship
together with the divine.

> There appeared to him a small globe of fire which rose from the
> earth to the upper regions of the air to be united with another
> globe which was larger and more luminous, then these two
> became one, mounting even higher, entering and being incor-
> porated into yet another globe which was infinitely greater and
> more resplendent than the others. . . .[6]

NOTES

INTRODUCTION

1. By the contemplative tradition of the Christian church I mean generally that thread of thought and personal orientation through the church's history that has been primarily concerned with the personal relationship between the individual and the divine. The focus of this tradition is most often upon the growing intimacy of the individual and deity through the process of prayer. The contemplative life may or may not be lived out in an institutional setting. In the Christian past it typically has taken a monastic form.

2. The evolution of François de Sales in the context of the friendship has been treated by other authors. Henri Bremond is chief among these. See his *Histoire littéraire du sentiment religieux en France depuis la fin des guerres de religion jusqu'à nos jours*, Vol. II, *L'invasion mystique* (Paris: Bloud et Gay, 1921) pp. 537–84. English translation: *A Literary History of Religious Thought in France*, Vol. II, *The Mystic Invasion* (New York: Macmillan Co., 1980). Also see Bremond's *Sainte Chantal* (Paris: J. Gabalda, 1912).

3. See Carolyn Walker Bynum, *Jesus as Mother, Studies in the Spirituality of the High Middle Ages* (London: Univ. of California Press, 1982) pp. 7, 17ff, 110–69, 170–262. The ability to identify with images of either sex in one's devotional life must be set against the context of the equalitarian anthropology that the early Christian community appears to have cultivated and which was retained in the contemplative tradition.

Certainly it is valid to argue for a distinctive feminine piety or mysticism and to try to chart its outlines [see Michael Goodich, "The Contours of Female Piety in Later Medieval Hagiography" in *Church History*, Vol. 50 (1981) pp. 20–32 and Bynum, pp. 170–262] but it should not be assumed that women leaned more to female imagery or were more "feminine" (i.e., more affective or nurturing) in their devotion than men.

4. It is my impression that in general men and women in the contemplative tradition of the early seventeenth century could, like their early

Christian and late medieval counterparts, see themselves as realizing a vision of humanity beyond sexual differentiation. See Eleanor McLaughlin, "Women, Power and the Pursuit of Holiness in Medieval Christianty" in *Women of Spirit: Female Leadership in the Jewish and Christian Tradition,* ed. Rosemary Ruether and Eleanor McLaughlin (New York: Simon and Schuster, 1979) pp. 100–30; Elizabeth Schussler Fiorenza, "Word, Spirit and Power: Women in Early Christian Communities" in the same volume pp. 29–70; Jo Ann McNamara, "Sexual Equality and the Cult of Virginity in Early Christian Thought" in *Feminist Studies,* Vol. III, no. 3/4 (1976), pp. 145–58. In the case of Jeanne de Chantal, however, while she and her contemporaries accepted her quest for holiness as easily and equally as they might a man's, she herself seems much more defined by her female roles than many other women in the tradition. This is presumably because she did not enter religious life until the age of thirty-eight and had been wife, mother, companion and widow before this.

5. At times the language of hagiography seems the correct language of interpretation because of Jeanne's own self-understanding. I have steered away from psycho-history in the mode of Erik Erikson, although I have been somewhat influenced by Jean Leclercq's attempt at psychological probing found in *Monks and Love in Twelfth Century France: Psycho-historical Essays* (Oxford: Clarendon Press, 1979) to the extent that I have found, in his subtle phenomenology of the monastic set of mind, an authority to harken to when I attempt a description of Jeanne's orientation and point of view. But I agree with Carolyn Walker Bynum in her review of *Monks and Love* in *Speculum,* Vol. 55 (1980) pp. 595–97 that some of what Leclercq attempted in the psycho-historical realm is questionable and fraught with methodological problems.

6. The reader is referred to Leclercq's view of the problem of the contemporary interpreter's approaching a medieval religious figure: *Monks and Love,* introduction. Also, for an exploration of this theme using the imagery of the Christian contemplative tradition, see Wendy M. Wright, "The Feminine Dimension of Contemplation" in *The Feminist Mystic,* ed. Mary Giles (New York: Crossroad, 1982), pp. 103–119.

The danger of superimposing a psychological interpretation upon the spiritual friendships of the past is that too often such an attempt does not take into account the extent to which personal motives, actions and interpretations are deeply influenced and shaped by prevalent cultural expectations and assumptions. This study will proceed on the premise that the early seventeenth century Christian world's understanding of the nature of love is an appropriate "factual" basis for examining the spiritual friendships of that period. But the reader is referred to *Spiritual Pilgrims: Carl*

Jung and Teresa of Avila by John Welch (New York: Paulist Press, 1982) which correlates the language of the Swiss psychologist and the Spanish mystic.

7. For a slightly different but complementary perspective on the contemplative mode of perception see Walter H. Capps and Wendy M. Wright, "The Contemplative Mode" in *Studia Mystica*, Vol. I, No. 1 (1978). For a cross-cultural examination of the contemplative experience see Raimundo Panikkar, *Blessed Simplicity: The Monk As Universal Archetype* (New York: Seabury Press, 1982).

8. On this see Bynum, *Jesus as Mother*, p. 87. Her essay in this collection on "Did the Twelfth Century Discover the Individual?" (pp. 82–109) raises the issues about another conception of the individual that can be juxtaposed to the modern one. Her assertions seem accurate and, in a general sense, applicable to my definition of "the contemplative life" as well as to the twelfth century Christian.

9. For a multifaceted critique of this generally unquestioned assumption see *Mysticism and Philosophical Analysis,* ed. Steven T. Katz (New York: Oxford Univ. Press, 1978).

10. Bynum, *Jesus as Mother*, p. 90.

11. The article "Contemplation" in the *Dictionnaire de spiritualité mystique et ascétique,* Vol. II, pt. 2, pp. 1643–2194, contains a detailed analysis of the nature of contemplation in the Christian tradition and gives an excellent idea of the varied and changing conceptions of the term "contemplation" itself.

12. On the Catholic as lover of God cf. J. Calvet, *La littérature religieuse de François de Sales à Fénelon* (Paris: del Duca, 1956) p. 10.

13. For a discussion of the various, changing understandings of the nature of the human soul in the Catholic tradition see the article by L. Reypens, "Ame (son fond, ses puissances et sa structure d'après les mystiques)" in *Dictionnaire de spiritualité ascétique et mystique,* Vol. I, pp. 433–69.

14. E. M. Lajeunie in his *St. François de Sales et l'esprit salesian* (Bourges: Editions du Seuil, 1962) includes a helpful description of François de Sales' particular formulation of the Christian life and his understanding of the soul.

The reader is further referred to François de Sales, *Traité de l'amour de Dieu,* Chaps 12–13. French edition found in *Oeuvres. Edition complète d'après les autographes et les éditions originales,* par les soins des Religieuses de la Visitation du Premier Monastère d'Annecy (Annecy, 1892–1932), Tome IV, *Traité de l'amour de Dieu,* pp. 63–69.

15. This "fine point" of the soul is the Salesian variant of a mystical tradition which found its most articulate expression in the late medieval

Rheno-Flemish authors. See L. Reypens, 'Ame' article in *Dictionnaire de spiritualité* and Steven E. Ozment, *Homo Spiritualis. A Comparative Study of the Anthropology of Johannes Tauler, Jean Gerson and Martin Luther in the Context of Their Theological Thought* (Leiden: Brill, 1969).

16. See John G. Gager, *Kingdom and Community. The Social World of Early Christianity* (New Jersey: Prentice-Hall, 1975); Elisabeth Schussler Fiorenza, *In Memory of Her* (New York: Crossroad, 1983) and the same author's "Word, Spirit and Power: Women in Early Christian Communities" in *Women of Spirit. Female Leadership in the Jewish and Christian Traditions.* ed. Rosemary Ruether and Eleanor McLaughlin (New York: Simon and Schuster, 1979) pp. 29–70; Wayne Meeks, "The Image of Androgyne: Some Uses of a Symbol in Earliest Christianity" in *History of Religions*, Vol. 13, No. 3 (Feb. 1974), pp. 165–208; Robin Scroggs "The Earliest Christian Communities as Sectarian Movement" in *Christianity, Judaism and Other Greco-Roman Cults*, Part II *Early Christianity*, ed. Jacob Neusner (Leiden: E. J. Brill, 1975) pp. 1–23; Gerd Theissen, "Itinerant Radicalism: The Tradition of Jesus' Sayings from the Perspective of the Sociology of Literature" in *Radical Religion*, Vol. II, Nos. 2 & 3 (1975) (Berkeley: Community for Religious Research and Education), pp. 84–101; Elaine Pagels, *The Gnostic Gospels* (New York: Random House, 1979).

17. Raoul Mortley in his *Womanhood: The Feminine in Ancient Hellenism, Gnosticism, Christianity and Islam* (Sydney, Australia: Delacroix Press, 1981) makes a persuasive argument, from an historian of religion's point of view, that the Pauline text could not have any social implications and that whatever equality is referred to is a purely spiritual one. Stephen B. Clark's *Man and Woman in Christ. An Examination of the Roles of Men and Women in Light of Scripture and the Social Sciences* (Ann Arbor, Michigan: Servant Books, 1980) denies any equality from a different point of view. The reader is referred to a review of this large and in many ways impressive study by Reta Finger in *Sojourner's Magazine*, Vol. 10, no. 9 (Sept. 1981), pp. 31–32, which raises several fundamental questions about the assumptions underlying Clark's exegesis.

18. See especially Fiorenza, *In Memory*, pp. 108–18.

19. For a study of the ramifications of Paul's intention, see Tavard, *Women in the Christian Tradition* (Notre Dame, Indiana: Univ. of Notre Dame Press, 1973) pp. 28ff.

20. Found in *New Testament Apocrypha*, Vol. II (Philadelphia: Westminster, 1965) pp. 322–90. The book is discussed by both Fiorenza in "Word, Spirit and Power" and Rosemary Ruether in "Mothers of the Church" in *Women of Spirit*, pp. 72–97.

21. Cf. Rosemary Rader, *Breaking Boundaries: Male/Female Friendship in Early Christian Communities* (New Jersey: Paulist Press, 1983), pp.

18-31. Also, Derrick Sherwin Bailey, *Sexual Relation in Christian Thought* (New York: Harper and Row, 1959) pp. 1-7. Tavard, *Women in the Christian Tradition*, pp. 27ff, sees two strands of orientation toward the female coming from the Jewish tradition: one positive, one negative.

22. Aristotle's theories informed not only Christian theology but western medical assumptions about women. See Vern L. Bullough, "Medieval Medical and Scientific Views of Women" in *Viator*, Vol. 4 (1973) (Berkeley: Univ. of California Press) pp. 485-501.

23. See Fiorenza, "Word, Spirit and Power" and Tavard, *Women in the Christian Tradition*, pp. 28ff.

24. The most recent treatment of the "agapatae" is by Rosemary Rader, *Breaking Boundaries*, pp. 63ff. See also her article in *The Continuing Quest for God: Monastic Spirituality in Tradition and Transition* (Collegeville, Minnesota: The Liturgical Press, 1982), pp. 80-87. See too the older entry by H. Achelis in the *Hasting's Encyclopedia of Religion and Ethics*, pp. 177-180 and his *Virgenes Subintroductae* (Leipzig: J. D. Hinrich, 1902). He sees the origins of the phenomenon in the ascetic impulse, viewing it as an attempt on the part of the couple to practice a rigorous form of sexual denial. Pierre de Labriolle, in his "Le mariage spirituel dans l'antiquité chrétienne", *Revue Historique* 138 (1921) pp. 205-25, picks up where he leaves off.

25. Cf. A. Vööbis, *A History of Asceticism in the Syrian Orient, O, Corpus Scriptorum Christianorum Orientalium*, Subsidia 14 (Louvain, 1958), pp. 326-48.

26. Achelis claims that the custom of "syneisakte" was widespread in the Celtic church as do L. Gougaud *Les Chrétientés celtiques* (Paris, 1911) and Roger E. Reynolds, "Virgenes Subintroductae in Celtic Christianity," *Harvard Theological Review*, 61 (October 1968). Ludwig Bieler, *Ireland: Harbinger of the Middle Ages* (London: Oxford Univ. Press, 1963), p. 25, and Nora Chadwick, *The Age of Saints in the Early Celtic Church* (London: Oxford Univ. Press, 1961), dismiss the evidence put forward as not representative of true spiritual friendship.

27. See Rader, *Breaking Boundaries*, p. 66.

28. The Latin of Jerome's letters with French translation of the letter is found in *Saint Jérôme: Lettres*. Tome I (Paris: Société d'Edition "Les Belles Lettres," 1949), pp. 110-60 especially pp. 122-41. A translation of Chrysostom's treatises on the subintroductae can be found in Elizabeth A. Clark, *Jerome, Chrysostom and Friends: Essays and Translations* (New York: Edwin Mellen Press, 1979), pp. 158-248.

29. The early Christian communities in northern Mesopotamia were both communal and celibate and pre-date the monasteries of the fourth century. See A. Vööbus, *A History of Asceticism in the Syrian Orient*, pp. 68ff.

30. Thomas Merton describes the monk in this fashion.

31. Gager, *Kingdom and Community*, p. 49.

32. Elizabeth A. Clark bases her understanding of male/female friendships between two leading church fathers on this point: *Jerome, Chrysostom and Friends*.

For examples of this transsexual phenomenon (with an analysis that, to my mind, makes too much of the neurotic anti-feminism of monasticism and not enough of the philosophical and religious assumptions underlying the practice) see John Anson, "The Female Transvestite in Early Monasticism: The Origin and Development of a Motif" in *Viator*, Vol. 5 (1974), pp. 1–32.

33. Cf. *Athanasius. The Life of Antony and the Letter to Marcellinus*, trans. & intro. by Robert C. Gregg (New York: Paulist Press, 1980) pp. 2ff.

34. Ruether, "Mothers of the Church" in *Women of Spirit*.

35. On Jerome and women see Clark, *Jerome, Chrysostom and Friends*, as well as Jerome's letter to Eustochium (cf. note 27) and his funeral oration for Paula in *Saint Jérôme, Lettres,* Tome V, pp. 159–201. Cf. Rader, *Breaking Boundaries*, pp. 94ff.

36. The chief source for those figures is the *Life* of Melania the Younger. There are two versions: in Latin, *Analecta Bollandiana* VIII (Paris: 1889) pp. 16–63; in Greek, *ibid.*, xxii (1903) pp. 5–50.

37. See Clark, *Jerome, Chrysostom and Friends* for a translation of the *Life of Olympias*. Also refer to Henriette Dacier, *Saint Jean Chrysostome et la femme chrétienne au IV⁰ siècle de l'église grecque* (Paris: Librairie H. Falque, 1907) as well as to A. M. Malingrey, ed., *Jean Chrysostome: Lettres à Olympias* in *Sources chrétiennes*, ed. H. de Lubac, Vol. 13, Paris, 1942.

38. St. Augustine, *On the Holy Trinity*, trans. by A. W. Haddan and W. G. T. Shedd in *Select Library of Nicene Fathers* (Buffalo, 1887), III, p.159.

39. Bailey, *Sexual Relation*, pp. 69ff.

40. *Life of Saint Leoba* by Rudolf, Monk of Fulda, trans. C. H. Talbot in *The Anglo-Saxon Missionaries in Germany* (New York, 1954), pp. 205–26.

41. *Ibid.*, p. 222.

42. However, evidence shows that many of the Anglo-Saxon missioner priests did enjoy the friendships of their female counterparts. Cf. Comte de Montalembert, *Les moines d'occident* (Paris: J. Lecoffre, 1867), Tome 5, pp. 230ff. Eng. trans. *The Monks of the West* (New York: P. J. Kenedy & Sons, 1955) Vol. II, pp. 645ff.

43. For an older but still informative overview see Lina Eckenstein, *Woman Under Monasticism* (New York: Russell & Russell, 1963 reprint

of 1896 edition). Also for individual studies of a large number of medieval women consult *Medieval Religious Women*, ed. John Nichols, 3 vols. (Kalamazoo, Michigan: Cistercian Pub., 1984–85).

44. Cf. Eleanor McLaughlin, "Women, Power and the Pursuit of Holiness in Medieval Christianity" in *Women of Spirit*, pp. 100–30.

45. See Michael Goodich, "The Contours of Female Piety in Later Medieval Hagiography" in *Church History*, Vol. 50 (1981) pp. 20–32.

46. Bynum's *Jesus as Mother*, pp. 110–69, contains the best recent account of this, with excellent bibliographic references.

47. *Ibid.*

48. On the androgynous nature of medieval devotion see McLaughlin, "Women, Power." Also, for an example of an eleventh century theologian's positive treatment of both "the feminine" and particular women, see Jean Leclercq, "S. Pierre Damien et les femmes" in *Studia Monastica*, Vol. 15 (1973), pp. 43–56.

49. A clear discussion of Thomas' theological position on women is found in Eleanor Commo McLaughlin, "Equality of Souls, Inequality of Sexes: Woman in Medieval Society" in *Religion and Sexism*, pp. 213–66. This part of her article relies upon the scholarship of Kari Elisabeth Børresen, *Subordination et équivalence, nature et rôle de la femme d'après Augustin et Thomas d'Aquin* (Paris, 1963).

50. See Bullough, "Medieval Scientific Views."

51. See A. Hamilton Thompson, "Double Monasteries and the Male Element in Nunneries" in *The Ministry of Women. A Report by a Committee appointed by the Archbishop of Canterbury* (London: Society for Promoting Christian Knowledge; New York: Macmillan Co., 1919) pp. 145–64. Also, Mary Bateson, "Origin and History of Double Monasteries" in *Transactions of the Royal Historical Society*, 13 (1899) pp. 137–98.

52. R. W. Southern, *Western Society and the Church in the Middle Ages* (England: Hammondsworth, 1970) p. 314.

53. A rather dated but highly empathetic portrait of the relationship between Francis and Clare is to be found in Le P. Léopold de Chérancé, *Sainte Claire d'Assise* (Paris: Librarie Charles Poussielque, 1901). See also *The Legend and Writings of St. Clare of Assisi* (St. Bonaventure, New York: The Franciscan Institute, 1953).

54. On the relationship between these two Dominicans, see Gerald Vann, *To Heaven with Diana. A Study of Jordan of Saxony and Diana d'Andalo with a Translation of the Letters of Jordan* (Chicago: Henry Regnery Co., 1965) and *Love Among the Saints. The Letters of Blessed Jordan of Saxony to Blessed Diana of Andalo*, trans. Kathleen Pond (London: Bloomsbury Pub. Co., 1958).

55. Vann, *To Heaven with Diana*, p. 34.

56. For an excellent analysis of the correspondence between Abelard and Héloïse which places it in the context of the epistolary genre without which it is easily misunderstood, see R. W. Southern, "The Letters of Abelard and Héloïse" in his *Medieval Humanism and Other Studies* (Oxford: Basil Blackwell, 1970) pp. 86–104. The reader is also referred to the classic study by Etienne Gilson, *Héloïse et Abelard* (Paris: Librairie Philosophique J. Vrin, 1948). A critical edition of the *Historia calamitatum* and of the correspondence between the two friends is available by J. T. Muckle C.S.B. See *Medieval Studies*, XII (1950) pp. 163–213; XV (1953), pp. 47–94; XVII (1955) pp. 249–81; XVIII (1956) pp. 241–92.

57. *The Life of Christina of Markyate: A Twelfth Century Recluse*, trans. and ed. by C. H. Talbot (Oxford: Clarendon Press, 1959).

58. *Ibid.*, p. 103.

59. Consult Augusta Theodosia Drane, *The History of St. Catherine of Siena and Her Companions* (London: Longmans, Green and Co., 1915).

60. Catherine of Genoa's work and life were made famous by Baron Friedrich von Hugel's study *The Mystical Element of Religion as Studied in Saint Catherine of Genoa and Her Friends*, 2 vols. (London: J. M. Dent & Co., 1909). On the friendship with Ettore Vernazza see pp. 145ff and 316–35.

61. On the controversy about women see Th. Schueller, *La femme et le saint: La femme et ses problèmes d'après saint François de Sales* (Paris: Les Editions ouvrières, 1970) pp. 36ff., and *Not In God's Image*, ed. by Julia O'Faolain and Lauro Martines (London: Temple Smith, 1973) pp. 169ff.

62. It has been shown that the ascetic tradition did have an offspring in the Radical Reformation in the Anabaptist communities. See Kenneth Ronald Davis, *Anabaptism and Asceticism. A Study in Intellectual Origins* (Scottsdale, Pennyslvania: Herald Press, 1974).

63. Roland Bainton, *Women of the Reformation, from Spain to Scandinavia* (Minneapolis: Augsburg Pub. House, 1977). Patrick Collinson "The Role of Women in the English Reformation Illustrated by the Life and Friendships of Anne Locke" in *Studies in Church History*, Vol. 2 (1965).

64. On the emergence of women's congregations see Ruth P. Liebowitz, "Virgins in the Service of Christ: The Dispute Over an Active Apostolate for Women During the Counter-Reformation " in *Women of Spirit*, pp. 131–52.

65. On the condition of French women during the seventeenth century see Henriette Houillon, "La femme en France aux XVIIe et XVIIIe siècles" in *Histoire mondiale de la femme*, publié sous la direction de Pierre Grimal (Paris: Nouvelle Librarie de France, 1966) pp. 9–98.

66. Bailey, *Sexual Relation*, p. 179.

67. This appearance may be due mainly to the labors of French scholars, especially Henri Bremond. See his *Histoire littéraire du sentiment religieux en France depuis la fin des guerres de religion jusqu'à nos jours*, 3 vols. (Paris: Bloud et Gay, 1916). Eng. trans.: *A Literary History of Religious Thought* (New York: Macmillian Co., 1930).

68. Cf. J. Calvet, *Louise de Marillac par elle-même* (Paris: Les Editions Montaigne, 1958). English language edition: *Louise de Marillac. A Portrait*, trans. G. F. Pullen (New York: P. J. Kenedy & Sons, 1959).

See also Saint Vincent de Paul. *Correspondence, Entretiens, Documents*, ed. publ. par Pierre Cost (Paris: Librairie Lecoffre J. Gabalda, 1923).

69. Bremond, *Histoire littéraire*, Vol. II, *L'invasion mystique*, pp. 186ff.

70. On Madame Acarie see *ibid.*, Vol. II, pp. 192ff.

71. *Ibid.*, pp. 27–54.

72. Quoted in *ibid.*, p. 31.

73. L'Abbé Huvelin, *Quelques directeurs d'âmes au XVIIe siècle* (Paris: Librarie Victor Lecoffre, J. Gabalda & Cie, 1911), pp. 79–134. Also consult Frédéric Monier, *Vie de Jean-Jacques Olier*, 2 vols. (Paris: Ancienne Librairie Poussielque, 1914).

74. Cf. Bremond, *Histoire littéraire*, Vol. III, *La Conquête mystique*, pp. 590ff and R. P. Emile Georges, *Saint Jean Eudes* (Paris: P. Lethielleux, Libraire-Editeur, 1925).

75. On Madame Guyon and Fénelon, refer to Michael de la Bedoyere, *The Archbishop and the Lady. The Story of Fénelon and Madame Guyon* (New York: Pantheon Books, 1956). Cf. also *Madame Guyon et Fénelon. La correspondence secrète*. Ed. Benjamin Sabler (Paris: Dervy-Levres, 1982). For the story of Angelique Arnauld and St. Cyran, consult Louis Cognet, *La Mère Angélique et Saint-Cyran (1634–1643)* (Paris: Editions Sulliver, 1953).

76. On these two friendships of Teresa's, consult *The Life of Saint Teresa* by Alice Lady Lovat (London: Simpkin, Marshall, Hamilton, Kent and Co., 1914), pp. 311ff, 360ff, 400ff, 439ff. Historical data that links the two saints is limited but the interaction between them has been analyzed by Maryvonne Bonnard "Les Influences réciproques entre sainte Thérèse et saint Jean de la Croix," in *Bulletin Hispanique*, Tome XXVII (1935), no. 2 (Avril–Juin), pp. 129–48 as well as by R. Garigou-Lagrange, "L'Accord et les différences de sainte Thérèse et de saint Jean de la Croix" in *La vie spirituelle, ascétique et mystique*, Supp., 1936, pp. 107–116.

77. On the "beatas" cf. M. Bataillon, *Erasme et l'Espagne: Recherches L'histoire spirituelle du XVIe siècle* (Paris: Librairie E. Droz, 1937), pp. 190ff. Another Spaniard of the period, Ignatius of Loyola, produced what amounts to a sizable volume of correspondence to women, but it is doubtful whether any of his relationships with these women could be considered

genuine spiritual friendships. See Saint Ignatius Loyola, *Letters to Women,* ed. Hugo Rahner (Edinburgh-London: Nelson, 1960).

78. Sister Colette Ackerman, O.C.D. and Father Joseph Healy, M.M., "Bonded in Mission: Reflections on Prayer and Evangelization" in *Spiritual Life,* Vol. 27, No. 2 (Summer 1981) pp. 90–104.

79. Ste. Thérèse de l'Enfant-Jésus, *Histoire d'une âme, écrite par elle-meme* (Lisieux et Paris: Office central de Lisieux, 1944). Eng. trans.: *Story of a Soul: The Autobiography of St. Thérèse of Lisieux,* trans. John Clark (Washington: ICS Publications, 1975), pp. 251ff. The saint's letters to her two spiritual brothers, Maurice Barthélemy-Bellière and Adolphe Roulland, are found in Sainte Thérèse de l'Enfant-Jésus et de la Sainte-Face, *Correspondance générale,* Tome II (Paris: Desclée de Brouwer, Editions du Cerf, 1972).

80. *Letters of Herbert Cardinal Vaughn to Lady Herbert Lea, 1867–1903,* ed. Shane Leslie (London, 1942).

81. Pierre Teilhard de Chardin, *Lettres à Léontine Zanta* (Paris: Desclée de Brouwer, 1965) (English trans.: New York: Harper and Row, 1968).

82. Dorothy Day, *The Long Loneliness: The Autobiography of Dorothy Day* (New York: Harper, 1952).

83. Catherine de Hueck Doherty, *Poustinia: Christian Spirituality of the East for Western Man* (Notre Dame, Indiana: Ave Maria Press, 1975).

84. Thérèse of Lisieux may be quoted as an example of this spiritual understanding of the kingdom. "I understand, and I know by experience," she wrote, "that the kingdom of God is within us."

1. THE BEGINNING (1604–1605)

1. In reconstructing the progress of the friendship shared by Jeanne de Chantal and François de Sales, I have relied upon several sources. First, the Annecy edition of François de Sales' *Oeuvres. Edition complète d'après les autographs et les éditions originales,* par les soins des Religieuses de la Visitation du premier monastère d'Annecy (Annecy, 1892–1932), which is the standard critical edition, has been used when quoting the bishop's words. Jeanne's works are collected in an edition, *Sainte Jeanne-Françoise Frémyot de Chantal. Sa Vie et ses oeuvres* (Paris: Plon, 1874), which is neither critical nor complete. From the Plon volumes I have relied quite a bit upon the *Life* written by Mère Françoise-Madeleine de Chaugy which is found in Volume I. Mère de Chaugy was Jeanne's neice by marriage who took the veil at the Visitation. In 1632 she became her aunt's secretary and nearly constant companion until the foundress' death in 1641. Immediately after Jeanne's demise, the secretary took up her pen to affix her aunt's

memory in the minds of history. Her biography is thus informed by intimate contact with its central character as well as by her thorough familiarity with the life inaugurated by the woman she portrayed. Yet the *Life* has its drawbacks as a source. As it was intended to enroll Jeanne in the ranks of saintly individuals, it has some of the defects of hagiography as history. If this is kept in mind, the *Life* remains nonetheless an invaluable source of information and insight.

The translation from the French is my own. I bear the responsibility for whatever lack of grace or accuracy may occur. However, I have relied upon a very helpful glossary of François de Sales' spiritual vocabulary found in André Ravier's *François de Sales. Correspondance: Les lettres d'amitié spirituelle* (Paris, Desclée de Brouwer, 1980) pp. 761–872.

As of the writing of this piece, a new critical edition of the letters is in progress in the archives of the First Monastery of the Visitation in Annecy, France. It has yet to be published. The letters especially form the basis of my evaluation of Jeanne's personality. In them, she springs to life. While I remain responsible for many of the interpretations of Jeanne's motives and inner impulses, I have at all times tried to allow those interpretations to emerge naturally from the evidence. For confirmation and amplification of my views I remain indebted to Sr. Patricia Burns with whom I spent many hours in conversation during September 1981.

Some details in the narrative come from Elisabeth Stopp's contemporary biography of Madame de Chantal: *Madame de Chantal: Portrait of a Saint* (London: Faber and Faber, 1962). This fine piece of historical writing relied upon sources not possible for me to procure. Finally, a first-hand visit to the sites of Jeanne de Chantal's life, undertaken in the summer of 1981, supplied the innumerable observations and visual images that hopefully enliven the text.

2. *Mémoires sur la vie et les vertus de Sainte Jeanne-Françoise Frémyot de Chantal.* Par la Mère Françoise-Madeleine de Chaugy, in *Sa Vie et ses oeuvres*, Tome I, p. 40.

3. Jean Calvet, *La littérature religieuse de François de Sales à Fénelon* (Paris: del Duca, 1956), pp. 38–39.

4. François de Sales was indeed a master-craftsman in the art of preaching. For his own description of his craft, see François de Sales, *Oeuvres*, Tome XII, Lettres 2, p. 321. The letter has been translated into English and the saint as a preacher discussed by John K. Ryan, *On the Preacher and Preaching: A Letter by Francis de Sales* (U.S.A.: Henry Regnery Co., 1964).

5. *Sa vie et ses oeuvres*, Chaugy, p. 51.

6. *Oeuvres*, Tome XII, Lettres 2, p. 262.

7. On the Catholic Reformation in France see especially Louis Prunel, *La renaissance catholique en France au XVIIe siècle* (Paris: Desclée de Brouwer, 1921). More generally, consult *Jean Delameau, Le catholicism entre Luther et Voltaire* (Presses Universitaires de France, 1971). English translation: *Catholicism Between Luther and Voltaire: A New View of the Counter-Reformation,* (London: Burns and Oates, 1977) and John C. Olin in his *The Catholic Reformation: Savanrola to Ignatius Loyola,* (New York: Harper and Row, 1969).

8. Herbert Jedin, *A History of the Council of Trent* (St. Louis, Mo.: B. Herder Book Co., 1957).

9. The observance among the laity was essentially a matter of parochial conformity according to John Bossy in his article "The Counter-Reformation and the People of Catholic Europe" in *Past and Present,* no. 47 (May 1970), pp. 51–70.

10. The term "devout humanism" was coined by Henri Bremond in his *Histoire littéraire du sentiment religieux en France depuis la fin des guerres de religion jusqu'à nos jours,* Vol. I, *L'Humanisme dévot (1580–1660)* (Paris: Bloud et Gay, 1921). English translation: *A Litercry History of Religious Thought in France from the Wars of Religion down to Our Own Times* (New York: Macmillan Co., 1930). Bremond distinguishes between "devout" and "Christian" humanism by deeming the latter primarily speculative and aristocratic, the former practical and popular. There is a discussion of this distinction in Julian Eymard d'Angers' work, *L'humanisme chrétien au XVIIe siècle: St. François de Sales et Yves de Paris* (La Haye: Martinus Nijhoff, 1970). His conclusion is that the distinction is spurious, that there is one Christian humanism presented, sometimes theologically, sometimes as praxis. It is this view of the issue that is assumed in the present piece.

11. There has also been a scholarly debate as to whether François de Sales should be located on the map of Christian humanists. With Eymard, the present piece will place the saint clearly within the confines of the Christian tradition.

12. On the Christian humanism practiced by the Jesuits see Louis Cognet's *De la dévotion moderne à la spiritualité française* (Paris: Librairie Arthème Fayard, 1958), pp. 65ff. An exhaustive history of the Jesuits in France has been accomplished by Le P. Henri Fouqueray, *Histoire de la Compagnie de Jésus en France des origines à la suppression (1528–1762)* (Nendeln/Liechtenstein: Kraus Reprint, 1972).

13. Like the classical authors, the biblical texts, at least within the Catholic camp, were not read unreservedly. Reading was selective and in keeping with the medieval exegetical tradition; the biblical words were understood in a spiritual as well as literal manner. In the Catholic world,

unlike the Protestant, unguided reading of Scripture was not encouraged, nor was translation of the Vulgate into the vernacular. See the section "Histoire spirituelle de la France" in the article "France" in *Dictionnaire de spiritualité ascétique et mystique,* Tome V, col. 785–1004.

14. On the teaching of humanist disciplines and scholasticism consult Paul Oskar Kristeller, *Renaissance Thought: The Classic, Scholastic and Humanist Strains* (New York: Harper and Row, 1961).

15. Anton C. Pegis' "Molina and Human Liberty" in *Jesuit Thinkers of the Renaissance,* edited by Gerald Smith (Milwaukee, Wisconsin: Marquette Univ. Press, 1939), pp. 75–131, has a useful discussion of Molinism. Also see Joseph H. Fichter, *Man of Spain: Francis Suarez* (New York: Macmillan Co., 1940).

16. Bremond, *Histoire littéraire* Vol. II, *L'invasion mystique,* is best on this flowering.

17. On Lefèvre d'Etaples' circle see Eugene F. Rice, Jr., "The Humanist Idea of Christian Antiquity: Lefèvre d'Etaples and His Circle" in *Studies in the Renaissance,* Vol. IX, 1962, pp. 126–160.

18. Prunel is good on the active apostolate in France.

19. Louis Cognet's survey, *Les origines de la spiritualité française au XVIIe siècle,* (Paris: La Colombe, 1949), provides a concise overview of the sources of French spirituality of the period being considered.

20. Jean Dagens, *Bibliographie chronologique de la littérature de spiritualité et de ses sources (1501–1610)* (Paris: Desclée de Brouwer, 1952).

21. On this monastic renewal refer to Vol. II, *L'invasion mystique* of Bremond's *Histoire littéraire.*

22. For information on the "abstract school" consult P. Renaudin, *Un maître de la mystique française: Benoît de Canfeld,* (Spes, 1956).

23. Two useful works on Bérulle's spirituality are: Michel Dupuy, *Bérulle: Une spiritualité de l'adoration* (Tournai, Belgium: Desclée et Co., 1964) and Jean Orcibal, *Le Cardinal de Bérulle: Evolution d'une spiritualité* (Paris: Les Editions du Cerf, 1965).

24. The best biography of Jeanne de Chantal in English, and perhaps in any language, is Elisabeth Stopp's *Madame de Chantal. Portrait of a Saint* (London: Faber and Faber, 1962).

25. Henriette Houillon, "La femme en France aux XVIIe et XVIIIe siècles," pt. 1 of *Histoire mondiale de la femme,* publiée sous la direction de Pierre Grimal (Paris: Nouvelle Librairie de France, 1966), pp. 9–98.

26. When Christophe retired from public life and returned to Bourbilly, he wrote a poem of farewell to the ladies of the court telling them that a life of solitude with his beloved wife far outweighed any charms they might have to offer him. Jeanne kept the poem after she became a nun. However, Christophe was very much a man of the world, and society at

the time did tolerate what we would call a "double standard" in regard to the conduct of men and women. According to Sr. Patricia Burns, the present archivist of the Annecy Visitation, Christophe did have an illegitimate daughter (Claudine was her name) who was possibly for a time under the charge of Jeanne de Chantal. Whether he fathered this child before or after his marriage to Jeanne is difficult to determine.

27. *Sa vie et ses oeuvres*, Chaugy, p. 32.

28. This fact has not always been obvious to scholars. Her strength of character has been unflatteringly contrasted with the gentle disposition that François de Sales represents. M. l'Abbé Em. Bougaud's presentation of her in his *Histoire de sainte Chantal et des origines de la Visitation* (Paris: Librarie de Mme Vᵉ Poussielque-Rusand, 1863), 2 vols., is at the root of this misapprehension.

29. This aspect of Jeanne's personality is brought out in Sr. Patricia Burns' article "La tendresse en Ste. Jeanne de Chantal" in *Annales Salesiennes*, No. 3, 1972, pp. 10–11.

30. *Sa vie et ses oeuvres*, Chaugy, p. 36.

31. In the eyes of the law, women were definitely subject to their male counterparts. In terms of actual, direct influence in French society and on mores, nonetheless, the legal status of woman did not correspond to the reality. The period of the wars of religion in France had seen the corruption of the moral fabric of society. It was the women that set about to restore the integrity of French life. In their salons (both aristocratic and bourgeoise) they introduced a new polite society and the art of conversation. They were the leaders in the upsurge of devotion and active charity then in vogue. They had great influence in both religious and political circles. Moreover, they as a class were not limited to the work of householding. Some women had active professional lives. Consult Houillon, "La Femme en France."

32. This included the housekeepers' children as well as possibly Christophe's illegitimate daughter Claudine and her deceased sister Marguerite's two boys.

33. *Oeuvres*, Tome XII, Lettres 2, p. 264.

34. We do not know her motives for this but among them must have been her own desire for privacy and her concern that her revelations might be misunderstood and cause scandal for the man she hoped would be canonized during her lifetime. Stopp in her biography of Ste. Chantal has a thoughtful discussion of her motives on pp. 190–94.

35. See Francis Vincent, *Saint François de Sales, Directeur d'âmes: L'education de la volonté* (Paris: Gabriel Beauchesne, 1923).

36. *Oeuvres*, Tome XII, Lettres 2, pp. 263–67.

37. The most recent study is Gustave Durham (and others), *Saint Claude: Vie at Présence* (P. Lethielleux, 1960).

38. *Sa vie et ses oeuvres*, Chaugy, p. 41.

39. *Ibid.*, p. 62.

40. *Ibid.*, p. 65.

41. See Ruth Kleinman, *Saint François de Sales and the Protestants* (Genève: Librairie E. Droz, 1962), for a reevaluation of the saint's image as the "gentle missionary."

42. *Oeuvres*, Tome XII, Lettres 2, p. 354.

43. She testifies to this fact in her *Déposition pour la canonisation de S. François* found in *Sa vie et ses oeuvres*, Tome III, p. 125.

44. *Oeuvres*, Tome XII, Lettres 2, p. 356.

45. Jeanne, after her mentor's death, recounted that he frequently bestowed this type of advice upon those who came to consult him. Cf. *Déposition*, pp. 199–200.

46. For various views on François de Sales as a Christian humanist, consult Henri Bremond, *Autour de l'humanisme d'Erasme à Pascal* (Paris: Editions Bernard Grasset, 1937) as well as his *L'Humanisme dévot (1580–1660)*, Vol. II of *Histoire littéraire;* Julian Eymard d'Angers, *L'humanisme chrétien au XVIIe siècle;* Cecilian Streebing, *Devout Humanism as a Style: St. François de Sales' Introduction à La Vie Dévote*, (Washington, D.C., Catholic Univ. of America Press, 1954).

47. *Oeuvres*, Tome XII, Lettres 2, p. 359.

48. *Sa vie et ses oeuvres*, Chaugy, p. 73.

49. On the literary sources of his teaching: Antanas Liuima, *Aux sources du Traité de l'amour de Dieu de St. François de Sales*, 2 parts (Rome: Librairie Editrice de l'Université Grégorienne, 1960). Also: Antoine Joseph Daniels, *Les rapports entre Saint François de Sales et les Pays-Bas. 1550–1700* (Nijmegen: Centrale Drukkerij N.V., 1932); Alphonse Vermeylen, *Sainte Thérèse en France au XVIIe siècle. 1600–1660* (Louvain: Université de Louvain, 1958); Mother Mary Majella Rivet, *The Influence of the Spanish Mystics on the Works of Saint Francis de Sales* (Washington, D.C.: Catholic University Press, 1941). A more general overview of the sources of the spirituality of the period can be gained by reading Dom J. Huyben's article "Aux sources de la spiritualité française du XVIIe siècle" in *Vie Spirituelle (supplément études et documents)*, XXV, Dec. 1930, pp. 113–139, and XXVI, Jan. 1931, pp. 17–49, Feb. 1931, pp. 75–111, May 1931, pp. 20–42.

50. Vermeylen, pp. 92ff.

51. *The Spiritual Combat*, attributed to Lorenzo Scupoli, Maryland (New York: John Murphy Co.). Scupoli was an Italian Theatine writer.

Scholarship has suggested that he was but a final editor of the work, its birthplace being Spain.

52. *Sa vie et ses oeuvres*, Tome III, *Déposition*, pp. 124–25.

53. *Ibid.*, p. 148.

55. *Sa vie et ses oeuvres*, Tome III, *Déposition*, p. 221.

55. On his aesthetic: Th. Schueller, *La femme et le saint: La femme et ses problèmes d'après saint François de Sales* (Paris: Les Editions Ouvrières, 1970), pp. 55–104.

56. This contrast, however, should not be overstated. See note 28.

2. HIDDEN GROWTH (1606–1610)

1. See Schueller, *La femme et le saint*, especially pp. 55–104.

2. In a society that did not instill a sense of independence in its female population, this could be a problem. The reader is referred to Chapter II.

3. *Oeuvres*, Tome XIII, Lettres 3, p. 82.

4. The area around Lake Annecy had been settled during pre-Christian times. Excavations show the remains of a typical Roman provincial town including an amphitheater and temples.

5. *Sa vie et ses oeuvres*, Tome II, *Petit Livret*, p. 12–13.

6. *Oeuvres*, Tome XIII, Lettres 3, pp. 67–68.

7. *Ibid.*, p. 141.

8. This motto "Vive, Jésus" came to be inscribed at the head of all the letters Jeanne and her nuns in the Order of the Visitation were later to write.

9. *Oeuvres*, Tome III, *L'introduction à la vie dévot*, pp. 216–17.

10. Bougaud, upon whose authority the portrait of Jeanne as a harsh personality depends, highlighted the incident.

11. *Oeuvres*, Tome XIII, Lettres 3, p. 76.

12. *Ibid.*, p. 75.

13. Women in seventeenth century France were not encouraged to make life decisions for themselves. Choices of occupation and spouse were usually left up to parents. Jeanne, before she entered the religious life, had to obtain the approval of both her father and her brother who, though he was younger than she, was legally her guardian once her husband and father had died.

14. *Oeuvres*, Tome XII, Lettres 2, p. 397.

15. *Oeuvres*, Tome XIII, Lettres 3, pp. 383–85.

16. The reader is referred to the article "Jeanne de Chantal: The Two Faces of Christ" by Wendy M. Wright in *Medieval Religious Women*, Vol.

2, ed. by John Nichols (Kalamazoo, Michigan: Cistercian Publications, 1985).

17. *Oeuvres,* Tome XIII, Lettres 3. p. 186.

18. *Ibid.,* p. 147.

19. *Oeuvres,* Tome XII, Lettres 2, p. 287.

20. In the Christian tradition the term meditation is generally used to describe the mental consideration, often in a disciplined manner, of the various mysteries of the faith. It is distinguished from contemplation.

21. *Oeuvres,* Tome XIII, Lettres 3, p. 123.

22. *Ibid.,* p. 162.

23. Bremond in particular saw things this way; but his assertion rests upon Catholic assumptions held in the modern era, not necessarily in the seventeenth century. The definition of "contemplative" prayer has not remained constant throughout the Christian centuries. By the early seventeenth century, the idea that contemplation was a fairly advanced "stage" of prayer that a chosen few were called to by God had become standard in some quarters. It was felt that meditation, or discursive prayer, could be practiced by anybody. But at a certain stage, the person ceased to be the agent in prayer and became a vessel for the inflowing of the divine. This view of the life of contemplative prayer became the standard Catholic view of the interior life until the mid-twentieth century. The idea of contemplation as a specific high stage of prayer open to only an elect few was not familiar to the early church or to the medieval world. (See the article "Contemplation" in *Dictionnaire de spiritualité ascétique et mystique,* Tome III, columns 1643–2194.) In the early centuries, especially among the desert fathers, contemplation was understood as "wisdom"—a knowing that went beyond intellectual knowledge. Contemplation involved for them a wholistic grasp of truth that could be achieved only through prayer. This wholistic understanding of contemplation persisted through the centuries. It is interesting to note that François de Sales, although he had read Teresa and was strongly influenced by her in his conceptions of prayer (consult Vermeylen, *Sainte Thérèse en France . . . ,* pp. 146ff), did not draw a sharp distinction between meditation and contemplation. For him, the latter was a natural evolution from the former.

24. By Louis Cognet in his *Les origines de la spiritualité française au XVII*ᵉ *siècle,* (Paris: La Colombe, 1949), pp. 33–52. See also the same author's *De la dévotion moderne à la spiritualité française* (Paris: Librarie Arthème Fayard, 1958). The editors of the Annecy edition of François de Sales' *Oeuvres* assumed that the advice was Carmelite in tone. See *Oeuvres,* Tome XIII, Lettres 3, p. 162, footnote #1.

25. The prayer is referred to as "l'oraison de simple remise." Cf. *Sa vie et ses oeuvres,* Tome II, p. 9, sect. 25.

26. ". . . simple et unique regard en Dieu, par une totale remise de l'âme entre ses mains." *Sa vie et ses oeuvres*, Tome VI, Lettres 3, p. 537.

27. Pierre Serouet has an analysis of Jeanne's prayer in *De la vie dévote à la vie mystique. Ste. Thérèse d'Avila et St. François de Sales* (Paris: Desclée de Brouwer, 1958, pp. 246–58.)

28. *Sa vie et ses oeuvres*, Tome II, *Entretien* 36, p. 352.

29. The term "virtues" has a specific meaning in the Christian context. There were understood to be three "theological" virtues, faith, hope and charity. There were also four "natural" or "cardinal" virtues: prudence, temperance, fortitude and justice.

30. *Oeuvres*, Tome XIII, Lettres 3, pp. 263–64.

31. *Ibid.*, p. 263.

32. *Sa vie et ses oeuvres*, Chaugy, p. 94.

33. See Emile Mâle, *L'art religieux de la fin du XVIe siècle du XVIIe siècle et du XVIIIe siècle* (Etude sur l'iconographie après le Concile de Trente) (Paris: Librairie Armand Colin, 1951), pp. 19–107.

34. *Sa vie et ses oeuvres*, Chaugy, pp. 95–96.

35. He was acquainted with a community for women, the Torre de Specchi, founded by Frances of Rome in the fifteenth century, which operated without vows or cloister. Likewise Charles Borromeo, in the sixteenth century had organized in Milan a house of Ursulines with a mitigated cloister.

36. *Sa vie et ses oeuvres*, Tome II, *Entretiens* and *Exhortations*, p. 305 and p. 186.

37. *Sa vie et ses oeuvres*, Chaugy, p. 101.

38. *Ibid.*, p. 101.

39. Eleven was the minimum age at which a girl was considered marriageable. Still, it was somewhat young for the practice of the period, but Marie-Aymée was considered mature for her age. Nonetheless, it was considered essential that she set up housekeeping within the purview of an older female family member.

40. *Oeuvres*, Tome XXV, p. 214.

41. The first convent of the Visitation took in several other young charges after Madame de Chantal's progeny were no longer in evidence, an enterprise which was not always successful.

42. On the complex relationship that existed between monastic foundations and society in the seventeenth century and the practice of patterns of giving dowries in Visitation communities see Roger Devos, *Vie religieuse féminine et société: Les Visitandines d'Annecy, aux XVIIe et XVIIIe siècles* (Annecy: L'Académie Salesienne, 1973).

43. *Sa vie et ses oeuvres*, Chaugy, pp. 111–12.

44. *Ibid.*, pp. 113–14.

45. *Ibid.*, p. 116.

46. *Oeuvres*, Tome XIV, Lettres IV, p. 211.

47. *Ibid.*, p. 214.

48. *Sa vie et ses oeuvres*, Chaugy, p. 129.

49. *Ibid.*, p. 129.

50. Elizabeth Stopp, *Madame de Chantal*, p. 111, has a fine analysis of the boy's display. She puts the histrionics in the context of the literature that, as an impressionable schoolboy, Celse-Bénigne would have been reading—Plutarch, for instance—with its stories of heroism and dramatic exploit.

Celse-Bénigne was apparently not adversely affected in his own mind by his mother's desertion to the monastery. Years later, after she had painstakingly arranged a very good marriage for him, he wrote to her that she could not have cared for him any better than she did if she had been living a less singular life.

3. FRIENDSHIP (1610–1614)

1. *Oeuvres*, Tome XIV, Lettres 4, p. 254.

2. *Oeuvres*, Tome XII, Lettres 2, p. 262.

3. *Ibid.*, p. 263.

4. *Ibid.*, p. 285.

5. For two good survey treatments of the terms in Christian thought see *Dictionnaire de spiritualité ascétique et mystique* on "Amitié" by G. Vansteenberger, Vol. I, pp. 500–29 and "Charité," Vol. II, pt. 1, pp. 509–691. Another invaluable source for understanding friendship, especially in the patristic and medieval monastic worlds, is Adele M. Fiske, *Friends and Friendship in the Monastic Tradition* (Cuernavaca, Mexico: Cido Cuaderno no. 51, 1970). The reader is also referred to Jean Leclercq's article, "Amicizia" in *Dizionario degli instituti di perfezione*, Vol. I, pp. 516–20.

6. The analysis of friendship among the Greek philosophers is based upon Elizabeth A. Clark's treatment in *Jerome, Chrysostom and Friends* (New York: Edwin Mellen Press, 1979) p. 35ff.

7. Plato, *Lysis*, 212–215.

8. The references are to Chrysippus, and *Vatican Sayings*. See Clark, *Jerome, Chrysostom*, pp. 36–37.

9. Aristotle's discussions of friendship are to be found in *Nicomachean Ethics*, *Eudemian Ethics*, and *Magna Moralia*.

10. Cicero, *On Old Age and On Friendship*, trans. Frank O. Copley (Ann Arbor: Univ. of Michigan Press, 1967), Sec. VI.I.

11. Jean Leclercq, "L'amitié dans les lettres au Moyen Age" in *Revue de Moyen Age Latin*, Vol. I (1945), pp. 391–410.

12. Fiske, *Friends and Friendship*, p. 0/13 and 2/1–2/9 as well as Leclercq, "L'Amitié" p. 401.

13. Clark, *Jerome, Chrysostom*, pp. 41ff.

14. For Jerome on friendship generally consult Fiske, *Friends and Friendship*, pp. 1/1–1/20. For his friendships with women and the theory and practice that supported them see Clark, *Jerome, Chrysostom* and Henriette Dacier, *Jean Chrysostome et la femme chrétienne au IVe siècle de l'église grecque* (Paris: Librarie H. Falque, 1907).

15. Clark, *Jerome, Chrysostom*, p. 42.

16. Jerome's famous friendship turned enmity for Rufinus can be cited in this regard. Moreover both of the fathers referred to were publicly condemned for their friendly associations with women. Jerome was forced to leave Rome because of his feminine friendships and Chrysostom was publicly charged with meeting women alone, a practice frowned upon for a man in his position.

17. Leclercq, "L'Amitié," and Fiske, *Friends and Friendship*, pp. 2/1–2/9, have discussions about Augustine on friendship.

18. Daniel Day Williams, *The Spirit and the Forms of Love* (New York: Harper and Row, 1968), pp. 2ff.

19. This distinction is developed by Williams to clarify a different issue.

20. Anders Nygren's influential book *Agape and Eros* (Philadelphia: Westminster Press, revised edition 1953) proposes that these two types of love are in opposition in the Christian tradition. For criticisms of Nygren's position see Williams, *The Spirit and Forms of Love* and M. C. Darcy, *The Mind and Heart of Love* (London: Faber and Faber, 1947).

21. On this see Williams, *The Spirit*, pp. 34–51.

22. Derrick Sherwin Bailey, *Sexual Relation in Christian Thought* (New York: Harper and Row, 1959), pp. 8–18.

23. See Williams, *The Spirit*, pp. 8ff on Augustine. Also Walter H. Capps and Wendy M. Wright, *Silent Fire, An Invitation to Western Mysticism* (New York: Harper and Row, 1977) pp. 10–18.

24. Thomas F. Martin, "A Heart in God for Others: St. Augustine and the Christian Life" in *Spirituality Today*, Vol. 33 no. 4 (Dec. 1981), pp. 318–28.

25. Caroline Walker Bynum discusses this in an essay on "The Cistercian Conception of Community" in her *Jesus as Mother* (Berkeley: Univ. of California Press, 1982), pp. 59–81. She shows that it was only with the Cistercian renewal of the twelfth century that there was much

concern with personal relationships within community in monastic thought.

26. Consult Fiske, *Friends and Friendship*, pp. 3/1–3/16. See also R. W. Southern, *Saint Anselm and His Biographer* (Cambridge: Univ. Press, 1963), pp. 67–76, "The Letters of Friendship," on Cassian's contribution to later theories of friendship.

27. *Rule of St. Benedict*, trans. Anthony C. Meisel and M. L. del Mastro (Garden City, New York: Image Books, 1975), ch. 1–2, pp. 47–51.

28. Bynum, *Jesus as Mother*, pp. 76–77.

29. Jean Cassien, *Institutions cénobitiques*, Livre II, Chap. 15, pp. 85–6, in *Sources chrétiennes* no. 109, ed. H. de Lubac and J. Daniélou.

30. *Conférences*, Vol. II. No. XVI, pp. 222–47 in *Sources chrétiennes*, no. 54.

31. See Fiske, *Friends and Friendship*, p. 3/8. Fiske relates the two "traditions" of friendship juxtaposed in Cassian to the Ciceronian ideal of friendship as social and practical and the ideal of friendship as a spiritual bond that comes from the Platonic mystical tradition and Evagrius (p. 3/10).

32. Cf. Joseph de Guibert, "Les amitiés dans la vie religieuse" in *Gregorianum*, XXII (1941), pp. 171–190. More recently, the role of friendship in the spiritual life has been given a more positive evaluation. For an example of this contemporary thinking see Alan Jones, *Exploring Spiritual Direction. An Essay on Christian Friendship* (New York: Seabury Press, 1982); Yves Raguin, *Celibacy for Our Times*, trans. Sister Mary Humbert Kennedy (St. Meinrad, Indiana: Abbey Press, 1974), pp. 73ff; R. Murray, "Spiritual Friendship" in *Way*, Supplement 10 (1970), pp. 62–65; P. M. Conner, *Friendship Between Consecrated Men and Women and the Growth of Charity* (Rome, 1972) and Andrew Greeley, *The Friendship Game* (New York: Doubleday, 1971). There is also an interesting issue of *Humanitas, Journal of the Institute of Man*, Vol. 6, no. 2 (1970), which contains a number of articles on friendship as explored from the psychoanalytic and anthropological points of view.

33. To my knowledge, only Jean Leclercq in his *Love of Learning and the Desire for God*, trans. Catherine Mishraie (New York: Fordham Univ. Press, 1961) and F. C. Gardiner, *A Pilgrimage of Desire: A Study of Theme and Genre in Medieval Literature* (Leiden: E. J. Brill, 1971) have given Gregory's language and its influence on western thought adequate consideration. Leclercq's treatment is rich in suggestions and questions. Gardiner develops his ideas more explicitly in relation to one particular genre of Latin liturgical drama: the Emmaus story.

34. Gardiner, *Pilgrimage of Desire*, P. 20. (I have replaced "men" with "persons" here.) The discussion of Gregory is based on Gardiner's interpretation.

35. Leclercq, *Love of Learning*, pp. 45ff.

36. On Gregorian language and letters of friendship see Gardiner, *Pilgrimage of Desire*, pp. 53–75.

Also, Leclercq points out in *Love of Learning*, pp. 32–33, that Gregory was one of the most popular authors of the Middle Ages, in both the eastern and western churches and that he was still widely read up through the seventeenth century.

37. Jean Leclercq, "Le genre épistolaire au Moyen Age" in *Revue de Moyen Age Latin*, II (1946) pp. 63–70. For treatments of these authors and friendship without reference to the Gregorian language see: on Isidore of Seville, Fiske, *Friends and Friendship*, pp. 4/1–4/6; on Alcuin, *ibid.*, pp. 8/1–8/26; on Anselm, *ibid.*, pp. 15/1–15/32 and Southern, *Saint Anselm*, pp. 67–76.

38. Gardiner, *Pilgrimage of Desire*, p. 72.

39. Bynum, *Jesus as Mother*, pp. 59–81. On some of the implications for spirituality of the recruiting of adults into the Cistercians see Jean Leclerq, *Monks and Love in the Twelfth Century. Psychohistorical Essays* (Oxford: Clarendon Press, 1979), especially pp. 9–26.

40. See Marvin Pope's commentary in *The Anchor Bible*, 7C, *Song of Songs*, pp. 80–229.

41. The reader is referred to Bernard of Clairvaux, *Commentary on the Song of Songs* (Kalamazoo, Michigan: Cistercian Publications) and to the commentary of his friend William of St. Thierry, *Exposition on the Song of Songs*, trans. Mother Columba Hart (Shannon: Irish Univ. Press, 1970) as well as John of Ford's exposition, *Sermons on the Final Verses of the Song of Songs* (Kalamazoo, Michigan: Cistercian Pub., 1977).

42. Leclercq, *Monks and Love*, p. 103.

43. Bynum, *Jesus as Mother*, pp. 59–81.

44. For an analysis of Bernard on friendship see Fiske, *Friends and Friendship*, pp. 16/1–16/41. She also has a section on William of St. Thierry. pp. 17/1–17/23.

45. The reader is referred to Aelred of Rievaulx, *On Spiritual Friendship* (Washington D.C.: Cistercian Publications, Consortium Press, 1974).

46. Even the article "L'amitié" in the *Dictionnaire de spiritualité* essentially ends its theoretical discussion of friendship with Aelred.

47. Aelred of Rievaulx, *On Spiritual Friendship*, sects. 1:69 and 1:70, pp. 67–68.

48. The Latin text of this work with French translation is: Pierre de Blois, *Un traité de l'amour du XIIe siècle*, ed. M. M. Davy (Paris: Bocard, 1932).

49. *Ibid.*, ch. III, p. 121.

50. Richard Rolle of Hampole, *Fire of Love (Incendium Amoris)*, trans. Frances M. M. Comper (London: Methuen and Co., 1914), Bk. II, chap. 9.

51. Teresa of Jesus, *The Complete Works of Teresa of Jesus*, trans. E. Allison Peers (London: Sheed and Ward, 5th impression 1957), Vol. II, *Book Called Way of Perfection*, P. 17. At the same time Teresa was not, at a different point in her life, unaware of the benefits of friendship. See Teresa of Jesus, *The Collected Works of St. Teresa of Avila*, trans. Kieran Kavanaugh and Otilio Rodriguez (Washington D.C.: ICS, Publications, Institute of Carmelite Studies, 1976), Vol. I, *Life*, pp. 64–65.

52. "L'amitié" in *Dictionnaire de spiritualité*, col. 522.

53. Bernardino of Siena, *Beatitudes* quoted in Luis Rouzic, *Essai sur l'amitié* (Paris: P. Lethielleux, 1906), p. 17.

54. As far as I know there is no study of friendship as a component of the religious life of either the Beguines or the Devotio Moderna or any other religious community following the twelfth century.

55. See "L'amitié" *Dictionnaire de spiritualité*, cols. 523–24 and Guibert, "Les amitiés dan la vie religieuse."

56. Jean-Joseph Surin, *Questions importantes à la vie spirituelle sur l'amour de Dieu* (Paris: Pierre Tequi, 1930), p. 31.

57. Saint Vincent de Paul, *Correspondence, Entretiens, Documents* ed. J. Gabalda (Paris: Librairie Lecoffre, 1923), Vol. X, pp. 458–74 and 486–501 and vol. XIII, pp. 551–56.

58. *Oeuvres*, Tome VI, *Entretiens* IV.

59. *Sa vie et ses oevres*, Tome II, *Exhortations*, pp. 100–01.

60. *Oeuvres*, Tome III, *L'Introduction*, p. 195.

61. *Ibid.*, p. 203–04.

62. *Ibid.*, p. 202–03.

63. See Jean Gautier, introduction to Marcelle Georges-Thomas, *Sainte Chantal et la spiritualité salesienne* (Paris: Edition Saint-Paul, 1963), pp. 9–18.

64. Schueller, *La Femme*, p. 106.

65. *Oeuvres* Tome IV, *Traité*, pp. 5–6. Aelred of Rievaulx's treatise was not known but an abridged version, attributed to Augustine, was read by St. François. See *Oeuvres*, Tome XV, Lettres V. p. 94, marginal note. On *De amicitia liber unus*, attributed to Augustine see *Dictionnaire de spiritualité* article on Augustine, Tome I.

66. *Oeuvres*, Tome IV, *Traite*, p. 9.

67. For a discussion of the relationship between religious language and mystical experience (in our case, the argument could easily be extended to include relational experience of a spiritual nature) consult various articles in *Mysticism and Philosophical Analysis,* ed. by Stephen T. Katz (New York: Oxford Univ. Press, 1978).

68. On the primacy of love in Salesian thought: Lajeunie, *Saint François de Sales: L'homme, la pensé, l'action,* vol. II, pp. 223ff. Also Michael Muller, *La joie dans l'amour de Dieu* (Paris: Fernand Aubier, 1935) and Etienne Delarulle, "La dialectique de l'amour de Dieu chez St. François de Sales," in *Saint François de Sales: maître spirituel* (Paris: Spes, 1960), pp. 21–40 as well as Schueller, *La femme,* pp. 105–54. The bishop of Geneva may have preached the primacy of love and cast his treatise in the form of a tracing of the progress and decline of love, but this does not mean that, in his thought, reason is either unimportant or excluded. One must know God as well as love Him, and the education of the intellect is as much a part of the journey as the education of the will.

69. In the *Treatise on the Love of God* he asserts that charity is "principal et plus éminent de tous les amours": *Oeuvres,* Tome IV, *Traité,* p. 73. Also, at the time of his death, he was planning to write a book entitled *Traité des Quatre Amours* dealing with how one loves God, self, friends and enemies. Cf. *Sa vie et ses oeuvres,* Tome IV, Lettres I, p. 543.

70. Jean Pierre Camus, bishop of Belley, *The Spirit of St. Francis de Sales,* trans. C. F. Kelley of 1631 edition (New York: Harper and Bros., 1952) p. 30.

71. *Oeuvres,* Tome XXVI, p. 79.

72. This principally negative evaluation of the purpose of marriage has its roots in patristic thought.

73. *Oeuvres,* Tome III, l'Introduction, pp. 270–76.

74. *Ibid.,* pp. 264–66.

75. *Oeuvres* XII, Lettres 2, p. 354.

76. *Ibid.,* p. 288.

77. *Oeuvres* XIII, Lettres 3, p. 113.

78. *Ibid.,* p. 147.

79. *Ibid.,* p. 52.

80. *Ibid.,* p. 295.

81. *Ibid.,* pp. 260–61.

82. *Oeuvres,* Tome XIV, Lettres 4, pp. 229–30.
The Holy Shroud and the Blessed Sacrament referred to are the Shroud of Besancon (to be distinguished from the Shroud of Turin) and a devotion to the Eucharist at Dole popular since the occurence there of a miracle in the fifteenth century involving two consecrated hosts. On his

voyage in 1609 François de Sales passed through Besancon and Dole and prayed for Jeanne at the two holy sites.

83. *Oeuvres*, Tome XIII, Lettres 3, p. 84 and Tome XIV, Lettres 4, p. 252.

84. *Oeuvres*, Tome XII, Lettres 2, p. 399.

85. A fine collection of the letters he sent to his many friends has been edited and annotated by André Ravier, *François de Sales, Correspondance: Les Lettres d'amitié spirituelle.* (Bibliothèque Européenne: Desclée de Brouwer, 1980).

86. *Oeuvres*, Tome XIV, Lettres 4, p. 34.

87. *Ibid.*, p. 80.

88. For biographies of the first Visitation sisters see Françoise-Madeleine de Chaugy, *Les vies des quatres premières mères de l'ordre de la Visitation Sainte-Marie* (Paris: 1659, reprinted 1892).

89. *Sa vie et ses oeuvres*, Chaugy, pp. 133–34.

90. *Ibid.*, p. 134.

91. *Ibid.*

92. *Ibid.*, p. 139.

93. On the sociological patterns of monastic recruitment in the first century see Roger Devos, *Vie religieuse féminine et société. Les Visitandines d'Annecy aux XVIIᵉ et XVIIIᵉ siècles (Annecy: 1973).*

94. The following portrait of the early Visitation is something of a composite portrait drawn from the information available about the first five to ten years of the group's existence. Since they rapidly became a formal order in 1618, the original nature of the community was not long maintained. Since it is not intended here to write a developmental history of the Visitation, something of a foreshortened view of its beginning emerges.

The rule of the Order was based upon the "rule" of St. Augustine, which was simply a statement of the spirit of communal life rather than a rule in the strict sense.

The definitive form of the constitutions was not drawn up until 1618. The earlier versions, in spirit and as it concerned most domestic matters, differed only slightly. The major change in 1618 was to be found in the transformation of the congregation into an order, a process begun in 1614. Regulations about cloister, vows and dowries were drastically affected by this alteration.

95. Christian monastic practice included the recitation of the Divine Office, taken from Scripture, daily at seven intervals. The "Little Office of Our Lady" was a shortened and simplified version of this which originated in the tenth century.

96. The out-sisters were not included in the three ranks.

97. In the beginning, the Visitation sisters did not work to support themselves as they do now, the material support for the houses being supplied by the dowries of the entrants. This was the common practice of the day, the Visitation being quite modern in that it accepted some women who evidenced a strong spiritual vocation but who had little or no dowry to offer and did not accept women with large dowries who had no visible vocation. Cf. *Vie religieuse féminine* as well as the same author's "La correspondance de sainte Jeanne de Chantal: son intérêt du point de vue de l'histoire sociale des mentalités" in *Congrès des Sociétés savantes de Savoie/ La vie culturelle et artistique en Savoie* (Chambéry, 1972), pp. 101–114.

98. *Oeuvres, Constitutions,* Tome XXV, p. 113.

99. The Jesuits early on, possibly as early as 1615, became the mainstays of the priestly ministry to the Visitation. Since they were also under episcopal jurisdiction they could safeguard the Visitation's rights of self-determination.

François did plan to institute a men's foundation but the Visitation was not intended to be under its jurisdiction.

100. *Oeuvres, V, Traité,* p. 6.

101. In the following discussion I am relying upon suggestions and interpretations made by Schueller, pp. 55–104. What Schueller has given in germ I amplify with my own analysis.

102. His aesthetic was given formation both at Paris and Padua. Among the figures that influenced him were Zabarella, and, through him, François Suarez. It is also possible that he knew Giovanni della Casa's *Galatée,* a manual of European civility which seems to have influenced his thought. Renaissance canons of aesthetics broke with the Middle Ages by introducing purely plastic considerations into the ideals of beauty. This emphasis on proportion, etc., can be seen in spiritual writers like Bellarmine and François de Sales.

103. *Oeuvres,* Tome XXII, *Exercises spirituels,* p. 34.

104. *Oeuvres,* Tome III, *Introduction,* pp. 227–28.

105. *Oeuvres,* Tome XIV, Lettres 4, p. 35.

106. John Berger in the book *Ways of Seeing* (Great Britain: British Broadcasting Corporation and Penguin Books 1972) analyzes the social presence of the female in Western European art and determines: "A woman must continually watch herself. She is almost continually accompanied by her own image of herself. . . . Her own sense of being in herself is supplanted by a sense of being appreciated as herself by another. . . . Women watch themselves being looked at. This determines not only most relations between men and women but also the relation of women to themselves" (pp. 45–47).

107. *Oeuvres,* Tome XIII, Lettres 3, p. 211.

108. Kenneth Clark is quoted as making the distinction between nudity and nakedness in Bergers, *Ways of Seeing* p. 53–54.

In this section, I have advanced ideas set forth by Schueller but I have gone well beyond them by introducing the naked/nudity distinction. This also amplifies the intent of Salesian teaching rather than reproducing that teaching in its exact vocabulary. I have felt that, for the purposes of this piece, the distinction is helpful and faithfully captures the spiritual vision of the bishop.

109. Later, the practice of revolving rooms grew up. Likewise, each year the sisters took a new saint for patron, thus even disallowing clinging to a devotional figure.

110. *Oeuvres,* Tome XVI, Lettres 6, p. 122.

111. Jeanne herself, after the Visitation was launched, observed the three-year tenure of office rule despite the affectionate objections of the sisters, a testimony to her faithfulness of the spirit of the community.

112. *Oeuvres,* Tome XXV, p. 216, Constitutions, 1613.

113. *Sa vie et ses oeuvres,* Tome II, *Entretiens,* p. 478.

114. Cf. Georges-Thomas, *Sainte Chantal.*

115. For a review of Saint Chantal's very original contributions to the structure and genius of the Visitation see two pieces by Roger Devos, *Vie religieuse féminine,* chap. "Ste. Jeanne de Chantal, interprète de la tradition Salesienne," pp. 38–43, and "Le testament spirituel de sainte Jeanne-Françoise de Chantal et l'affaire du visiteur apostolique" in *Revue d'histoires de la spiritualité,* vol. 48 (1972), pp. 453–76 and Vol. 49 (1973) pp. 119–226 and 341–66.

116. "Simple regard" and "simple remise." See Part III.

117. *Sa vie et ses oeuvres,* Tome I, p. 341.

118. *Responses,* pp. 517–24, quoted in R. P. Mezard, *Doctrine spirituelle de sainte Jeanne-Françoise de Chantal* (Paris: Monastère de la Visitation. 1980 reprint of 1927 edition).

119. *Sa vie et ses oeuvres,* Tome III, *Conseils de Direction,* p. 337.

120. See Chaugy, pp. 66ff, and Bremond, *Histoire littéraire,* Vol. II on the flowering of mysticism in the Visitation until approximately 1650. It should be noted that they were not alone in feeling the mystic upsurge that swept France in the early seventeenth century. Yet it remains true that the Visitation had a special gift.

121. It is interesting to note that Jeanne considered Chapter Nine to be a depiction of François' inner state. See *Sa vie et ses oeuvres,* Tome III, p. 250.

122. Tome XVI, Lettres 6, p. 129.

123. From an unpublished manuscript in the Archives of the Monastery of the Visitation, Annecy, entitled "Avis à une Supérieure par Notre Sainte Mère," pp. 1–3.

124. *Ibid.*, pp. 3–4.

125. *Ibid.*, pp. 20–21.

126. See Sr. Patricia Burns, "La tendresse en Ste. Jeanne de Chantal," pp. 10–11.

127. The best treatment of this process is found in Devos, *Vie religieuse féminine et société*, Chap. IV, "Ste. Jeanne de Chantal, interprète de la tradition Salesienne," pp. 38–43.

128. A one year novitiate was common practice at the time. Of course, being novice, novice mistress and mother superior at one and the same time, as Jeanne was, was highly unusual. Also, because Visitation vows were to be simple and not solemn, the ceremony was known as oblation not profession.

129. *Sa vie et ses oeuvres*, Tome IV, Lettres 1, pp. 4–5.

130. *Ibid.*, p. 155.

131. *Ibid.*

132. *Sa vie et ses oeuvres*, Chaugy, p. 157.

133. *Sa vie et ses oeuvres*, Tome IV, Lettres 1, pp. 5–6.

134. *Oeuvres*, Tome 15, Lettres 5, p. 21.

135. *Oeuvres*, Tome XV, Lettres 5, p. 98.

136. *Ibid.*, p. 102.

137. *Sa vie et ses oeuvres*, Tome IV, Lettres 1, p. 26.

138. The bishop affectionately referred to Charlotte as his "niece."

139. *Oeuvres*, Tome XVI, Lettres 6, p. 331.

140. *Oeuvres*, Tome XIV, Lettres 4, p. 320.

141. *Oeuvres*, Tome XV, Lettres 5, p. 76.

142. *Sa vie et ses oeuvres*, Chaugy, p. 321.

143. *Ibid.*, pp. 356–57.

144. *Oeuvres*, Tome XV, Lettres 5, pp. 197–98.

145. *Sa vie et ses oeuvres*, Tome IV, Lettres 1, pp. 20–21.

146. *Sa vie et ses oeuvres*, Tome VI, Lettres 3, p. 114.

147. *Sa vie et ses oeuvres*, Tome IV, Lettres 1, pp. 13–14.

4. BOND OF PERFECTION (1615–1622)

1. Cf. Devos, *Vie religieuse féminine*, pp. 27–35.

2. Bremond is responsible for initiating this interpretation which has been much taken up.

3. *Sa vie et ses oeuvres*, Tome V, Lettres 2, p. 306.

4. *Oeuvres*, Tome V, *Traité*, p. 346.

5. From *Depositions des Contemporaines de la Sainte* quoted in *Sa vie et ses oeuvres,* Chaugy, pp. 164–65, note 1.

6. *Oeuvres,* Tome XVII, Lettres 7, p. 190.

7. The article "L'Amitié" in *Dictionnaire de spiritualité,* by Mgr. Van Steenberghe, p. 528, suggests that François severed the bonds of friendship because the relationship had become an obstacle to his own spiritual advancement. It seems to me this interpretation is lacking in sensitivity to the equality and vision of perfection that the two friends shared, as well as reflecting a basic mistrust of male and female relations on the part of the author.

8. *Sa vie et ses oeuvres,* Tome II, *Questions,* p. 39.

9. *Sa vie et ses oeuvres,* Tome IV, Lettres 1, pp. 109–111.

10. *Oeuvres,* Tome XVII, Lettres 7, pp. 214–15.

11. *Sa vie et ses oeuvres,* Tome IV, Lettres, pp. 112–13.

12. The Sulamite referred to is the bride of the Song of Songs.

13. François de Sales held the theological opinion that Mary was perpetually a virgin and had been predestined for divine motherhood from the beginning of time. This means that, when he was inside her, Christ did not open Mary's womb or occupy any place in the human manner of maternity. Her virgin integrity, in François' mind, was in no way compromised by the ordinary process of maternity. She was predestined not to undergo the physical process of childbearing. See Edward J. Carney, *The Mariology of St. Francis de Sales* (Eichstatt: Franz-Sales-Verlag, 1963).

14. *Oeuvres,* Tome XVII, Lettres 7, pp. 216–17.

15. François' physician and the doctor for the Visitation as well.

16. *Sa vie et ses oeuvres,* Tome IV, Lettres 1, pp. 115–17.

17. *Oeuvres,* Tome XVII, Lettres 7. pp. 218–19.

18. *Sa vie et ses oeuvres,* Tome IV, Lettres 1, pp. 149–50.

19. For a complete account of the lives of Jeanne de Chantal's two daughters see Ctesse. Alexandre de Menton, *Les deux filles de Sainte Chantal* (Annecy: Monastère de la Visitation, 7th ed., 1913).

20. *Sa vie et ses oeuvres,* Chaugy, p. 188.

21. *Ibid.,* p. 189.

22. *Ibid.,* p. 190.

23. *Sa vie et ses oeuvres,* Tome IV, Lettres 1, pp. 223–24.

24. Henri Bremond, *Sainte Chantal* (Paris: J. Gabalda, 1912) p. 169.

25. Carolyn Walker Bynum points to this fact in her essay on the nuns of Helfta of the thirteenth century. Bynum also shows that the use of feminized language and the view of parental authority as nurturing rather than disciplining comes, in the High Middle Ages and the Cistercian tradition at least, more from men who are abbots than from women who are abbesses and derives more from an ambivalence about exercising authority than the

possession of a certain gender. See her *Jesus as Mother,* pp. 110–69 and 170–262.

As for the seventeenth century, it was the reforming abbesses who were in the forefront of religious activism in the early part of the century (cf. Bremond, *Histoire littéraire,* Vol. II) and, to my knowledge, there was at that time no great emphasis on the "feminine" qualities of being that these women were supposed to exhibit.

26. Bynum, *Jesus as Mother,* points out that perhaps it is a fairly modern distinction that limits men to the expression of "masculine" traits and women to the cultivation of "feminine" ways of being than was often the case earlier in western civilization.

27. *Sa vie et ses oeuvres,* Tome IV, Lettres 1, p. 81.

28. *Sa vie et ses oeuvres,* Tome IV, Lettres 1, pp. 549–51.

29. The reader is referred to the article "Contemplation" in *Dictionnaire de spiritualité* and to Butler's *Western Mysticism.*

30. *Sa vie et ses oeuvres,* Tome IV, Lettres 1, pp. 568–69.

31. The founder was opposed to this and wished the institute to be responsible to the Holy See and the bishops alone. On Jeanne's later heroic defense of this principle after François' death see Roger Devos, "Le testament spirituel de sainte Jeanne-Françoise de Chantal et l'affaire du visiteur apostolique," in *Revue d'histoire de la spiritualité,* Vol. 48 (1972) pp. 453–76 and Vol. 49 (1973), pp. 199–226 and 341–66.

32. *Sa vie et ses oeuvres,* Chaugy, p. 211.

33. *Ibid.*

34. *Ibid.,* p. 214.

35. *Ibid.,* p. 188.

36. *Ibid.*

37. In fact, there was something of a conflict over the disposition of the remains of the bishop. The populace of Lyon claimed the body because it was in their town that its owner had died. It took a great deal of political maneuvering and an actual escape in the dead of night to get the body back to Savoy.

38. *Sa vie et ses oeuvres,* Tome V. Lettres 2, pp. 103–04.

39. *Ibid.,* Tome V, Lettres 2, p. 90.

40. *Ibid.,* pp. 90–92.

41. Cf. Devos, *Vie religieuse féminine et société,* pp. 38–43.

42. Cf. Devos, "Le testament spirituel de Sainte Jeanne-Françoise de Chantal."

43. The deposition is found in *Sa vie et ses oeuvres,* Tome III, *Oeuvres Diverses 2,* pp. 82–247. For an excellent English translation, see Elisabeth Stopp. *St. Francis de Sales: A Testimony by St. Chantal* (London: Faber and Faber, 1967).

44. *Sa vie et ses oeuvres*, Chaugy, p. 336, note.

45. *Ibid.*, p. 317.

THE NATURE OF SPIRITUAL FRIENDSHIP

1. For an example of this point of view see de Guibert, "Les amitiés dans la vie religieuse."

2. *Oeuvres*, Tome II, *Introduction*, pp. 181–84 and 197–202.

3. *Ibid.*, Tome XIII, Lettres 3, p. 242.

4. *Sa vie et ses oeuvres, Déposition*, p. 149.

5. Carol Gilligan, "Woman's Place in Man's Life Cycle" in *Harvard Educational Review*, Vol. 49, No. 4 (Nov. 1979), pp. 431–46 and the same author's "In a Different Voice: Women's Conceptions of Self and of Morality" in *Harvard Educational Review*, Vol. 47, No. 4 (Nov. 1977), pp. 481–517.

6. *Sa vie et ses oeuvres*, Chaugy, p. 336, note.

BIBLIOGRAPHY

JEANNE DE CHANTAL AND FRANÇOIS DE SALES

A. Primary Sources

Oeuvres de Saint François de Sales. Edition complète d'après les autographes
et les éditions originales. Par les soins des Religieuses de la Visitation
du Premier Monastère d'Annecy. 26 vols. Annecy, 1892–1932.
Vol. 1: *Les Controverses.* 2: *Défense de l'Estendart de la Sainte Croix.*
3: *Introduction à la Vie Dévote.* 4 and 5: *Traité de l'Amour de Dieu.* 6:
Les Vrays Entretiens Spirituels. 7–10: *Sermons.* 11–21: *Lettres.* 22–26:
Opuscules.
St. François de Sales. *Oeuvres.* Ed. André Ravier et Roger Devos. Paris:
Bibliothèque de la Pléiade, Editions Gallimard, 1969.
François de Sales. Correspondance: les lettres d'amitié spirituelle. Ed. André
Ravier. Paris: Bibliothèque Européenne, Desclée de Brouwer, 1980.
Ste. Jeanne-Françoise Frémyot de Chantal. Sa vie et ses oeuvres. Edition
authentique publiée par les soins des Religieuses du Premier Monas-
tère de la Visitation Sainte-Marie d'Annecy. 8 vols. Paris: Plon, 1874–
79.
Vol. 1: *Mémoire sur la vie et les vertus de sainte Jeanne-Françoise Fré-
myot de Chantal.* Par la Mère Françoise-Madeleine de Chaugy. 2 and
3: *Oeuvres diverses.* 4–8: *Lettres.*
"Avis à une supérieure." Pub. in 17th c., n.d., n.p. Reprinted in *Recueil de
ce qui est marqué dans nos écrits pour la supérieure.* Lyon: Sauvignet,
1835.
*Responses de nostre très-honorée et digne Mère Jeanne Françoise Fremiot sur
les règles, constitutions et coustumier de nostre ordre de la Visitation
Sainte-Marie.* Paris, 1632.
Chaugy, Françoise-Madeleine de. *Les vies des quatres premières mères de
l'ordre de la Visitation Sainte-Marie.* Paris, 1659. Reprinted as Vol. I
of *Oeuvres historiques de la Mère Françoise-Madeleine de Chaugy.* Paris,
1892.

240

Constitutions de l'ordre de la Visitation Sainte-Marie. Annecy, 1979.

Mission et esprit de l'ordre de la Visitation Sainte-Marie selon St. François de Sales et Ste. Jeanne de Chantal. Annecy, 1979.

B. Translations

Francis de Sales, St. *Introduction to the Devout Life.* Trans. John K. Ryan. New York: Doubleday, 1982.

————. *Treatise on the Love of God.* 2 vols. Trans. John K. Ryan. Rockford, Illinois: TAN Books and Publ., 1974.

Letters from a Saint: The Great Christian Guide to Peace of Mind and Soul. Ed. George T. Eggleston. New York: 1957.

Library of St. Francis de Sales. Trans. and ed. H. B. Mackey. London, 1873–1910.

Vol. 1: *Letters to Persons in the World.* 2: *Treatise on the Love of God.* 3: *The Catholic Controversy.* 4: *Letters to Persons in Religion.* 5: *Spiritual Conferences.* 6: *Mystical Explanation of the Cross of Christ* and *Deposition of St. Jeanne de Chantal.* 7: *The Spirit of St. Francis de Sales* by his friend Pierre Camus, bishop of Belley.

On the Preacher and Preaching. A Letter by Francis de Sales. Trans. John K. Ryan. Chicago: Henry Regnery Co., 1964.

St. Francis de Sales in His Letters. Ed. by the Sisters of the Visitation, Harrow-on-the-Hill. St. Louis, Mo.: B. Herder Book Co., 1933.

St. Francis de Sales. Selected Letters. Trans. Elisabeth Stopp. New York: Harper and Bros., 1960.

A Selection from the Spiritual Letters of St. Francis de Sales. Trans. by the author of "Life of St. Francis de Sales" (Mrs. Sidney Lear). London, Oxford, Cambridge: Rivingtons, 1871.

The Spiritual Conferences of St. Francis de Sales. Trans. Abbot Gasquet and the late Canon Mackey. Westminster, Maryland: Newman Bookshop, 1943.

Answers of the Blessed Mother Jane Frances Frémiot. Georgetown: Joshua N. Rend, 1834.

Answers of Our Holy Mother St. Jane Frances Frémiot on the Rules, Constitutions and Book of Customs of the Institute. Trans. from the French. Annecy: 1849.

St. Francis de Sales. A Testimony by St. Chantal. Trans. Elisabeth Stopp. London: Faber and Faber, 1967.

Saint Jane Frances Frémyot de Chantal. Her Exhortations, Conferences and Instructions. Trans. from the Paris 1975 ed. Chicago: Loyola Univ. Press, 1928.

The Spirit of St. Jane Frances de Chantal as Shown in Her Letters. Trans. by the Sisters of the Visitation, Harrow-on-the-Hill. London, New York: Longmans, Green and Co., 1922.

The Spiritual Life. A Summary of the Instructions on the Virtues and on Prayer, Compiled from the Writings of St. Jane Frances de Chantal. Compiled by the Sisters of the Visitation, Harrow-on-the-Hill. London: Sands and Co., 1928.

C. Secondary Sources

Bedoyere, Michael de la. *François de Sales.* New York: Harper and Brothers, 1960.

Berliet, Julie. *Les amis oubliés de Port-Royal.* Paris: Dorbon-Aîne, n.d.

Bordeaux, Henry. *Saint François de Sales et notre coeur de chair.* Paris: Plon, 1924.

Bougaud, M. L'Abbé Em. *Histoire de sainte Chantal et des origines de la Visitation.* 2 Vols. Paris: Librarie de Mme. Ve Poussielque-Rusand, 1863.

Bremond, Henri. *Autour de l'humanisme de'Erasme à Pascal.* Paris: Editions Bernard Grasset, 1937.

―――――. *Histoire littéraire du sentiment religieux en France depuis la fin des guerres de religion jusqu'à nos jours.* 3 Vols. Paris: Bloud et Gay, 1921. English trans.: *A Literary History of Religious Thought in France from the Wars of Religion Down to Our Own Times.* 3 Vols. New York: Macmillan Co., 1930.

―――――. *Sainte Chantal.* Paris: J. Gabalda, 1912.

Burns, Sr. Patricia. "La tendresse en Ste. Jeanne de Chantal." In *Annales Salesiennes,* No. 3 (1972), pp. 10–11.

Busson, Henri. *La pensée religieuse française de Charron à Pascal.* Paris: Libraire Philosophique, J. Vrin, 1933.

Calvet, J. *La littérature religieuse de François de Sales à Fénelon.* Paris: Les Editions Mondiales, 1956.

Camus, Jean Pierre (Bishop of Belley). *The Spirit of St. François de Sales.* Trans. C. F. Kelley. New York: Harper and Bros., 1952.

Carney, Edward J. *The Mariology of St. François de Sales.* Eichstatt: Franz-Sales-Verlag, 1963.

Cognet, Louis. *De la dévotion moderne à la spiritualité française.* Paris: Librarie Arthème Fayard, 1958.

―――――. *La Mère Angélique et Saint François de Sales. 1618–1626.* Paris: Editions Sulliver, 1951.

Dagens, Jean. *Bibliographie chronologique de la littérature de spiritualité et de ses sources (1501–1610).* Paris: Desclée de Brouwer, 1952.

Daniels, Joseph. *Les rapports entre Saint François de Sales et les Pays-Bas. 1550–1700.* Nigmegen: Centrale Drukkeri; N.V., 1932.

Delaruelle, Etienne, Joseph Perret, Claude Roffat. *Saint François de Sales: maître spirituel.* Paris: Spes, 1960.

Devos, Roger. "La correspondance de sainte Jeanne de Chantal: son intérêt du point de vue de l'histoire sociale des mentalités." In *Congrès des Sociétés savantes de Savoie/La vie culturelle et artistique en Savoie.* Chambéry, 1972, pp. 101–14.

————. "Le testament spirituel de Sainte Jeanne-Françoise de Chantal et l'affaire du visiteur apostalique." In *Revue d'Histoire de la Spiritualité,* Vol. 48 (1972), pp. 453–76 and Vol. 49 (1973), pp. 199–266 and 341–66.

————. *Vie religieuse féminine et société: les Visitandines d'Annecy aux XVIIe et XVIIIe siècles.* Annecy. Mémoires et documents publiés par l'Académie Salesienne, Tome LXXXIV, 1973.

Georges-Thomas, Marcelle. *Sainte Chantal et la spiritualité Salésienne.* Paris: Edition Saint-Paul, 1963.

Henry-Coüannier, Maurice. *Saint François des Sales et ses amitiés.* Paris, Tournai, Casterman, n.d.

Huvelin, Abbé. *Quelques directeurs d'âmes au XVIIe siècle. Saint François de Sales, M. Olier, saint Vincent de Paul.* Paris, 1911.

Huyben, Dom. J. "Aux sources de la spiritualité française du XVIIe siècle." In *Vie spirituelle* (supplement études et documents) XXVI, Dec. 1930, pp. 113–139; Jan. 1931, pp. 17–46; Feb. 1931, pp. 75–111; May 1931, pp. 20–42.

Jeu, Vicomte E. du. *Madame de Chantal. Sa vie dans le monde et sa vie religieuse.* Paris: Perrin et Cie Libraires Editeurs, 1927.

Julien-Eymard d'Angers. *L'humanisme chrétien au XVIIe siècle: St. François de Sales et Yves de Paris.* La Haye: Martinus Nijhoff, 1970.

Kleinman, Ruth. *Saint François de Sales and the Protestants.* Genève: Librairie E. Droz, 1962.

Lajeunie, E.-M. *Saint François de Sales et l'esprit salésien.* Bourges: Editions du Seuil, 1962.

————. *Saint François de Sales. L'homme, la pensée, l'action.* 2 Vols. Paris: Editions Guy Victor, 1964.

Lanson, Gustave. "Etudes sur les rapports de la littérature française et la littérature espagnole au XVIIe siècle (1600–1660)." In *Revue d'Histoire Littéraire de la France.* Paris, Vol. 3 (1896), pp. 45–70.

Leclercq, Abbé Jacques. *Saint François de Sales, docteur de la perfection.* Paris: Gabriel Bauchesne, 1928.

LeCouturier, E. *Lettres de direction et spiritualité de saint François de Sales.* Paris, Lyon: E. Vitte, 1952.

Lemaire, Henri. *Les images chez St. François de Sales.* Paris: Editions A. G. Nizet, 1962.

————. *Lexique des oeuvres complètes de François de Sales.* Paris: Editions A. G. Nizet, 1973.

LaVallée, F. *La Naissance de la Visitation.* Paris, Lyon, 1922.

Liuima, Antanas. *Aux sources du traité de l'amour de Dieu de St. François de Sales.* 2 Parts. Rome: Librairie Editrice de l'Université Grégorienne, 1960.

————. "St. François de Sales et les mystiques." In *Revue d'Ascétique et de Mystique,* Vol. XXIV (1948), pp. 220–39 and 376–85.

Menthon, Ctesse. Alexandre de. *Les deux filles de Ste. Chantal.* 7th ed. Annecy: Monastère de la Visitation, 1913.

Mezard, R. P. *Doctrine spirituelle de Sainte Jeanne-Françoise de Chantal.* 2nd ed. Paris: Monastère de la Visitation, 1980.

Müller, Michael. *Die Freundschaft des hl. Franz von Sales mit der hl. Johanna Franzista von Chantal.* München: Verlag Josef Kosel and Friedrich Dustet R-G., 1924.

————. *La joie dans l'amour de Dieu.* Trans. J. Peyraube. Paris: Fernand Aubier, Editions Montaigne, 1935.

Murphy, Ruth. *Saint François de Sales et la civilité chrétienne.* Paris: A. G. Nizet, 1964.

Papasogli, Giorgio. *Come piace a Dio. Francesco di Sales e la sua "grande figlia".* Roma: Città nuova editrice, 1981.

Perroy, Marguerite. *A l'école de sainte Chantal.* Paris: Editions Oeper, 1948.

Pocetto, Alexander T. "The Distinctive Spirit of a Religious Family and Christianity." In *Salesian Studies,* Vol. 3, no. 4 (Autumn 1966), pp. 68–77.

————. "An Introduction to Salesian Anthropology." in *Salesian Studies,* Vol. 6, no. 3 (Summer 1969), pp. 36–62.

Prunel, Louis. *La renaissance catholique en France au XVIIe siècle.* Paris: Desclée de Brouwer, 1921.

Ravier, André. *Ce que croyait François de Sales.* Paris: Nouvelles Editions Mame, 1976.

Rivet, Mother Mary Majella. *The Influence of the Spanish Mystics on the Works of Saint Francis de Sales.* Washington, D.C.: Catholic Univ. Press, 1941.

Roffat, Claude. *A l'ecole de saint François de Sales.* Paris: Editions Spes, 1948.

Sales, Charles-August de. *Histoire de bien-heureux François de Sales*. Lyon: Francois La Bottiere, 1634.

Sanders, E. K. *Sainte Chantal, 1572-1641: A Study in Vocation*. London: Society for Promoting Christian Knowledge, 1918.

Schueller, Th. *La Femme et le saint: la femme et ses problèmes d'après saint Francois de Sales*. Paris: Les Editions Ouvrières, 1970.

Serouet, Pierre. *De la vie dévote à la vie mystique: Ste. Thérèse d'Avila, St. François de Sales*. Paris: Les Etudes Carmelitaines chez Desclée de Brouwer, 1958.

Vidal, Chanoine F. *Aux sources de la joie avec St. François de Sales*. Paris: Nouvelle Librairie de France, 1974.

Vincent, Francis. *St. François de Sales, Directeur d'âmes: l'éducation de la volonté*. Paris: Gabriel Beauchesne, 1923.

Wright, Wendy M. "François de Sales." In *Spirituality of Western Christendom*. Vol. II. Kalamazoo: Cistercian Pub., 1984.

————. "Jeanne de Chantal. Two Faces of Christ." In *Medieval Religious Women*. Vol. 2. Kalamazoo: Cistercian Pub., 1985.

FRIENDS AND FRIENDSHIP

Acts of Paul and Thecla. In New Testament Apocrypha, Vol. II. Philadelphia: Westminster, 1965, pp. 322-90.

Abelard. *Historia Calamitatum*. Ed. J. T. Muckle. In *Medieval Studies*, XII (1950), pp. 163-213; XV (1953), pp. 47-94, XVII (1955), pp. 249-81 and XVIII (1956), pp. 241-92.

Achelis, H. "Agapatae." In *Hastings Encyclopedia of Religion and Ethics*, Vol. I, pp. 177-80.

————. *Virgenes Subintroductae*. Leipzig: J. D. Hinrich, 1902.

Ackerman, Sister Colette and Father Joseph Healy. "Bonded in Mission: Reflections on Prayer and Evangelization." In *Spiritual Life*, Vol. 27, no. 2 (Summer 1981), pp. 90-104.

Aelred of Rievaulx. *On Spiritual Friendship*. Washington, D.C.: Cistercian Publications, Consortium Press, 1974.

Aron, Margarite. *Lettres du Bienheureux Jourdain de Saxe à la Bienheureuse Diane d'Andalo*. Paris, 1924.

Bataillon, M. *Erasme et l'Espagne: recherches sur l'histoire spirituelle du XVI siècle*. Paris: Librairie E. Droz, 1937.

Bateson, Mary. "Origins and Early History of Double Monasteries." In *Transactions of the Royal Historical Society*, 13 (1899), pp. 137-98.

Bedoyere, Michael de la. *The Archbishop and the Lady. The Story of Fénelon and Madame Guyon*. New York: Pantheon Books, 1959.

Bieler, Ludwig. *Ireland: Harbinger of the Middle Ages*. London: Oxford Univ. Press, 1963.

Bonnard, Maryvonne. "Les influences réciproques entre sainte Thérèse de Jesus et saint Jean de la Croix." In *Bulletin Hispanique*, Tome XXXVII (1935), no. 2, pp. 129–48.

Bremond, Henri. *Histoire littéraire du sentiment religieux en France depuis la fin des guerres de religion jusqu'à nos jours*. 3 vols. Paris: Bloud et Gay, 1921. English trans.: *A Literary History of Religious Thought in France from the Wars of Religion Down to Our Own Times*. 3 vols. New York: Macmillan Co., 1930.

Calvet, J. *Louise de Marillac par elle-même*. Paris: Editions Montaigne, 1958. English trans.: *Louise de Marillac: A Portrait*. Trans. G. F. Pullen. New York: P. J. Kenedy and Sons, 1959.

Cassien, John. *Conférences* and *Institutions cénobitiques*. In *Sources chrétiennes*, Nos. 54 and 109. Ed. H. de Lubac and J. Danielou. Paris, 1942.

Chadwick, Nora. *The Age of Saints in the Early Celtic Church*. London: Oxford Univ. Press, 1961.

Chérancé, Léopold de. *Sainte Claire d'Assise*. Paris: Librairie Charles Poussielque, 1901.

Cicero. *On Old Age and On Friendship*. Trans. Frank O. Copley. Ann Arbor: Univ. of Michigan Press, 1967.

Clare, of Assisi. *The Legend and Writings of Saint Clare of Assisi*. St. Bonaventure, New York: The Franciscan Institute, 1953.

Clark, Elizabeth A. *Jerome, Chrysostom and Friends. Essays and Translations*. New York and Toronto: Edwin Mellen Press, 1979.

Collinson, Patrick. "The Role of Women in the English Reformation Illustrated by the Life and Friendships of Anne Locke." In *Studies in Church History*, vol. 2 (1965).

Cognet, Louis. *La Mère Angélique et saint Cyran (1634–1643)*. Paris: Editions Sulliver, 1953.

Conner, Paul M. *Friendship Between Consecrated Men and Women and the Growth of Charity*. Rome: Institutum Spiritualitatis Teresianun, 1972.

Dacier, Henriette. *Saint Jean Chrysostome et la femme chrétienne au IVe siècle de l'eglise grecque*. Paris: Libraire H. Falque, 1907.

Day, Dorothy. *The Long Loneliness: The Autobiography of Dorothy Day*. New York: Harper, 1952.

Dirvin, Joseph I. *Louise de Marillac*. New York: Farrar, Straus and Giroux, 1970.

Drane, Theodosia Augusta. *The History of St. Catherine of Siena and Her Companions*. 2 vols. London: Burns and Oates and Washbourne, Ltd., 1914.

Fiske, Adele M. *Friends and Friendship in the Monastic Tradition.* Cuernavaca, Mexico: Cidoc Cuaderno. no. 51, 1970.

Gardiner, F. C. *The Pilgrimage of Desire. A Study of Theme and Genre in Medieval Literature.* Leiden: E. J. Brill, 1971.

Garigou-Lagrange, R. "L'accord et les différences de Ste. Thérèse et des S. Jean de la Croix." In *La Vie spirituelle ascétique et mystique.* Supplément (1936), pp. 107–16.

Georges, R. P. Émile. *Saint Jean Eudes.* Paris: P. Lethielleux Libraire-Editeur, 1925.

Gilson, Etienne. *Héloïse et Abelard.* Paris: Librairie Philosophique J. Vrin, 1948.

Gougaud, L. *Les chrétientes celtiques.* Paris, 1911.

Greeley, Andrew M. *The Friendship Game.* New York: Doubleday, 1971.

Guibert, Joseph de. "Les amitiés dans la vie religieuse." In *Gregorianum,* XXII (1941), pp. 171–90.

Hausherr, I. "Le moine et l'amitié." In *Le message des moines à notre temps. Mélanges ... A Presse.* Paris, 1958, pp. 207–20.

Hericault, Charles Joseph, *Les amis des saints.* Paris, 1897.

Hueck Doherty, Catherine de. *Poustinia: Christian Spirituality of the East for Western Man.* Notre Dame, Indiana: Ave Maria Press, 1975.

Hugel, Baron Friedrich von. *The Mystical Element of Religion as Studied in Saint Catherine of Genoa and Her Friends.* 2 vols. London: J. M. Dent and Co., 1909.

Humanitas: Journal of the Institute of Man. Vol. 6, no. 2 (1970). Dusquenne: Univ. of Pittsburgh.

Hutter, Horst H. *Friendship in Theory and Practice: A Study of Greek and Roman Theories of Friendship in Their Social Settings.* Dissertation. Stanford Univ., 1972.

Huvelin, l'Abbé. *Quelques directeurs d'âmes au XVIIᵉ siècle.* Paris: Librairie Victor Lecoffre, J. Gabalda et Cie, 1911.

Jena-Nesmy, C. "Les amitiés du Christ." Dans *La Vie Spirituelle Ascétique et Mystique* 110 (1964), pp. 673–86.

Jerome. *Saint Jérôme: lettres.* Tomes I, V. Paris: Société d'Edition "Les Belles Lettres," 1949.

Jordan of Saxony. *Love Among the Saints: The Letters of Blessed Jordan of Saxony to Blessed Diana of Andalo.* Trans. Kathleen Pond. London: Bloomsbury Pub. Co., 1958.

Jones, Alan. *Exploring Spiritual Direction: An Essay on Christian Friendship.* New York: Seabury Press, 1982.

Kelly, J. N. D. *Jerome: His Life, Writings and Controversies.* London: Duckworth, 1975.

Kennedy, Eugene. *On Being a Friend.* New York: Continuum, 1982.

Labriolle, P. de, "Le mariage spirituel dans l'antiquité chrétienne." In *Revue Historique*. 136 (1921), pp. 204–25.

Leclercq, Jean. "Amicizia." In *Dizionairio degli Instituti di Perfezione*, Vol. I, pp. 516–20.

———. "L'amitie dans les lettres au Moyen Age." In *Revue de Moyen Age Latin*, Vol. I (1945), pp. 391–410.

———. "Le genre épistolaire au Moyen Age." In *Revue de Moyen Age Latin*. Vol. II (1946), pp. 63–70.

———. *Monks and Love in Twelfth Century France: Psycho-Historical Essays*. Oxford: Clarendon Press, 1979.

———. "S. Pierre Damien et les femmes." In *Studia Monastica*, 15 (1973), pp. 43–55.

Leech, Kenneth. *Soul Friend: The Practice of Christian Spirituality*. San Francisco: Harper and Row, 1980.

Letters of Herbert Cardinal Vaughn to Lady Herbert of Lea, 1867–1903. Ed. Shane Leslie. London, 1942.

Life of Christina of Markyate: A Twelfth Century Recluse. Trans. C. H. Talbot. Oxford: Clarendon Press, 1959.

Lovat, Alice Lady and R. H. Benson, *Life of St. Teresa*. London: Simpkin, Marshall, Hamilton, Kent and Co., 1914.

Malingrey, A. M., ed. *Jean Chrysostome: Lettres à Olympias*. In *Sources chrétiennes*, ed. H. de Lubac. Vol. 13. Paris, 1942.

McDonald, Kevin. "Friendship." In *Clergy Review*, Aug. 1982, pp. 274–78.

McGuire, B. P. "Friends and Tales in the Cloister. Oral Sources on Caesarius of Heisterbach's Dialogus Miraculorum." In *Analecta Cisterciensia*, 1980, pt. 2 July–Dec.

Meilaender, Gilbert C. *Friendship: A Study in Theological Ethics*. Indiana: University of Notre Dame Press, 1981.

Monier, Frédéric. *Vie de Jean-Jacques Olier*. 2 vols. Paris: Ancienne Librairie Poussielque, 1914.

Montalembert, Comte de. *Les Moines d'occident*. 5 vols. Paris: Jacques Lecoffre et Cie, Libraires-Editeurs, 1967. English trans.: *The Monks of the West From St. Benedict to St. Bernard*. New York: P. J. Kenedy and Sons, 1905.

Murray, R. "Spiritual Friendship." In *Way*. Supplement 10 (1970), pp. 62–75.

Pierre de Blois. *Un traité de l'amour du XIIᵉ siècle*. Trans. M. M. Davy. Paris: Boccard, 1932.

Rader, Rosemary. *Breaking Boundaries: Male/Female Friendship in Early Christian Communities*. New Jersey: Paulist Press, 1983.

————. "Syneisaktism: Spiritual Marriage." In *The Continuing Quest for God: Monastic Spirituality in Tradition and Transition*. Collegeville, Minnesota: The Liturgical Press, 1982.

Raguin, Yves. *Celibacy for Our Times*. Trans. Sr. Mary Humbert Kennedy. St. Meinrad, Indiana: Abbey Press, 1974.

Rahner, Hugo. *Ignatius von Loyola: Briefwechsel mit Frauen*. Frieburg: Herder, 1956. English trans.: *Saint Ignatius Loyola: Letters to Women*. Edinburgh-London: Nelson, 1960.

Reynolds, Roger E. "Virgenes Subintroductae in Celtic Christiantity." *Harvard Theological Review*, 61 (October, 1968).

Rolle, Richard, of Hampole. *The Incendium Amoris of Richard Rolle of Hampole*. Ed. Margaret Deanesly. Manchester: The Univ. Press, London, New York: Longmans, Green and Co., 1915.

Rouzic, Louis. *Essai sur l'amitié*. Paris: P. Lethielleux, 1906.

Rudolf, Monk of Fulda. *Life of St. Leoba*. Trans. C. H. Talbot. In *The Anglo Saxon Missionaries in Germany*. New York, 1954, pp. 205–26.

Sabatier. *Life of St. Francis of Assisi*. Trans. Louise Seymour Houghton. New York: Charles Scribner's Sons, 1907.

Sahler, Benjamin, ed. *Madame Guyon et Fénelon. La correspondence secrète*. Paris: Dervy-Livres, 1982.

Savigny-Vesco, Marguerite. *L'amour et l'amitié chez les saints*. Paris: Bonne-Prisse, 1947.

Southern, R. W. "The Letters of Abelard and Heloise." In *Medieval Humanism and Other Studies*. Oxford: Basil Blackwell, 1970, pp. 86–104.

————. *Saint Anselm and His Biographer*. Cambridge: Univ. Press, 1963.

Surin, Jean-Joseph. *Questions importantes à la vie spirituelle sur l'amour de Dieu*. Paris: Pierre Tequi, 1930.

Teilhard de Chardin, Pierre. *Lettres à Léontine Zanta*. Paris: Desclée de Brouwer, 1965. English trans.: *Letters to Leontine Zanta*. New York: Harper and Row, 1968.

Teresa of Avila. *The Collected Works of St. Teresa of Avila*. Trans. Kieran Kavanaugh and Otilio Rodriguez. Washington: ICS Publ., 1976.

Thérèse de l'Enfant Jesus. *Correspondence générale*. 2 vols. Paris: Editions du Cerf, Desclée de Brouwer, 1973.

————. *Histoire d'une âme, ecrite par elle-même*. Lisieux et Paris. Office central de Lisieux, 1944. English trans. *Story of a Soul: The Autobiography of St. Therese of Lisieux*. Washington: ICS Publ., 1975.

Thompson, A. Hamilton. "Double Monasteries and the Male Element in Nunneries." In *The Ministry of Women. A Report by a Committee Appointed by the Archbishop of Canterbury*. London: Society for Promoting Christian Knowledge, New York: Macmillan Co., 1919.

Vann, Gerald. *To Heaven with Diana. A Study of Jordan of Saxony and Diana d'Andalo with a Translation of the Letters of Jordan.* Chicago: Henry Regnery, 1965.

Steenberghe, Mgr. "Amitié." In *Dictionnaire de spiritualité ascétique et mystique,* Vol. I, pp. 500–30.

Vincent de Paul. *Correspondence, Entretiens, Documents.* Paris: Librairie Lecoffre, J. Gabalda, éd., 1923.

Vööbis, A. *A History of Asceticism in the Orient, I. Corpus Scriptorum Christianorum Orientalium,* Subsidia 14. Louvain, 1958, pp. 326–48.

OTHER WORKS CONSULTED

Anson, John. "The Female Transvestite in Early Monasticism: The Origin and Development of a Motif." In *Viator,* Vol. 5 (1974), pp. 1–32.

Athanasius. *The Life of Antony and the Letter to Marcellinus.* Trans. Robert C. Gregg. New York: Paulist Press, 1980.

Augustine. "On the Holy Trinity." Trans. A. W. Hadden and W. G. T. Shedd. In *Select Library of Nicene Fathers.* Buffalo, 1887.

Bailey, Derrick Sherwin. *Sexual Relation in Christian Thought.* New York: Harper and Row, 1959.

Bainton, Roland. *Women of the Reformation from Spain to Scandinavia.* Minneapolis: Augsburg Pub. House, 1977.

Bardeche, Maurice. *Histoire des femmes.* Paris: Stock et Maurice Bardeche, 1968.

Benton, John F. "Individualism and Conformity in Medieval Western Europe." In *Individualism and Conformity in Classical Islam.* Ed. Amin Banani and Speros Vryonis, Jr. Wiesbaden: Otto Harrassowitz, 1977, pp. 145–58.

Børresen, Kari Elisabeth. *Subordination et équivalence, Nature et rôle de la femme d'après Augustin et Thomas d'Aquin.* Paris, 1963.

Bossy, John. "The Counter-Reformation and the People of Catholic Europe." In *Past and Present,* no. 47 (May 1970), pp. 51–70.

Bouyer, Louis. *A History of Christian Spirituality.* 3 vols. New York: Desclée Company, 1963–1969.

Bullough, Vern L. "Medieval Medical and Scientific Views of Women." In *Viator,* vol. 4 (1973), pp. 485–501.

Butler, Dom Cuthbert. *Western Mysticism: The Teachings of Augustine, Gregory and Bernard on Contemplation and the Contemplative Life.* 2nd edition. New York: Harper Torchbooks, 1966.

Bynum, Carolyn Walker. *Jesus as Mother. Studies in the Spirituality of the High Middle Ages.* London: Univ. of California Press, 1982.

————. Review of Jean Leclercq's *Monks and Love*. *Speculum*, Vol. 55 (1980), pp. 595–97.

Cabassut, André. "Une dévotion médiévale peu connue; la dévotion à 'Jésus Notre Mère'." In *Revue d'Ascétique et de Mystique*, Vol. 25 (1949), pp. 234–45.

Clark, Stephen B. *Man and Woman in Christ: An Examination of the Roles of Men and Women in Light of Scripture and the Social Sciences*. Ann Arbor, Michigan: Servant Books, 1980.

Capps, Walter H. and Wendy M. Wright. "The Contemplative Mode." In *Studia Mystica*, Vol. I, no. 1 (1978).

————. *Silent Fire: An Introduction to Western Mysticism*. San Francisco: Harper and Row, 1978.

"Charité." In *Dictionnaire de spiritualité ascétique et mystique, doctrine et histoire*, Vol. II, pt. 1, pp. 509–691.

"Contemplation." In *Dictionnaire de spiritualité ascétique et mystique, doctrine et histoire*, Vol. 2, pt. 2, pp. 1643–2194.

D'Arcy, M. C. *The Mind and Heart of Love: Lion and Unicorn, A Study in Eros and Agape*. London: Faber and Faber, 1945.

Davis, Kenneth Ronald. *Anabaptism and Asceticism: A Study in Intellectual Origins*. Scottsdale, Pennsylvania/Kitchener, Ontario: Herald Press, 1974.

Daniel-Rops, Henri. *The Catholic Reformation*. 2 vols. Garden City, New York: Doubleday and Co., 1969.

Dejob, Charles. *De l'influence du concile de Trente sur la littérature et les beaux-arts chez les peuples catholiques*. Genève: Slatkine Reprints, 1969.

Delameau, Jean. *Le Catholicisme entre Luther et Voltaire*. Paris: Presses Universitaires de France, 1971. English trans.: *Catholicism Between Luther and Voltaire: A New View of the Counter-Reformation*. London: Burns and Oates, 1977.

Dupuy, Michel. *Bérulle: une spiritualité de l'adoration*. Tournai, Belgium: Desclée et Co., 1964.

Eckenstein, Lina. *Woman Under Monasticism*. New York: Russell and Russell, 1963 reprint of 1896 edition.

Evennett, H. Outram. *The Spirit of the Counter-Reformation*. Cambridge University Press, 1968.

Fichter, Joseph H. *Man of Spain: Francis Suarez*. New York: Macmillan Co., 1940.

Fiorenza, Elisabeth Schüssler. *In Memory of Her*. New York: Crossroads, 1983.

Gager, John G. *Kingdom and Community: The Social World of Early Christianity*. New Jersey: Prentice-Hall, 1975.

Gilligan, Carol. "In a Different Voice: Women's Conceptions of Self and of Morality." *Harvard Educational Review,* Vol. 47, No. 4 (Nov. 1977), pp. 481–517.

──────. "Woman's Place in Man's Life Cycle." *Harvard Educational Review.* Vol. 49, No. 4 (Nov. 1979), pp. 431–46.

Goodich, Michael. "The Contours of Female Piety in Later Medieval Hagiography." In *Church History,* vol. 50 (1981), pp. 20–32.

Janelle, Pierre. *The Catholic Reformation.* Milwaukee: Bruce Publ. Co., 1949.

Jedin, Herbert. *A History of the Council of Trent.* 2 vols. Trans. from German by Dom Ernest Graf. St. Louis, Mo.: B. Herder Co., 1957.

Houillon, Henriette. "La femme en France aux XVIIᵉ siècle" Pt. I, *Histoire mondiale de la femme.* Publiée sous la direction de Pierre Grimal. Paris: Nouvelle Librairie de France, 1966.

Jesuit Thinkers of the Renaissance. Ed. Gerard Smith. Milwaukee, Wis.: Marquette Univ. Press, 1939.

Kristeller, Paul Oskar. *Renaissance Thought: The Classic, Scholastic, and Humanist Strains.* New York: Harper and Row, 1961.

Leclercq, Jean. *The Love of Learning and the Desire for God.* Trans. Catherine Mishrai. New York: Fordham Univ. Press, 1961.

──────. "Modern Psychology and the Interpretation of Medieval Texts." In *Speculum,* no. 48 (1973), pp. 476–90.

──────. *Monks and Love in Twelfth Century France: Psycho-historical Essays.* Oxford: Clarendon Press, 1979.

──────. *Nouveau visage de Bernard de Clairvaux: approches psycho-historiques.* Paris: Les Editions du Cerf, 1976.

Mâle, Émile. *L'art religieux de la fin du XVIᵉ siècle du XVIIᵉ siècle et du XVIIIᵉ siècle. Etude sur l'iconographie après le concile de Trente.* Paris: Librairie Armand Colin, 1951.

Mandrou, R. "Les femmes dans l'histoire." Dans *Revue Historique,* vol. 242 (Oct–Dec 1969), pp. 339–46.

Martin, Thomas F. "A Heart in God for Others: St Augustine and Christian Life." In *Spirituality Today,* vol. 33, no. 4 (Dec. 1981), pp. 318–28.

Meeks, Wayne. "The Image of Androgyne: Some Uses of a Symbol in Earliest Christianity." In *History of Religions,* vol. 13, no. 3 (Feb. 1974), pp. 165–208.

McNamara, JoAnn. "Sexual Equality and the Cult of Virginity in Early Christian Thought." In *Feminist Studies,* vol. III, no. 3/4 (1976), pp. 146–58.

Medieval Religious Women. 3 vols. Ed. John Nichols. Kalamazoo: Cistercian Pub., 1984-85.

Mortley, Raoul. *Womanhood: The Feminine in Ancient Hellenism, Gnosticism, Christianity and Islam.* Sydney, Australia: Delacroix Press, 1981.

Mysticism and Philosophical Analysis. Ed. Steven T. Katz. New York: Oxford Univ. Press, 1978.

Not in God's Image. Ed. Julia O'Faolain and Lauro Martines. London: Temple Smith, 1973.

Nygren, Anders. *Agape and Eros.* Trans. Philip S. Watson. Philadelphia: Westminster Press, 1953.

Olin, John C. *The Catholic Reformation: Savonarola to Ignatius Loyola.* New York: Harper and Row, 1969.

Orcibal, Jean. *Le cardinal de Bérulle: évolution d'une spiritualité.* Paris: Les Editions du cerf, 1965.

Ozment, Steven E. *Homo Spiritualis: A Comparative Study of the Anthropology of Johannes Tauler, Jean Gerson and Martin Luther (1509–16) in the Context of Their Theological Thought.* Leiden: Brill, 1969.

Pagels, Elaine. *The Gnostic Gospels.* New York: Random House, 1979.

Panikkar, Raimundo. *Blessed Simplicity: The Monk as Universal Archetype.* New York: Seabury Press, 1982.

Pope, Marvin H. *Song of Songs: A New Translation with Introduction and Commentary.* Vol. 7C of *The Anchor Bible.* Garden City, New York: Doubleday and Co., 1977.

Pourrat, Pierre. *La spiritualité chrétienne.* Paris, 1927–28. English trans.: *Christian Spirituality.* 3 vols. Trans. W. H. Mitchell and S. P. Jacques. London: Burns, Oates and Washbourne, 1922–27.

Rice Eugene F., Jr. "The Humanist Idea of Christian Antiquity, Lefevre d'Etaples and His Circle." In *Studies in the Renaissance,* vol. IX, pp. 126–60.

Religion and Sexism: Images of Women in the Jewish and Christian Traditions. Ed. Rosemary Radford Ruether. New York: Simon and Schuster, 1974.

Reypens, L. "Ame (son fond, ses puissances et sa structure d'après les mystiques)." In *Dictionnaire de spiritualité ascétique et mystique, doctrine et histoire,* vol. I, pp. 433-69.

Scroggs, Robin. "The Earliest Christian Communities as Sectarian Movement." In *Christianity, Judaism and Other Greco-Roman Cults.* Pt. II. Ed. Jacob Neusner. Leiden: E. J. Brill, 1975, pp. 1–23.

Southern, R. W. *The Making of the Middle Ages.* New Haven and London: Yale Univ. Press, 8th ed., 1963.

————. *Western Society and the Church in the Middle Ages*. England: Hammondsworth, 1970.

Scupoli, Lorenzo. *The Spiritual Combat and a Treatise on Peace of the Soul* (by Juan Bonilla). Trans. William Lester and Robert Mohan. Westminster, Maryland: Newman Bookshop, 1947.

Sichel, Edith. *Women and Men of the French Renaissance*. New York, London: Kennikat Press, 2nd ed. 1970.

Tavard, George H. *Women in the Christian Tradition*. Notre Dame, Indiana: Notre Dame Press, 1973.

Theissen, Gerd. "Itinerant Radicalism: The Tradition of Jesus' Sayings from the Perspective of the Sociology of Literature." In *Radical Religion*, vol. II, nos. 2 and 3 (1975–76), pp. 84–101.

Vermeylen, Alphonse. *Sainte Thérèse en France au XVIIᵉ siècle 1600–1660*. Louvain: Université de Louvain, 1958.

Williams, Daniel D. *The Spirit and the Forms of Love*. New York: Harper and Row, 1968.

Women of Spirit: Female Leadership in the Jewish and Christian Tradition. Ed. Rosemary Ruether and Eleanor McLaughlin. New York: Simon and Schuster, 1979.

Wright, Wendy M. "The Feminine Dimension of Contemplation." In *The Feminist Mystic*. Ed. Mary Giles. New York: Crossroad, 1982, pp. 103–19.

·